HEMAYA

Islam - A Profound

ISLAM
A Profound Insight

Ahmad M. Hemaya

TODAY

one finds in almost every library in the West books on Islam. Many authors attempt to either attack or glorify the religion to the highest degree. Most of these books are not written by experts. At the same time, bad translations of texts can lead to misunderstandings, which are adopted by the media and present an incorrect image of Islam. As a result, the West understands Islam differently from Muslims in Islamic countries, where people obtain their Islamic knowledge from traditional sources such as imams and Islamic schools.

This informative book objectively presents Islam as it is understood by "traditional imams", and offers its reader an authentic, comprehensive, deeper insight into Islam.

AHMAD HEMAYA

was born in 1979 in Cairo, Egypt. For 17 years, he studied at Al-Azhar and obtained knowledge from 72 scholars. Al-Azhar is the oldest and most renowned religious institution in the Islamic world.

Before and during his studies of the Islamic Law at Al-Azhar University of Cairo, he wrote and published several books in different languages about Islam, history, economics and geography. For his book "The way of the true life", he was awarded an honorary doctorate in Ireland in 2002. Since 2003, Hemaya has pursued his function as an imam and as a community adjudicator concerning personal matters for Muslims in Germany, where he was also involved in intercultural dialogue.

He speaks Arabic, German and English fluently. In addition to his work as director of a cultural project, the author is currently the imam of the famous Sultan Hasan mosque in Cairo, and offers free counseling in the subject-matters of religion, family and Arabic literature on his website (www.hemaya.info).

The book is also available in other languages
Official website of the book:

www.mercy4all.com

Cover concept: Ahmad Hemaya
Design and composition: www.zaun-design.de
Original German Title:
Islam -Wieso? Weshalb? Warum?
Ein Tiefgründiger Einblick
Translated from German by: Dr. Silvia Hernandez
Edited by: Brian Wright
Printing & Binding: Zamzam Presses, Cairo
Printed in Egypt
Reg.-Nº of the Egyptian Book Bureau: 14243/2010

ISBN 978-977-449-066-8

بسم الله الرحمن الرحيم

AL - AZHAR AL - SHARIF
ISLAMIC RESEARCH ACADEMY
GENERAL DEPARTMENT
For Research, Writting & Translation

الأزهــــر الشريف
مجمـع البحـوث الاسلامية
الادارة العــامـة
للبحــوث والتأليف والترجمـة

الســـيد / أحمد محمود حمايـة ....

السلام عليـكم ورحمــة اللـه وبركاتـه ــ وبعـد :

فبناء على الطلب الخاص بفحص ومراجعة كتاب : " نظرة معمقة فى الإسلام "
فى ١٦٦٠. صفحة. تأليف : سيادتكم بـاللغة الانجليزية " Islam: A Profound insight "

نفيد بأن الـكتاب المذكور ليس فيه ما يتعارض مع العقيدة الاسلامية ولا مانع
من طبعـــه ونشره على نفقتـكم الخاصــة .

مع التـأكيد على ضرورة العنـاية التامـة بكتـابة الآيات القـرآنية والأحاديث
النبوية الشريفة والالتزام بتسليم ٥ خمس نسخ لمكتبة الأزهر الشريف بعد الطبـع .

واللــــه المـــوفـق ،،،

والسلام عليـكم ورحمــة اللـه وبركاته ،،،

ادارة الترجمة

حبشى محمد حبشى

تحريرا فى ١٠ / ٥ / ١٤٣٢ هـ
الموافق ١٢ / ٤ / ٢٠١١ م

مــدير عـــام
ادارة البحوث والتـأليف والترجمـة

CONTENTS

Foreword ... 20

CHAPTER ONE | FROM WHERE? ... 23

1   Where Does The Universe Come From? ... 24

1.1   The Beginning – Where and When? ... 24
1.2   Further Expansion – How and Who? ... 26
1.3   The Clock and its Manufacturer ... 26
1.4   The Universe: Perpetuum mobile? ... 27
1.5   Order and Harmony in the Universe ... 29
1.6   Beauty in the Universe ... 30

2   Where Do Man and Life Come from? ... 31

2.1   Who Steers the Atoms? ... 31
2.2   Infinite Knowledge and Precision ... 32
2.3   A System Without an Inventor? ... 32
2.4   Raw Materials and Nutrients ... 35
2.5   The Cleverly-Devised Protective System Conclusion ... 36
2.6   Pre-requisites to Life ... 38
2.7   Chance or Calculation ... 40
        Conclusion ... 43
2.8   Evolution or Creation? ... 44
        2.8.1   The Theory of Evolution and God? ... 47
        2.8.2   What Did Darwin Believe In? ... 48
2.9   Deep Knowledge Leads to God ... 49

3   There Is Only One God ... *51*

3.1   Harmony in the Overall Picture ... *51*
3.2   The Chain of Interdependencies ... *51*
3.3   Independent Power and Knowledge ... *52*
3.4   One Center and One Boss ... *53*
3.5   A Soccer Team with no Coach ... *53*
3.6   The Conductor's Baton ... *54*
3.7   A Question of Boundaries ... *55*

CHAPTER TWO | TO WHERE...?
LIFE IN THE HEREAFTER ... *59*

1   The Logic of the Heart ... *60*

1.1   Concern with Man's Needs ... *60*
1.2   Needs in this Life and in the Afterlife ... *62*
1.3   Longing for Immortality ... *64*
1.4   Unlimited Human Capabilities ... *65*
1.5   Eternal Effect ... *66*
1.6   The Art Exhibit ... *66*
1.7   Divine Justice ... *67*
1.8   A Theater Play ... *68*
1.9   Winter Will Be Followed by Spring ... *69*
1.10 The Honorable Promise ... *70*

2   Logic and Science ... *71*

2.1   The Invisible ... *71*
2.2   Certainty about Non-Existence? ... *74*
2.3   Who Wins and Who Loses? ... *74*
2.4   What Does Death Mean? ... *75*

2.4.1   Body and Soul ... *75*

2.4.2   Further Thoughts ... *76*

2.4.3   'Different Thinkers' Views About Death ... *78*

2.5   The Soul in the Eyes of Research ... *80*

2.6   Another Path to the Truth ... *84*

2.7   What Does the Belief in an Afterlife Serve? ... *85*

3   What Will Happen after Death? ... *88*

3.1   Good News for the Muslim on His Deathbed ... *88*

3.2   Festive Procession in the Heavens ... *90*

3.3   The Last Trial ... *90*

3.4   Waiting in Barzakh ... *91*

4   Outline of the Day of Resurrection ... *93*

4.1   The Gigantic Outcry ... *94*

4.2   And God Will However Call Man Back to Life ... *97*

5   Accountability and the Entrance into Janna (paradise) ... *99*

5.1   On the Field of the Gathering ... *99*

5.2   The Declaration of the Eternal Fate ... *102*

5.3   Leaving the Gathering Field ... *105*

5.4   Crossing Jahannam ... *106*

5.5   Salvation of Acquaintances ... *107*

5.6   The Prophet Intercedes for the Salvation of Mankind ... *108*

5.7   Salvation of the Remaining Muslims ... *109*

5.8   The Last Person Saved from Jahannam ... *110*

6   Overview of Janna ... *113*

6.1   The Entrance of People into Janna ... *114*

6.2   Women in Janna ... *117*

6.3   Promenades in Janna ... *117*

6.4   The Death of Death ... *119*

6.5   God's Well-Pleasing in Janna ... *119*

6.6. The Levels in Janna ... *120*

7   Jahannam (Hell) ... *122*

Summary of Chapter 2 and Outlook ... *122*

A.   In Janna: Body or Soul? ... *123*

B.   Why does Jahannam Exist? ... *123*

C.   To Love God or to Fear Him? ... *124*

**CHAPTER THREE | PROPHET
MUHAMMAD WHO? WHAT? WHY?** ... *128*

1   The Prophets ... *130*

1.1   Why Did God Send Prophets? ... *131*

1.2   On Angels and Prophets ... *131*

1.3   The Miracles of the Prophets ... *132*

2   Muhammad, Prophet or Liar? ... *133*

2.1   Muhammad — Who? ... *134*

2.1.1   In Macca ... *134*

2.1.2   In Madina ... *136*

2.2   Muhammad's Character — How? ... *138*

2.2.1   The Prophet's Benevolence and Gentleness ... *138*

2.2.2   Muhammad's Honesty ... *140*

2.2.3   No Personal Gain ... *141*

2.3   Muhammad's Deeds — What? ... *141*

2.3.1   The Broad and Fast Spread of Islam ... *141*

2.3.2   The Swift Abolishment of Bad Habits ... *143*

2.3.3   Changing the Way of Life of Many Nations ... *144*

2.3.4   Muhammad as Pioneer for the
Renovation of the World ... *145*

2.4   The Miracles of Prophet Muhammad ... *145*

2.4.1   The Multiplication of Water ... *146*

2.4.2   The Multiplication of Food ... *146*

2.4.3   The Weeping Tree Trunk ... *147*

2.4.4   The Speaking Spiny-tailed Lizard ... *147*

2.4.5   The Healing of the Ill ... *148*

2.4.6   The Acceptance of His Supplication ... *149*

2.4.7   Prophecies ... *150*

2.4.8   Other Miracles ... *151*

2.5   Muhammad, Truthful and Unique ... *152*

CHAPTER FOUR | THE QURAN, THE LAST LETTER FROM GOD ... *167*

1   The Linguistic Miracles of the Quran ... *171*

1.1   No Imitation Possible ... *171*

1.2   The Quran's Rhetoric and Inimitable Style ... *173*

1.3   The Quran's Particular Influence ... *174*

1.3.1   In Private ... *175*

1.3.2   Warning the Guests ... *176*

1.3.3   The Tempting Offers ... *177*

1.3.4   Another Attempt to Stop the Message ... *178*

2   The Scientific Wonders of the Quran ... *179*

2.1   The "Roots" of the Mountains ... *179*

2.2   The Primitive Phase of Galaxies ... *180*

2.3   The Existence of Individual Orbits of Planets ... *181*

2.4   The Size of the Universe ... *182*

2.5   The Description of the Developmental Phases of the Embryo ... *183*

Embryo - Partially Formed and Partially Unformed ... *185*

2.6   "Haman" and Ancient Egyptian Inscriptions ... *186*

3   The Quran from the Perspective of Intellectuals and Scientists ... *187*

**CHAPTER FIVE | WHY?
SENSE AND MEANING OF LIFE AND
WORSHIP IN ISLAM** ... *194*

1   The Value of Man in Islam ... *196*

2   The Meaning of Our Existence in Islam ... *197*

2.1   The Story about the King and His Palace ... *198*

3   Man and Sin in Islam ... *200*

4   Sex in Islam ... *203*

5   Morality in Islam ... *205*

6   The Reliance on God (Tawakkul) ... *207*

7   What Do We Need Islam For? ... *210*

8   Spiritual Bliss Through Islam ... *213*

9   Aging From the Islamic Perspective ... *218*

10 Death From the Islamic Perspective ... *220*

    10.1   The Gate to an Illuminated World ... *221*
    10.2   Release ... *223*
    10.3   Reunion ... *224*
    10.4   Unbearable Difficulties ... *224*
    10.5   The Return of Youth ... *225*

11 Prayer ... *226*

    11.1   The Dawn Prayer ... *229*
    11.2   The Noon Prayer ... *230*
    11.3   Late afternoon Prayer ... *231*
    11.4   The Sunset Prayer ... *232*
    11.5   The Night Prayer ... *234*

12 Supplication (Do'a) ... *235*

13 The Meaning of the Pilgrimage in Islam ... *237*

14 Why Does God Let All of This Happen? ... *239*

    14.1   Behind Every Event Is a Meaning ... *240*
    14.2   Injustice in This Life ... *243*
    14.3   Generous Redemption ... *244*
    14.4   Where Things March To the Beat of a
           Different Drum ... *245*

15 The General Characteristics of Islam ... *246*

CHAPTER SIX | CRITICAL QUESTIONS ... 249

1   Islam as the Only Way to Paradise ... 250

1.1   The Caravan of Humanity ... 252

2   The True Teaching of Jesus, According to the Quran and the Bible ... 256

2.1   What Did Jesus Invite Us To? ... 257

2.2   Jesus Says: I Am a Messenger of God ... 259

2.3   Jesus, the Man ... 260

2.4   In the Bible It Is Said: God Cannot Be Seen ... 260

2.5   To Worship the Same God as Jesus ... 261

2.6   Jesus' Explanation of Salvation ... 262

2.7   The Quran Makes an Appeal to Mankind ... 262

2.8   The Love of Muslims for Jesus ... 264

3   Women ... 265

3.1   The Status of Women in Pre-Islamic Cultures ... 265

3.1.1   Women in Ancient Greece ... 266
(approx. 750 BC − 30 BC)

3.1.2   Women in Ancient Rome ... 267
(approx. 750 BC − 500 AD)

3.1.3   Women in Hinduism ... 269

3.1.4   The Abortion of Girls in India ... 270

3.1.5   Women in the Middle Ages ... 272
(approx. 500 AD − 1500 AD)

3.1.6   The Bible and the Status of Women ... 274

3.2   Women in Islam ... 276

3.2.1   Rules and Measures to Improve their Position ... 276

3.2.2   Prophet Muhammad Speaks About Women ... 282

3.2.3   Islamic Influence on the Position of Women ... *283*

3.2.4   Muslim Women in Today's World ... *287*

3.2.5   The Headscarf ... *289*

3.2.6   The Inheritance of Women in Islam ... *290*

3.2.7   Polygamy ... *292*

3.2.8   Genital Circumcision ... *293*

4   Religion, State and Civilization ... *294*

4.1   Knowledge in the Islamic Civilization ... *296*

4.2   Islamic Contributions to Civilization ... *297*

4.3   The Forgotten Legacy ... *305*

4.4   Downfall ... *311*

4.5   The End of the Islamic Civilization in Spain ... *312*

4.6   The Ability to Re-Establish Oneself ... *314*

5   What is the Position of Islam towards People of Different Religions? ... *314*

5.1   The Position of the Quran ... *316*

5.2   The Position of the Hadiths ... *319*

5.3   In the Books of Islamic Law (Sharia) ... *320*

5.4   The Practical Interaction with People of ... *323*
Different Religions

5.4.1   Protection and Preservation of Other
Religions ... *324*

5.4.2   Examples from the Time of the First Caliph ... *326*

5.4.3   Examples from the Time of the Second Caliph ... *326*
People Are Born Free

5.4.4   Egypt ... *329*

5.4.5   One Century after the Prophet ... *330*

5.4.6   Examples since the 10th Century ... *331*

5.4.7   Under the Ottoman Caliphate (1299-1923) ... *332*

5.4.8   Aid and Support for the Jews ... *333*

6   Jihad, a Free Ticket for Suicide Bombers? ... *336*

6.1   The Morality of Battle in Islam ... *341*

How Does a Person Become a Muslim? ... *343*

Final Remarks on Chapter Six ... *344*

Websites ... *345*
Books ... *345*

The Central points of Islam ... *346*

Glossary ... *351*

Hadith ... *351*
Remarks ... *352*
Janna (Paradise) ... *352*
Jahannam (Hell) ... *353*
Sharia (Islamic Law) ... *353*
ieman ... *353*

References ... *354*

Internet References ... *362*

List of Illustrations ... *365*

FOREWORD

Who among us has not wondered, "where do I come from, and where does this world come from? Why am I here? and where will I go after I die?"

Based on these key questions about our existence, we attempt in the present book to explore, from the Islamic perspective, how a harmonic relationship between man and the universe exists, and how a balance between the needs of the soul and the needs of the body is established. The reasons for inner peace and spiritual tranquility, as rooted in Islam, will also be closely examined.

This book is not a crash course on Islam, for there are already many; on the contrary, here the reader will be provided with a profound insight into the structure and way of reasoning of Islam, whereby emphasis will be laid on the "Why?", as well as on the "How?"
This work is the result of a deepened insight into Islam, which was established through the study of Islamic sciences and acquiring knowledge from more than 72 scholars over 17 years.

The following brief description of the chapters represents only part of the subject-matters handled, and serves to convey a first impression.

In addition to exploring the key questions posed above in Chapters 1 and 2, and part of Chapter 5, the book conveys a detailed description of paradise (Janna) in Islam.
Chapter 3 highlights what kind of person Muhammad was, and how he treated children, women, and non-Muslims around him. Through the latter, one discovers how he managed to obtain such great influence on the history of the world and billions of people.
Chapter 4 addresses the question of what the Quran is, and how it

has been identically preserved, down to the very last letter, for over 1400 years, in each and every single one of its copies.

The position of Islam about controversial topics such as sex, sin and violence is explored in Chapter 5, which also provides an explanation of aging and death. It will also be explained why God allows injustice and sorrow, while being considered merciful and just at the same time. Here we will also discover the deeper meaning of prayer in Islam, and we will also find out the reasons for their chronological shifting.

In the sixth and final chapter, the topics that currently dominate the image of Islam in the media will be taken up and discussed. These issues will be explained and defined using Islam's original sources – the Quran, Sunnah (Prophet Muhammad's sayings and living habits) and Sharia (Islamic Law). Additionally, the everyday application of these issues in Muslim societies throughout history will be discussed. Here, the position of women in Islam will be addressed first, followed by the relation between freedom, civilization and Islam as a state system.

The position of Islam towards other religions and the interaction of Muslims with religious minorities throughout history will also be described. Finally, the Jihad and its plural meanings will be illustrated.

I wish you an enlightening and informative read, for the information contained here represents, even to Muslims, the answer to many of life's important questions.

Ahmad Mahmoud Hemaya

Chapter 1
From Where?

"Something obviously exists now, and something never sprang from nothing."
Epicurus

1 WHERE DOES THE UNIVERSE COME FROM?

Where does the Universe come from?

1.1 The Beginning — Where and When?

Science explains how matter changes from one form to another, but it does not explain where the matter that exploded in the Big Bang originated from and how it got there. With the Big Bang theory, science describes the beginning of the Universe. However, it does not reveal under which circumstances this explosion came to being, and why it did so at a specific time.

 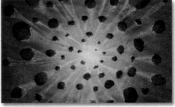

Would a common explosion (see figure on the right) produce all these beautiful planets, and complex galactic and solar systems?

Dr. Andrei Linde

Dr. Andrei Linde[1], professor of physics, says about the Big Bang: *"The first problem, and at the same time the main problem, is the happening of the Big Bang itself. One wonders what there was before the Big Bang. If space and time were not given, how could they emerge from nothing? What emerged first, the Universe, or the laws that determined*

---

1 Andrei **Linde** is a Russian cosmologist and one of the founders of the theory of inflation of the universe. He studied physics at Lomonosov Moscow State University and then worked at the Lebedev Physical Institute, where he was also a professor from 1985 to 1989. Since 1990, he has taught as a professor of Physics at Stanford University in California

the beginning of the Universe? The most difficult question of modern astronomy is this unique beginning: where and when did everything begin?"[1] This problem was taken on by Anthony Kenny from the

University of Oxford. He writes: *Anthony Kenny*
  "A proponent of the Big Bang theory, at least if he is an atheist, must believe that the universe came from nothing and by nothing."[2]

But this hypothesis does not make any sense. From nothing comes nothing. Then why does the Universe exist instead of just nothing? Where did it come from?

> *"Were they (the humans) created of nothing, or were they themselves the creators?"*
>
> The Quran, 52:35

There must be something which caused the Universe to exist. This thing must be independent, changeless, timeless, and supernatural (not part of the material Universe).

It must be independent because there cannot be an infinite regress of causes. It must be timeless and therefore changeless because time came to being only when the Universe was created. Space did not exist before either, and hence this being is also supernatural.

Stephen Hawking

Stephen Hawking[3] summarizes: *"It would be very difficult to explain why the Universe should have begun in just this way, except as the act of a God who intended to create beings like us."*[4]

---

1 **Linde,** Andrei: The Self-Reproducing Inflationary Universe. Scientific American, November 1994, p. 48.

2 **Kenny,** Anthony: The Five Ways, New York 1969, p. 66.

3 Stephen **Hawking,** (born in 1942) is a British astrophysicist, and was the Lucasian Professor of Mathematics at the University of Cambridge from 1979 to 2009, the title once held by Sir Isaac Newton and Paul Dirac.

4 **Hawking,** Stephen: A Brief History of Time, New York 1988. p. 127.

1.2 Further Expansion – How and Who?

Astronomers theorize that the Universe is always expanding. In physics, this means that the density of matter in the Universe continuously decreases, because matter must fill an ever-expanding space. Astronomers however reject this notion and believe that the density of matter in the Universe remains constant. As an attempt to solve this problem, astronomers assume that new matter emerges as the Universe expands.

Science, however, has still not answered the question: Where does this new matter come from?

"With the power
and skill did We (God)
construct the Firmament.
Verily, We extend the vastness of space"

The Quran, 51:47

"And He creates
(other) things
of what ye have no knowledge"

The Quran, 16:8

1.3 The Clock and its Manufacturer

A clock with the most precise clockwork and a finely chiseled case cannot exist without the perfection and knowledge of a manufacturer.

Similarly, the processes and particularities of nature, perfected to such a degree and harmonized with one another – which is increasingly demonstrated by scientific insights and discoveries –, cannot have emerged without conscious action and extensive knowledge.

our planet

our solar system

our galaxy

galaxies in the space

Our galaxy (the Milky Way), with its diameter of 100.000 light years and its approx. 300 billion stars, reaches a dimension that is very difficult for us to imagine. In spite of its size, it is only one of the 100 billion galaxies supposed to exist in the visible Universe

The Universe: Perpetually mobile?

1.4 The Universe: Perpetually mobile?

If one considers the unimaginable size and structure of outer space, many questions come to mind: What moves the moon around the earth? What moves the earth around the sun? What moves the sun, with its solar system, around the center of the galaxy? Physicists know, and it is indisputable, that the earth moves around the sun on a fixed orbit, because there are two forces acting against each other. The first force is the gravitational force exerted by the sun, which attracts the earth from one side. The other force is the centrifugal force, which pushes the earth outwards – away from the sun –, towards outer space. The counteraction of these forces makes it possible for the earth to remain on its orbit. But is this the whole truth?

Bringing them into motion – in the right direction

Newton's first law of motion indicates that an object at rest stays at rest and an object in motion stays in motion with the same speed and in the same direction unless a force acts upon it. So, who got the moon, the earth, the sun and its entire system rolling, and gave them that initial push in the right direction? And who coordinates the gravitational and centrifugal forces and holds a balance between them?

The creation of the Universe, with its balanced system, indispensably requires a single "general planner", who must possess the following:

1. Oversight, to determine the orbits of all moons, planets, stars and galaxies, so that they do not collide with one another.
2. Comprehensible knowledge, to calculate the exact distance between the earth and the sun, so that life is possible on earth. If the gravitational force of the sun were to increase, the earth would burn up at the sun. If, on the other hand, the centrifugal force of the earth were to augment, then it would collide with other planets and freeze.

3. Enormous power, to be able to implement these calculations. The same relation of balance exists between the sun and the center of the galaxy. In millions of other galaxies, the same balance between their suns and their planets exists, in spite of their different sizes and velocities.

Harmony in the Universe
1.5 Order and Harmony in the Universe

> " *Do they not look*
> *at the sky above them?*
> *How We have made it and adorned it,*
> *and there are no fissures in it?*
> *And the earth!*
> *We have spread it out,*
> *and set thereon mountains standing firm,*
> *and produced therein*
> *every kind of beautiful growth (in pairs)*
> *– An insight and a Reminder*
> *for every slave turning*
> *(to God)."*
>
> *The Quran, 50: 6-8*

In nature we find a very complex and well harmonized order. In the Universe, everything correlates in such a wonderful fashion that a dignified environment for the harmonic structures, life and people is created. In nature we find astounding unity and harmony. Where do they come from? Natural laws and phenomena do not have intelligence themselves, and they cannot strive for a conscious goal. Therefore they do not constitute sufficient grounds for an explanation for the origin of the universe.

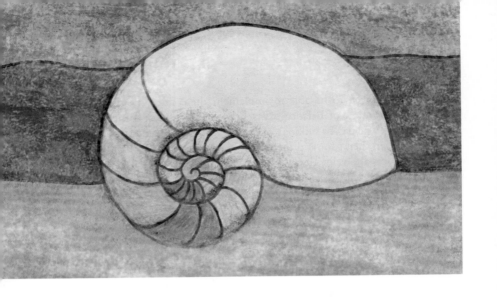

1.6 Beauty in the Universe

A child that is talented in painting, one day sits down in his room and begins to paint a landscape. After being engaged with brushes, canvas and colors for many hours, he becomes tired and walks to the door, sees the sky, the trees, the flowers, and spontaneously exclaims:

"Oh yeah, this is so much more beautiful than what I am painting and will ever paint! Who is the painter of all these things?"

How is it that birds, flowers and fish glow with such beautiful colors? The enchanting view of nature was and is often a source of revelations for many artists. If one wants to create an image of nature with its harmonic interplay of colors and forms, one may not focus on only one of the elements of the picture, for one needs an overview over the whole. Therefore, it is impossible that the beauty and harmony of nature were created by blind atoms and cells, or by chance. They all lack both intelligence and oversight. Furthermore, they do not possess a way to communicate to reach this goal.

Beauty in the Universe

2 WHERE DO MAN AND LIFE COME FROM?

Where do man and life come from?

2.1 Who Steers the Atoms?

Some people, who rejected the idea that God had created the entire Universe, asked a Muslim to set a date to have a debate about Creation. The meeting place was by a river. When they wanted to return home from the river, after vainly waiting for the Muslim, the latter showed up on a beautiful boat.

- *"Why are you so late?"*

- *"I was on the other side of the river, and didn't find a boat to cross it. But suddenly, as I was standing there, a large tree exploded, and it was divided into many small planks, it made this beautiful boat out of them, and it glided onto the water. So I got in the boat and came to you."*

- *"Excuse me. Who built this boat?"*

- *"Why do you not believe that a tree exploded into pieces and formed the boat? But you believe that something exploded in the Big Bang and that the Universe formed itself, even though it is even more beautiful and organized than a boat!"*

2.2 Infinite Knowledge **and Precision**

Imagine a huge drug store. Inside it, there are thousands of different medications which were composed by innumerable chemists in many laboratories and factories. It is clear that thousands of brains participated in these highly-technological research processes, and that countless experiments took place over the years. Medical effects had to be verified, and unwanted side-effects had to be studied. It was not until the latter was done that these drugs could be brought to the market.

Just as in this example of the drug store, the "earth laboratory" contains more than 2 million[1] different animal and plant species. Many species feature such complex and finely structured construction, that they remind us of complex synthetic chemicals. In comparison to the endless multiplicity of flora and fauna, the latter shows that enormous knowledge and great precision were required for the creation of Earth.

2.3 A System **without an Inventor?**

Let us look at our favorite toy, the computer. Invented over 60 years ago as a huge calculator that occupied an entire room, the computer eventually developed to the highly-efficient, pocket-sized PC that we know today, combined with the increased power of the

---

1 Prof. Dr. STREIT, Bruno: Biozahl 2006 – 2 Millionen-Grenze erreicht, Natur und Museum, Frankfurt am Main 2005/06, Nº 136, p. 131-134.

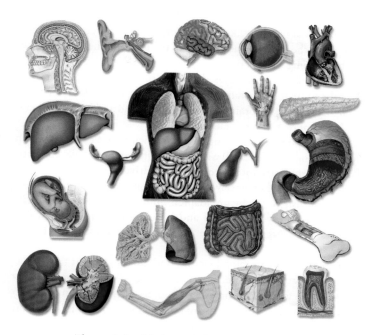

The complexity of the human body, its organs and systems

internet, fingerprint readers and Bluetooth.

This system was perfected by countless engineers and computer scientists over the decades. The idea occurred first, which then had to be materialized, tested, and always improved on.

The operating system of a computer has to be revised and re-engineered regularly by its manufacturers, in order to correct the errors of the old version. If one was to say that this system arose serendipitously, without human control and out of the blue, who would believe it?

But we know of something far more complex than the computer, with controls and functions that run without any updates or new versions: the human body.

The human brain is like the memory of a computer; the eyes correspond to the camera, and the ears to the microphone. Data reaches the brain using these ways.

As a computer translates data into bits (numerical values), so does the human body transform sound waves and images to chemical signals so that the brain can store, understand and interpret them.

Let us draw further parallels:

No component of a computer works without electricity, which flows through cables and wires with different, specific currents. These currents vary for processors, hard drives, cameras and printers – each one of them receives the corresponding kilowatt amounts, which are distributed by an adapter. Similarly, the body has a circulatory system with its small and large arteries and veins, which supplies each organ with the corresponding amount of blood.

In addition to the blood circuit, one can also look at the regulation of body temperature, which constantly lies at approximately 37° C. If the weather becomes hotter, pores open, the skin begins to sweat and thus prevents the rise of body temperature. If it is cold, on the contrary, pores contract to prevent the dissipation of heat. Who developed this system and how does it measure body temperature? And who supplied the body with the glands that prompt the pores in the skin to discharge sweat?

A computer possesses neither feelings nor senses; it lacks will, reason of its own, and an individual character. The human psyche and physique therefore allude to a builder with more extensive knowledge than a group of engineers.

> *"You can see no flaws*
> *in the creations of (God)*
> *the Most Gracious.*
> *So turn Thy vision again:*
> *Can you see any rifts?"*
>
> The Quran, 67: 3

> *"And also in your*
> *own selves.*
> *Will you not then see?"*
>
> The Quran, 51: 21

2.4 Raw Materials and Nutrients

A car cannot function with crude oil. Petroleum has to be refined through many steps in order to separate the precious raw material from secondary chemicals that can damage a car's motor.

Likewise, nutrients in the body are filtered by means of a complex digestive system; waste products are excreted, and useful items such as carbohydrates, proteins, fats, minerals, vitamins and water are broken down, distributed amongst all body parts according to their requirements, and the remaining energy is stored for future use.

The fuel indicator alerts the driver when there is not enough gas in the tank. The human body signals when it needs nourishment by means of hunger, and when it needs fluid by means of thirst. Is it possible that the fuel indicator in cars was invented, tested and developed by mechanical engineers, and that the alert functions of the body came to being without an inventor?

2.5 The Cleverly-Devised Protective System

The Cleverly-Devised Protective System

The location of each organ was chosen so that it can operate optimally and is at the same time protected. Some of them are located rather externally, while others are in the most internal parts of the body, in order to be safe from possible impacts. Thus, the heart beats enclosed in the rib cage, and the brain is surrounded by strong cranial bones.

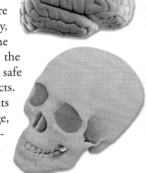

Protective cage for the heart, the lungs, and the brain

↻ Conclusion

Thus, we arrive at the clarification of the question posed at the beginning of the second subchapter: "From Where?" in regards to man. We have looked at man and his characteristics from multiple perspectives. For that purpose, examples were presented in an everyday, down-to-earth context, in order to provide the reader with an initial approach.

By comparing these miracles to human inventions, we are hoping to create a connection with items that people are accustomed to admiring.

But how much greater would the amazement and rejoicing be if people were aware of the miracle of God's creation and how it surpasses that of man!

"And how many Signs
in the heavens and the earth do they pass by?
Yet they turn away from them!"

The Quran, 12:105

"There are only two ways to live your life. One is as though nothing is a miracle. The other is as though everything is a miracle."
Albert Einstein [1]

Albert Einstein

Albert Einstein

---

1 Albert **EINSTEIN** (1879-1955), German-American physicist, founder of the theory of relativity and Nobel laureate

2.6 Pre-requisites to Life

In the following paragraphs we will seek the answer to the **"From Where"** for life, and we will ask:

What pre-requisites are needed to allow for life to be created on Earth? Could they arise by chance?

Scientists once believed that, regardless of the initial conditions of the Universe, intelligent life could emerge. However, today we know that the existence of intelligent life depends on the interaction of initial conditions, and that it must take place at a level of highest refinement.

The laws of nature are often expressed as mathematical equations, and certain constants can be derived from them (i.e. the gravitational constant). These constants are not determined by the laws of nature. However, the laws of nature are consistent with a wide range of these constants.

In addition to these constants, there are arbitrary quantities, which were established as initial conditions to enable the functioning of the laws of nature, i.e. the amount of entropy or the equilibrium between matter and anti-matter in the Universe. All these constants and quantities fall into an extraordinarily narrow range of values, necessary for the origin of life.

P.C.W. Davies

The physicist P. C. W. Davies calculated that a differnce of $1:10^{100}$ in the magnitude of the gravitational force would be enough to make life in the Universe impossible.

Roger Penrose

Roger Penrose from the University of Oxford also calculated[1] that the chances for an accidental form of existence in conditions of

---

1 cp. PENROSE, Roger: Time-Asymmetry and Quantum Gravity, in: Quantum Gravity 2, Editor C. J. Isham, R. Penrose, and D. W. Sciama, Oxford 1981, p. 249.

low entropy after the Big Bang are 1 out of 10^{10} (That's one chance in 10 with 10 zeroes.). Hence, not only must each constant and its values be finely adjusted, but their ratios to one another must also be in accord. So improbability is multiplied by improbability by improbability until our minds are reeling in incomprehensible numbers.[1]

Stephen Hawkins

The scientist Stephen Hawkins also comments on this:

"The laws of science, as we know them at present, contain many fundamental numbers, like the size of the electric charge of the electron and the ratio of the masses of the proton and the electron

[...] The remarkable fact is that the values of these numbers seem to have been finely adjusted to make the development of life possible. For example, if the electric charge of the electron had only been slightly different, stars either would have been unable to burn hydrogen and helium, or else they would not have exploded."[2]

Fred Hoyle

The astronomer and writer Fred Hoyle states that the characteristics of the elements carbon and hydrogen (on which the makeup of our body is based) suggest the conclusion that they were intentionally composed the way they are, and he infers that:

"A common sense interpretation of the facts suggests that a super intellect has monkeyed with physics, as well as with chemistry and biology, and that there are no blind forces worth speaking about in nature.

The numbers one calculates from the facts seem to me so overwhelming as to put this conclusion almost beyond question."[3]

---

1 cp. Dr. **CRAIG,** William Lane: Does God Exist?, www.leaderu.com/offices/billcraig/docs/craig-pigliucci1.html (Accessed: December 1st 2009).

2 **HAWKING,** Stephen: A Brief History of Time, New York 1988, p. 125.

3 **HOYLE,** Fred: The Universe- Past and Present Reflections. Engineering and Science, November 1981, p. 8–12.

Another example is given to us by DNA. It is a bio-molecule found in all living creatures that carries genetic information. It is also present, in its complete form, in every cell of an organism. The human genome, i.e. the entire genetic information contained in a cell, contains about 3.2 billion DNA base pairs.

Jonathan Gallagher

Jonathan Gallagher further explains: *"Just a quick look at the amazingly intricate structure of DNA gives pause for thought. When you discover that this 'double helix' design contains around 100 million twists and 100 billion atoms, and realizing that DNA is essential to life itself, it seems quite absurd to even consider the possibility that it could 'self-arrange' or come about by accident!*

In fact, the idea that DNA could have come about accidentally has been called a 'non-scientific absurdity.' [...] Even the humble bacterium is made up of some 25 million molecules — which need to be produced and organized."[1]

According to Fred Hoyle, chances against the accidental generation of DNA are of 10^{40}: 1, which corresponds to a very low probability of one chance in 10 with 40 zeroes.[2]

Chance or Calculation

2.7 Chance or **Calculation**

A. Cressy Morrison

A. Cressy Morrison, former president of the New York Academy of Sciences, argues: *"Suppose you put ten pennies, marked from one*

1 **GALLAGHER,** Jonathan: The Universe and the existence of God, URL: www.pineknoll.org/jg/45-god-in-other-words/173-jonathan-gallagher-the-universe-and-the-existence-of-god (Accessed: April 25th 2009).

2 cp.: **HOYLE,** Fred: The Universe. Past and Present Reflections, Engineering and Science, n.l. 1981. in: FERRIS, Timothy: The World Treasury of Physics, Astronomy and Mathematics, London 1991, p. 392.

to ten, into your pocket and give them a good shuffle. Now try to take them out in sequence from one to ten, putting back the coin each time and shaking them all again. Mathematically we know that your chance of first drawing number one is one in ten; of drawing one and two in succession, one in 100; of drawing one, two and three in succession, one in 1000, and so on; your chance of drawing them all, from number one to number ten in succession, would reach the unbelievable figure of one in ten billion.

By the same reasoning, so many exacting conditions are necessary for life on earth that they could not possibly exist in proper relationship by chance. The earth rotates on its axis 1000 miles an hour at the Equator; if it turned at 100 miles an hour, our days and nights would be ten times as long as they are now, and the hot sun would likely burn up our vegetation each long day, while in the long night any surviving sprout might well freeze.

Yet again, the sun, the source of our life, has a surface temperature of approx. 5500 °C degrees, and our earth is just far enough, so that the sun warms us just enough and not too much! If the sun gave off only one half of its present radiation, we would freeze, and if it gave as much more, we would roast.

The slant of the earth, tilted at an angle of 23 degrees, gives us our seasons; if the earth had not been so tilted, vapors from the ocean would move North and South, piling up continents of ice for us. If our moon were, say, only 50000 miles away instead of its actual distance, our tides might be so enormous that twice a day all continents would be submerged; even the mountains would soon be eroded away. If the crust of the earth had only been ten feet thicker, there would be no oxygen, without which animal life must die. Had the ocean been a few feet deeper, carbon dioxide and oxygen would have been absorbed and no vegetation could exist. "[1]

1 **MORRISON,** A. Cressy: Seven Reasons Why a Scientist Believes in God, URL: www.dlshq. org/messages/sciblgod.htm (Accessed: April 25th 2009).

Would we believe that a small child would always draw a sewing needle of the same color from a bag full of sewing needles of different colors, 30 times in a row, without looking? Or that he throws each needle 10 meters away, and that each needle accidentally lands in the eye of another?[1]

Was the eye created without knowledge of optics, and the ear without comprehension of sound?

And is it possible that the ability of seeing of living creatures was created by someone who could not see? Were the ears and hearing created by someone who could not hear? Or could someone who does not have a complete intelligence and a perfect perception of feelings create reason, sensory perception and feelings?

Sir Isaac Newton

In order to bring the question about chance or calculation to an end, Sir Isaac Newton[2] says:

"Whence arises this uniformity in all their outward shapes but from the counsel and contrivances of an Author? Whence is it that the eyes of all sorts of living creatures are transparent to the very bottom, and the only transparent members in the body, having on the outside a hard transparent skin, and within transparent humors, with a crystalline lens in the middle, and a pupil before the lens, all of them so finely shaped and fitted for vision, [...] Did blind chance know that there was light, and what was its refraction, and fit the eyes of all creatures, after the most curious manner, to make use of it? These, and suchlike considerations, always have, and ever will prevail with mankind, to believe that there is a Being who made all things, and has all things in his power, and who is therefore to be feared."[3]

---

1 cp. **AL-GESR**, Nadeem: Kissatul-Ieman, Tripoli, n.d., p. 291.

2 Sir Isaac **NEWTON** (1643- 1727), English philosopher, physicist and mathematician.

3 cp.: **BREWSTER**, D.: Life of Sir Isaac Newton, London 1831, Vol. II, p. 347-348.

⟳ Conclusion

Discoveries in different fields of physics and astrophysics, classic cosmology, quantum mechanics and biochemistry consistently show that the existence of intelligent life on earth, which is carbon-based, depends on a very fine balance of physiologic and cosmologic magnitudes. The slightest alteration would destroy this equilibrium, and life could no longer exist.[1]

Apart from the origin of life, in order to produce the right conditions for the existence of the Universe, everything had to be balanced and adjusted from the moment of its formation. The only reasonable conclusion from this is that creation came about intentionally.[2]

"It is He who hath created for you
all things that are on earth"

The Quran, 2: 29

"Yet there are among men
those who dispute about God,
without knowledge and without guidance,
and without a Book
to enlighten them!"

The Quran, 31: 20

1 cp. Dr. **Craig,** William L.: The Teleological Argument and the Anthropic Principle, URL: www.conservapedia.com/Evidence_for_intelligent_design_in_cosmology (Accessed: November 21st 2009).

2 cp. **Gallagher,** Jonathan: The Universe and the existence of God, URL: www.pineknoll. org/jg/45-god-in-other-words/173-jonathan-gallagher-the-universe-and-the-existence-of-god (Accessed: November 21st 2009).

2.8 Evolution **or Creation?**

In the course of our explanations about Creation we cannot possibly leave out Darwin's theory of evolution.

Nonetheless, this should not be about emphasizing the importance of his observations and his theory, but rather making some of their less noted elements to our focal point. Because they have been ignored for years, the general idea has been established that Darwin was an atheist who wanted to replace God with the theory of evolution.

Darwin

- The theory of evolution describes the development of living creatures, but it does not occupy itself with the question about the origin of the world and the Universe.
- Darwin did not find an explanation for that which gave the spark of life to the earth, made out of mere lifeless matter, and of why life in the Universe is so extremely rare.
- The theory of evolution explains the development of species as a result of natural selection. It was not until after Darwin that modern genetic research discovered that it is only through alterations in the DNA of a living creature that changes in the following generations can occur.

Today we also know that the human genome, i.e. the total extent of our DNA, comprises approximately 3.2 billion DNA base pairs. DNA does not only contain the information about the differences between species, but it also determines the character and the qualities of the living creature. In order to develop the countless genetic information of DNA in its complexity, the following is necessary:

1. Comprehensive overview of the governing environmental conditions of each living creature, in order to have sensibility for necessary changes.

2. In order to make these necessary changes, creative thought is required, as well as the competence to filter the finely-adjusted and most advantageous solution out of all the possible ones.

3. The newly found design must be, from the very first moment, so perfect and adapted to the new environment that it does not require any further modifications.

4. Finally, one must know the point on the DNA strand where the change has to be made. A little mistake can lead to body deformities.
   Neither the accidentally occurring evolution factors[1] nor the

---

1 Today, scientists speak of four basic evolution factors, which lead to the change and development of a living creature. These four evolution factors are in actuality, as one can clearly see, nothing more than accidental events and circumstances:

1. Mutations: They occur by chance. By means of a mutation, the information comprised in DNA is altered. Single genes or entire chromosomes may be affected. Even though the mutation rate, regarded for a single gene, is relatively low, it is considerable if one takes into account the entirety of genes in a population.

2. Genetic recombination: It is a process through which paternal and maternal chromosomes are haphazardly distributed, which leads to new gene combinations and genetic diversity.

3. Selection factors: These are environmental influences that affect the reproduction rate of different individuals in different ways, for instance cold, predators, etiologic agents and preys. These environmental factors also occur accidentally.

4. Genetic drift: Defined as "the change in the genetic pool of a population due to chance" cp. Lara, B.: Evolutionsfaktoren, ULR: www.webmic.de/evolutionsfaktoren.htm, home.arcor.de/paflitschek/ppt/Selektion_und_Gendrift.ppt (Accessed: May 9th 2009)).

living creatures themselves possess the required knowledge, precision and consciousness to carry out countless DNA modifications so successfully for each and every living creature throughout the ages. It requires even higher capabilities than the construction of a computer-driven robot.

Can an analphabet decipher the DNA of a person (see figure DNA) and for instance recognize and change the information of one's eye color?

In spite of his human intelligence and his sense of beauty, he is not able to do so.

Chance cannot do all of this, either.

The structure of a section of a DNA. 20 bases lie horizontally between the two spiralling strands.

2.8.1. The Theory of Evolution and God?

The theory of evolution is no substitute for God's Creation, but it is an explanation for the Laws of God that prevail in nature. In other words: it does not explain how species evolve, but rather it describes the system of laws God applied in developing these species. Intelligent design[1] described herewith points to the fact that the laws of nature created by God do not function by themselves, because they are dependent upon God's knowledge and God's intention. The evolution of successive "versions" of species is a description of the fact that God invents a new and creative design for his creatures in each environment.

Equus
2 million - today

Pliohippus
5-2 million years ago

Merychippus
25-20 million years ago

Mesohippus
35-30 million years ago

Hyracotherium
50 million years ago

The evolution of the horse: a work of art in each version

Instead of simply being in awe at God's creativity in designing and creating millions of living creatures and plants, the theory of evolution explains that God continuously shows His creativity by designing and crafting different "versions" of each such species.

---

1 At this point, one must address the possible confusion of the term "intelligent design" with the so-called "intelligent design movement" as a form of creationism, from which this book wishes to separate itself. Creationists deny the theory of evolution, which is clearly affirmed here, and which does not contradict the Islamic theology of Creation. Hence, creationists also have a different explanation and concept of Creation itself. Intelligent design only takes place within the framework of Islamic belief.

2.8.2 What Did **Darwin Believe In?**

Darwin never saw his theory as a replacement for God.
His opinion remained that God was the absolute lawmaker of nature[1], and in the year 1879 (three years before his death) he even stressed that he was never an atheist, and that he had never denied the existence of God.[2]

He opened his most significant work "On the Origin of Species" with a quote by Francis Bacon, through which he implied that the contemplation of nature shall lead to God: *"To conclude, therefore, let no man out of a weak conceit of sobriety, or an ill-applied moderation, think or maintain, that a man can search too far or be too well studied in the book of God's word, or in the book of God's works; divinity or philosophy; but rather let men endeavor an endless progress or proficiency in both."*[3]

In spite of the accusation from Church leaders that he was an atheist, Darwin said: *"When I wrote 'The Origin of Species', my belief in God was stronger than that of a bishop."*[4]

He explains that the belief in God does not contradict natural causes, if one understands God as the initiator of them:

"We can explain how nature produced these adaptations to the environment. We can explain how the beauty of a butterfly is useful to that butterfly in pursuing its way of life. I can come up with causes for this and it's up to you to believe that God created these things through these causes or not."[5]

---

1 von **Sydow,** Momme: Darwin – A Christian Undermining Christianity? On Self-Undermining Dynamics of Ideas Between Belief and Science, Burlington 2005, p. 146-151.

2 Anonymous: Belief. Historical essay, What did Darwin believe? URL: www.darwinproject.ac.uk/content/view/130/125/. (Accessed: May 9th 2009).

3 cp. **Darwin,** Charles: On The Origin Of The Species, London 1859.

4 **Moore,** James: Evolution and Wonder - Understanding Charles Darwin. Speaking of Faith (2006) in: American Public Media (Series), URL: http://speakingoffaith.publicradio.org/programs/darwin/transcript.shtml (Accessed: April 25th 2009).

5 cp. idem

2.9 Deep Knowledge **Leads to God**

*"And those
who have been given knowledge
see that what is revealed to you (O Muhammad)
from your Lord is the truth,
and guides to the Path of the Exalted in Might,
Owner of all praise."*

The Quran, 34: 6

Francis Bacon[1], a philosopher in the 16th century, established:
"A little philosophy inclineth man's mind to atheism, but depth in philosophy bringeth men's minds about to religion."[2]

---

1 Francis **Bacon** (1561-1626), English philosopher, scientist and statesman.

2 **Bacon,** Sir Francis: The Essays: Of Atheism, URL: http://bacon.thefreelibrary.com/The-Essays/16-1 (Accessed: December 17th 2009).

Werner Heisenberg

The physicist Werner Heisenberg[1] also stated four centuries later:
"The first sip from the cup of natural science makes one an atheist, but at the bottom of the cup, God awaits."

Wernher von Braun

The belief in the existence of God becomes larger the more our insight into our complex universe - drafted with great detail - our earth and our humanity grows.[2] Therefore, high-ranking scientists do not doubt this belief, and they freely say, like Wernher von Braun[3]:
"I find it difficult to understand a scientist who does not acknowledge the presence of a superior rationality behind the existence of the universe."[4]

Albert Einstein

Thus, Albert Einstein, known as a natural scientific genius, manifested:
"The common idea, that I would be an atheist, is based on a great error,"

Lord Kelvin

and Lord Kelvin[5] acknowledged that:
"The more thoroughly I conduct scientific research, the more I believe that science excludes atheism."[6]

1 Werner **Heisenberg** (1901-1976), German physicist and Nobel laureate.

2 cp. **Gallagher,** Jonathan: The Universe and the existence of God, URL: www.pineknoll.org/jg/45-god-in-other-words/173-jonathan-gallagher-the-universe-and-the-existence-of-god (Accessed: April 25th 2009).

3 Wernher von **Braun** (1912-1977) German-American missile inventor.

4 von **Braun,** Wernher: My Faith, American Weekly, February 10, 1963.

5 William **Thomson** (later Lord Kelvin) (1824 – 1907) British physicist and one of the most famous scientists of the second half of the 19th century.

6 **Thompson,** S. P.: The Life of William Thomson. Baron Kelvin of Largs, London 1859, p. 604-605.

3 THERE IS ONLY ONE GOD

There is only one God

3.1 Harmony in the Overall Picture

It is a fact that the Universe was created with precision and harmony between all its elements, all from one piece and thus all from one source. If it were not so, there would be no harmony, regularity and unity in the Universe. Let us imagine that ten artists, from the most diverse genres and with different painting and drawing methods, are all asked to draw on the same single canvas. Each one of them paints only on one tenth of the canvas, and can freely choose his subject-matter and his way of portraying it. How chaotic would the overall painting be?

The uniform creative style, which extends throughout the entire Universe, from atoms to galaxies, points to one and the very same creative Maker.

All creatures are built out of atoms. All living creatures are composed of cells. All planets, stars and galaxies have round or elliptic orbits.

3.2 The Chain of Interdependencies

The different elements and parts of creation are linked to one another, and they depend on one another – for instance, man needs animals, animals need plants, and plants need the sun and the air. We need the sun and the moon with their gravitational forces just as much as we need water to flow, which depends on many factors such as the structure of water and the soil, and the warmth

of the sun in relation to its distance from the earth. Planets need the gravitational force of the sun in order to remain in their orbits, and the sun equally needs the center of the galaxy, and so on.

Chain of dependencies

Each item is linked to the other, and is dependent on it, so that it would be inconceivable to think that the different parts of the Universe could have emerged from different sources.

Independent Power

3.3 Independent Power and Knowledge

The creator that could craft a galaxy must possess almighty power and endless knowledge, and thus He is completely independent of any kind of help from other possible supplementary deities.

In ancient times, some people believed that the sun was the greatest form of existence in the Universe.
Thus, they made it into a deity, and they worshipped it.

Nowadays we know that the sun is only a little star amongst billions of stars in the Universe.

3.4 One Center **and One Boss**

One Center and One Boss

The entire system of the Universe is constructed on the principle of one single boss and one single center, and it is based on an inner unity. Thus, each atom has a nucleus, each cell has a nucleus, and each galaxy has a center. If this relation is disrupted, these systems collapse into chaos, and they can even stop functioning. If all the single parts of the Universe are based on the principle of oneness, then how could the Universe have two Gods?

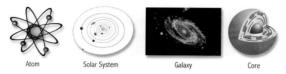

| Atom | Solar System | Galaxy | Core |

Everything is constructed on the principle of oneness

It is inconceivable that billions of atoms would build such a highly complex construct as the human body, if each atom moved according to its own perspective.

3.5 A Soccer **Team with no Coach**

A Soccer Team with no Coach

In order to guarantee the best game course to the eleven players of a soccer team, an experienced and committed coach is required. He trains, challenges and helps the players improve, devises new tactics and coordinates the team. If there was another coach in charge -who gave directions during the game course with equal authority- the game strategy, the movements and the actions of the players could no longer be in sync with one another. One can imagine the sort of defeat that the team would suffer, if, in addition, each and every player moved according to his own tactics and his own will.

A winning and high-scoring game would no longer be possible.

3.6 The Conductor's Baton

The Conductors 's Baton

An orchestra is composed of many musicians with different instruments. Their eyes are solely directed towards the conductor during a concert.

In addition to his interpretation, the conductor's role is mainly to develop the work with the musicians before their concert. He coordinates and provides them with the beat, so that a harmonic ensemble can be created.

What a disharmonious tumult would it be, if two conductors were to act at the same time in an orchestra!

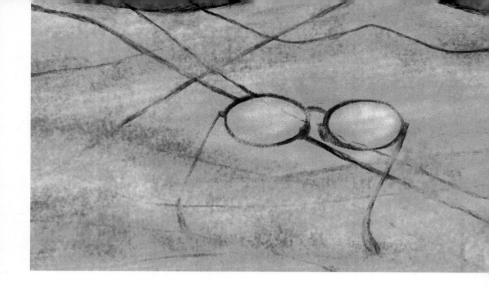

3.7 A Question of Boundaries

Albert Einstein

"When I sit engrossed in my calculations and watch a tiny insect landing on my paper, I feel like; Allah is great and we with all our scientific majesty remain helpless minuscule droplets."[1] Albert Einstein

If there is a God, then why do we not see him?

At this point, we will address one of the most frequently asked questions in religion.

If we are clear that some galaxies, as well as the smallest components of nature (atoms), are invisible to the naked eye or auxiliary means such as telescopes and microscopes, then it should also be understandable that we cannot see their Maker.

To expect man to perceive God comes close to the idea of

---

1 Albert **Einstein** quoted in German by: Prof. Dr. **Jaspers**, Karl: video recording, www.youtube.com/watch?v=pRCMQ3myf_w (Accessed: February 10th 2011). (Note: the Islamic word for God "Allah" was chosen and used in this quotation by Einstein himself).

expecting an ant to understand human circulation or the Pythagorean Theorem.

Ants were given sufficient perception and instinct to cope with their existence.

But the difference between God and man is much larger than the one this comparison between man and an ant allows us to presume[1].

Consequently, in spite of all our knowledge, we only have a very limited concept of Him, His knowledge and His wisdom.

Science can only examine things within our existing Universe and attempt to explain them. We cannot regard God as though He were subject to our own limitations, for it was Him who established these boundaries.

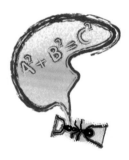

---

1 cp. **AL-GESR**, Nadeem: Kissatul-Ieman, Tripoli, n.d., p. 207.

We were born, and we will die.
We do not decide to live, and we cannot decide
what will happen to us afterwards.

Chapter 2

To Where...?
Life in the Hereafter

*"The sheer volume of evidence
for survival after death is so immense
that to ignore it is like standing
at the foot of Mount Everest and insisting that you cannot
see the mountain."*
Colin Wilson

1 THE LOGIC OF THE HEART

In our daily lives, we are used to seeking a reason for everything; why something happened in one way or another. Why should we remove ourselves from this natural logic when it comes to pondering where we came from and where we are going? Here, and especially here, there must also be a reason that can satisfy our rationality!

> *"I do admonish you on one (thing):*
> *that you do stand up before God in pairs,*
> *or singly – and reflect (within yourselves)"*
>
> The Quran, 34: 46

1.1 Concern with Man's Needs

From life's first moment, even as an embryo, man is protected from any kind of harmful substances in the womb by a fine shell, and at the same time he is provided with the necessary nutrients by means of the umbilical cord. When he is born as a small, defenseless creature, he finds the hearts of his parents full of love, and thus they provide for him and attend to all his needs.

God's preoccupation with the satisfaction of even the smallest of man's needs is also clearly recognizable in the way his body is built.

As an example, He created a small gland, not larger than a centimeter, in the middle of the brain for him. This gland, the pineal gland, produces the hormone melatonin[1] at night, in order to improve the quality of sleep and to avoid sleep disorders.

God's wish to fulfill man's needs goes so far that He gave man special characteristics that are secondary to the struggle for survival and the conservation of the species.

For instance, in order to beautify and individualize his appearance, God gave man external characteristics such as hair, nails, eyelashes and eyebrows, thin or thick lips, light or dark skin. Some of them have a positive effect on man's emotional state, since they allow him to modify himself according to his taste.

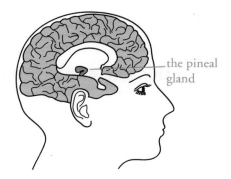

The pineal gland

Would it be logical for a king to build a large, magnificent castle, equipped with a cleverly-designed pipe system, a strategic defense system, and filled with many valuables, to pay attention to every architectural detail, and then forget about the roof, so that during the first storm this work of art is completely destroyed?

---

1 Melatonin is a hormone produced in the pineal gland especially known for regulating sleep. It brings mind and body to the right rhythm, and it participates in the regulation of many other hormones. Scientists point to a protective function of melatonin; it acts against the development of diverse diseases, such as cancer or arteriosclerosis. Low melatonin levels were found in women with breast cancer, and in men with prostate cancer. This hormone is not only found in humans, but also in almost all animals and many plants. During the nighttime hours, the pineal gland slowly begins the production of melatonin, and it reaches its production peak between 2:00 and 4:00 a.m. During the day, it stops production. The duration of daily melatonin secretion is directly proportional to the length of the night. The ability of the pineal gland to recognize light has led to it being called "the third eye". cp.: ZVEREV, A.: Melatonin. 2005, URL: www.egbeck.de/melatde.htm, (Accessed: April 25th 2009).

Accordingly, would it be possible for God to equip man with fine capillaries, organs, an immune system and feelings, to perfect him, to beautify him, and then leave this living work of art to melt like an ice sculpture? No. Instead, God guarantees the preservation of man by taking him to another life in the Afterlife. He thus gave His human work of art a roof, which stands here as a metaphor for Paradise.

1.2 Needs in this Life and in the Afterlife

Here we will assume that human needs can be divided into two categories:
1. The bodily, physical needs that reside in this world.
2. The spiritual needs, which correspond to both this life and the afterlife.

If one takes a closer look at man, one recognizes that the satisfaction of the physical needs of a healthy person is balanced out by the creation of organs and bodily alarm signals.

The different organs and systems function so that they correspond, in amount and in type, to the requirements of the body. Examples of the latter are the creation of different proteins and hormones, or the secretion of glands.

The secreted amount and the type of signal produced by these secretions also correspond to particular requirements, i.e. those signals sent by the brain for hunger, cold or pain. The feeling of hunger expands from a little hunger over a growling stomach to severe hunger pain. Cold sensation varies in gradual levels according to how much warmth is required for the body at that point: from a mild shiver over trembling to strongly freezing.

Sexual drive, maternity and the wish to have children are also part of those physical needs, and they all serve the realization of human reproduction.

In addition to these needs, man was given needs whose satisfaction goes beyond the limits of this life, i.e. wishes, hopes, and the longing for eternal life and eternal bliss.

This observation brings to mind the following questions:

1. If all alarm signals in our bodies were created with a specific purpose, how could spiritual needs emerge with no purpose and remain unfulfilled?
2. If God is concerned with even our smallest physical needs, how could He fail to fulfill the longing for eternal life?
3. If everything in our bodies has a function, how could man exist without divine intention?

If everything in our bodies has a function, how could man exist without Divine Intention?

1.3 Longing for **Immortality**

Longing for Immortality

Man is the only living creature aware of the limited nature of his life. The desire for immortality is at least as old as human civilization. In some of the most ancient cultures, people buried their dead with objects to prepare them for the afterlife.

Different peoples and cultures had different burial rites, but they all reflected a belief in an existence beyond death. One can thus rightly conclude that this belief is intimately linked to man's nature, and that there are actual reasons for it.

The fact that today many people find it easy to accept a complete extinction of life after death is based on the fact that they avoid thinking about it, rather than it being drawn from a deep conviction.

Norman V. Peale

Norman V. Peale accurately says in this regard: *"In fact, the instinctive feeling of the existence of another world after death is one of the strongest evidences of this existence. If God wants to convince people of something, He implants conviction of it in their hearts. Furthermore, the longing for an eternal life is a common feeling among people that cannot be taken lightly. Great truths like this cannot be accepted by way of proof or material confirmation, but through belief, inspiration and personal feeling. Inspiration is itself an important factor in the understanding of truth."*[1]

1.4 Unlimited Human Capabilities
Unlimited Human Capabilities

Man was given unlimited spiritual capabilities: zeal and ambition, fantasy and imagination that goes beyond the known material world, the ability to empathize, to give and receive love, the deep longing for eternal life and the strong desire for unyielding bliss.

This short life is not enough to experience and utilize all of man's unlimited spiritual capabilities and intellectual activities. They expand far beyond the dimension of this finite world, and they exceed the earthly boundaries of the senses.

They qualify man for life in the Afterlife, and they point to it. Only with eternal life, in Paradise, can they be utilized and fulfilled. Because man was made unique and extraordinary through these characteristics, which expand far beyond those of other living creatures, his future aptitude will not be disregarded, and his life will not be extinguished.

---

1 PEALE, Norman Vincent: Beyond Death There Is Life, Reader's Digest, October 1957; Vol. 71, N°. 426

> " *Did* you then think
> that We had created you in play,
> and that you would not be
> brought back to Us (for account)?"
>
> *The Quran, 23: 115*

> *"Does man think
> that he will be left Suda (neglected)?"*
>
> *The Quran, 75: 36*

1.5 Eternal **Effect**

The entire world is like a mirror that reflects divine characteristics to us such as mercy, generosity, and providence. These eternal attributes cannot be fully presented to man in this short life. Therefore, they require a corresponding eternal life, where they can continue to be bestowed upon man.

1.6 The **Art Exhibit**

The generosity and beauty that we can perceive in the nature that surrounds us point to an equivalent perfection of similar, or maybe even more beautiful works that lie beyond our cognition.

An art lover who visits an art show notices relatively quickly if the works therein were made by a skillful artist: he notices it in the sum of aesthetics, technical implementation, function and intention.

If an art lover is asked, at the end of the exhibit, what his expectations are for future works from this, he will say: from such an artist we can only anxiously await his succeeding works.

1.7 Divine **Justice** *Divine Justice*

Because God is just, an afterlife must exist.
There are wrongdoers whose unjust behavior is never punished, and their victims spend their entire lives searching for the person responsible for the injustice done unto them.

Let us imagine that a person has killed a thousand innocents in a horrendous way, and that he destroyed the lives of many other people because of it. However, he enjoyed prosperity and led a comfortable life.

To exonerate such a person is merciful to the murderer, but, at the same time, it is a great injustice towards the thousands killed and their loved ones.

On the day of Resurrection, God will let justice befall those who escaped their punishment on Earth, as well as those whose suffering was not avenged.

> " *Think not
> that God is unaware
> of that
> which the wrong-doers are doing.
> He but gives them
> respite against up
> to a Day
> when the eyes will fixedly stare*"
>
> The Quran, 14: 42

A state without such a system of justice and punishment would sooner or later collapse into chaos.

1.8 A Theater Play

To imagine this life with all its events without the Day of Resurrection is like imagining a play composed of two acts, missing the last one.

In the first act, the scene presented captured the audience: a villain who does much wrong, a hero who opposes him, and many more subplots with exciting scenes that require continuation after the intermission.

The director has carefully orchestrated all scenes and their plots, every little detail regarding the stage setting and the costumes are arranged to make a perfect production.

Such an act suggests that the director is so competent, that he was able to create suspense, which draws the audience in to the second act. Consequently, they expect the completion of the story in the last act. It is inconceivable that the curtain would not be drawn for a second act.

1.9 Winter Will Be **Followed by Spring**

Winter will be followed by Spring

When winter approaches, the majestic creatures of spring and summer are locked away in a divine treasure chest, and the sleeping earth is covered by snow as though it were a shroud.

The beautiful trees of spring now stand leafless and resemble lifeless skeletons. For months, they wait in this sad pose for the next spring to come, then they begin to awaken, come back to life, and they are newly dressed in fresh, green leaves. The seeds, which slept throughout the entire winter in the Earth, are also summoned back to life in the next spring. Like the seed that now germinates, so is man awoken to a new life after a long sleep in his grave.

He gives life to the Earth

> " *Then contemplate (O man!)*
> *To the symbols of God's! – how*
> *He gives life to the earth after its death:*
> *verily the Same shall indeed*
> *raise the dead,*
> *and He has power*
> *over all things.*"
>
> The Quran, 30: 50

1.10 The Honorable **Promise**

God has made a Promise to man thousands of times through His Prophets over thousands of years; He has promised to give man eternal bliss if he believes in Him and accepts His Prophets' messages. God does not break His Promise, for that would contradict His characteristic of perfection.

To extinguish man would be betrayal and deceit.

2 LOGIC AND SCIENCE

Logic and Science

2.1 The Invisible

"It gives me a deep comforting sense that 'things seen are temporal and things unseen are eternal'."
Helen Keller [1]

If we cannot see something, does it mean that it does not exist? Even if we cannot see in this earthly life the afterlife that awaits the dead, such as Paradise (Janna) or Hell (Jahannam), it does not mean that these things do not really exist.

In science, we are also confronted with the invisible: scientific studies and calculations over the past 20 years have shown that the truly visible part of the Universe is only 4% of it. The vast majority of 96% remains, in spite of modern technology, invisible. The latter is composed of the so-called dark matter and dark energy, which neither emit nor reflect light.[2]

And even on earth we find traces of invisible processes: after the huge wave of the tsunami in Asia at the end of 2004, which destroyed up to 3 kilometers deep into the Yala National Park in Sri Lanka, approximately 200 human bodies were found in the park, but no animal corpses. Animals seem to have mysteriously sensed the catastrophe, and therefore escaped it.

---

1 Helen Keller (1880 – 1968) was an American writer and the first deaf-blind person to obtain a B.A.

2 MINKEL L, J.R.: Mystery of Galaxies Full of Dark Matter Solved, Scientific American, Edition from February 16th 2007.

People died, animals survived

H.D. Ratnayake

"*There are no dead elephants, not even a dead hare or a dead rabbit*", said H.D. Ratnayake, vice-director of the environmental authorities of Sri Lanka.[1] Lately, odd behaviors have also been increasingly registered in captive animals (i.e. flight behavior), which remain a mystery to the scientists working there. Stories about dogs barking hysterically and panicking grazing livestock before an earthquake are also numerous.[2] Therefore, are there events or things before natural catastrophes that only animals perceive? Prophet Muhammad explained that animals can hear and see some things that come from the unseen world.

The Prophet said: "*If you hear the howling of dogs or the yelling of a donkey at night, then say Na-Uu-tho billah (We take refuge in Allah), for animals can see what you cannot.*"[3]

---

1 Anonymous: Wussten Tiere von dem Tsunami? URL: www.china-intern.de/page/wissenschaft-neue/1104343167.html (Accessed: April 25th 2009).

2 Anonymous: Erdbeben, URL: www.schlauweb.de/Erdbeben (Accessed: Oct. 15th 2010).

3 **ABO DAWOOD:** Assunan, Hadith Nº: 4439, **IBN HANBAL**, Ahmad: Al-Musnad, Hadith Nº: 13765, **ABDURRAZZAQ**: Al-Musannaf, Hadith Nº: 19872, **IBN-HIBBAN**: Assahih, Hadith Nº: 5609.

It is surely difficult to consider and understand the events of the afterlife, such as the resurrection, or Janna (Paradise) and Jahannam (Hell) according to our known physical measures and criteria. But if we can already establish that completely different rules apply to some parts of our universe, such as black holes, is it not conceivable that the standards in the afterlife are completely different, and that we do not know and cannot even imagine them on earth?

A black hole

The latest findings about black holes in the Universe turn our conception of measures and physics upside down: some scientists hypothesize that time can stop and even elapse backwards in black holes, because the space and time continuums coincide in them[1].

Carl Friedrich Gauss

Carl Friedrich Gauss[2] explains the following about the limits of science:

"That, in addition to this material world, a second, purely spiritual world order with equal multiplicities as the one in which we live exists,

1 **Travis**, John: Could a Pair of Cosmic Strings Open a Route Into the Past? Science Magazine, 04/10/1992, N° 256, p. 179-180.

2 Carl Friedrich Gauss (1777 – 1855), German mathematician, astronomer, geodesist and physicist. He greatly contributed to pure mathematics and established important practical laws for astronomy, geodesy and electromagnetism in the 20th century.

is strongly supported – of it we shall one day partake. There are questions on whose answers I would lay endlessly higher value than those of mathematics, for instance about ethics, about our relation to God, about our purpose and our future. There is, for the soul, a satisfaction of a higher kind, and for it I do not need the material. "[1]

2.2 Certainty about **Non-Existence?**

It is normally much easier to prove the existence of something if one has one single piece of evidence for it, than it is to prove its non-existence. This also applies for Janna (Paradise) and Jahannam (Hell): while it is impossible to prove they don't exist with our methods (without looking in every single galaxy known to us), their existence is guaranteed by God's message. Therefore, there is one piece of evidence for their existence against nothing for their non-existence.

There are two anecdotes about man's attempt to find God and Paradise: The Quran tells us about a pharaoh who built a high tower to look for Moses' God in the skies. Although we now understand that man's knowledge of the universe at that time was very limited, it is not much different from the case of former Soviet president Khrushchev, who instructed his cosmonaut Juri Gagarin to keep an eye out for Paradise during his space flight around the Earth in 1961.

2.3 Who Wins **and Who Loses?**

A Muslim has accepted the Message of God and is glad to belong to those who will be allowed to enter Paradise and saved from Hell. Let us picture two people: one is this Muslim, and the other one is a

---

1 **EINIGER,** Christoph: Die schönsten Gebete der Menschheit, München 1964, p. 201.

non-Muslim. Both have died. Who wins and who loses?

In the case where there is no paradise and no hell after death, neither one of them is a winner or a loser. But if Paradise and Hell do exist, the Muslim wins eternal blissful life, and the non-Muslim loses, for he will suffer eternal pain in Hell.

The Muslim can win and cannot lose. The non-Muslim cannot win and can lose. In addition to this win in the afterlife, the Muslim will also enjoy spiritual tranquility, bliss and contentment in this life.

2.4 What Does Death Mean?

2.4.1 Body and Soul

"Dust you are, and to dust you will return, was not spoken of the soul."
H.W. Longfellow

How can it be that a dead person, whose corpse was burnt and whose ashes were scattered, is not extinguished, but rather continues to exist, enjoying and suffering in spirit?

That which was burnt or decomposed was the body, which, after the soul had abandoned it, died. The soul is the secret to and the basis of life, and the material body is only its external, finite covering. Eyes and ears are only tools; however, sight and hearing, like all other senses and our personality, belong to the soul, and they are independent from the preservation of the body. Therefore, one can see, hear, feel and think after death, and thus one can continue to enjoy or to suffer. On the Day of Resurrection, the body will be rebuilt and rejoined with the soul. Thus, man can spend his eternal life with his body and his soul. Eternity exists beyond time, and this is why neither aging processes nor illness nor death exist in the afterlife.

2.4.2 Further **Thoughts** *Further Thoughts*

The topic handled here about the existence of the soul after death raises, after intensive preoccupation with it, the following continuing thoughts, which shall not be expanded on in this framework, but mentioned:

- Up until today, it has been impossible to construct life out of artificial components.
- Since the soul is not a product of physical processes in nature, it is not decomposed after death by physical processes.
- Since man is composed of both soul and body, the body of matter, and matter – as physics demonstrates – is not destroyed but only transformed, how could the soul be destroyed, even though it is not subject to the laws of matter and environmental conditions?
- Man can lose his consciousness by means of sleep, fainting and narcosis. Nonetheless, most times he wakes up with the same personality traits, memories and preferences. They do not stem from the body, even though the brain has specific areas responsible for thought and memories. The French philosopher Bergson said: *"The brain is the call-center between the body and something else*[(1)]*."*
- While we sleep, our bodies become inactive, and the soul becomes strong and active, for the effect of the body's restraint on the soul becomes weaker. And because the soul becomes active, we can have meaningful, enigmatic dreams. It happens all the time, all over the world, that people see the dead in their dreams, who tell them about future events, which take place exactly as they were foretold by them.
- As sleep does not abate the soul, only the body, the death of the body will neither weaken nor destroy the soul.

---

1 Henri Bergson (1859 – 1941), French philosopher, professor at the Collège de France and politician, who, after World War 1, also worked in the field of international relations.

- There are times when one is in a situation in which one forgets one's physical concerns or pain because of the strong spiritual bliss or sadness that one is experiencing. The latter suggests that psyche is stronger than physique.
- "I" stands for the soul, not for the body. The soul contains one's life within it, and it is the bearer of one's personality.
- A guest began screaming in the middle of the night. His host heard him and woke him up from his nightmare. The next day, during breakfast, the troubled host wanted to know why his friend had been screaming. The latter told him that, in his dream, someone was beating him with a stick so badly that he believed he was actually experiencing the pain.

This situation brings to mind many questions:

1. What would have happened if he would not have been able to wake up from his dream, or if he did not have a body to return to anymore?
2. If we can experience suffering and pain while asleep, how can we be sure that we could not experience something similar or maybe even worse in death, when we only know so little about the afterlife and its measures?
3. Can it be proved that people, after they die, could not have similar experiences?

Medicine and science do not know exactly what death is, or what happens in the transition between life and death. The soul, the essence of life, remains, in spite of scientific advances, enigmatic and unexplored.

Albert Einstein

"Do you remember how electrical currents and 'unseen waves' were laughed at? The knowledge about man is still in its infancy."
Albert Einstein

2.4.3 'Different Thinkers' Views About Death

Vladimir Nabokov
"Life is a great surprise. I do not see why death should not be an even greater one." - *Vladimir Nabokov*

Joseph H. Miller
"Life is a journey to death and death is a passport to life."- *Joseph H. Miller*

Davis Searls
"Seeing death as the end of life is like seeing the horizon as the end of the ocean." - *David Searls*

Benjamin Franklin
"A man is not completely born until he is dead." - *Benjamin Franklin*

Stephen Levine

"Death is just a change in lifestyles." - Stephen Levine

Tom Stoppard

"Every exit is an entry to somewhere else." - Tom Stoppard

Helen Keller

"Death is no more than passing from one room into another. But there's a difference for me, you know. Because in that other room I shall be able to see." - Helen Keller

Elisabeth Kübler-Ross

"Death is simply a shedding of the physical body like the butterfly shedding its cocoon. It is a transition to a higher state of consciousness where you continue to perceive, to understand, to laugh, and to be able to grow." - Elisabeth Kübler-Ross

2.5 The Soul in the Eyes of Research

In the past century, a very important and essential fact has been brought to light as a result of the efforts of scientific research to obtain more knowledge about the soul. This fact is that every living creature, human or animal, has an immaterial body, called ethereal or astral.

Moris Sharbel

According to Moris Sharbel: *"Modern science has accepted the idea that the human body is bound to something invisible. [...] A normal human being is understood as a body that disposes of an ephemeral soul. But the truth is that the human being is composed of a soul that disposes of an ephemeral body."*[1]

---

1 SHARBEL, Moris: Das Jenseits unter Wissenschaftlichem Licht, n.l., 1998, p. 176.

Baron Reichenbach.

In the early 1860s, Baron Reichenbach[1] was occupied with experiments about the radiation of living bodies. For this purpose, he invited especially sensible people to his castle, who could see a glowing liquid, in the form of halos, around living bodies in complete darkness. He called this glowing liquid "Od". This designation means in Sanskrit: *"Thing that penetrates it all"*. Such halos were neither smoke nor fume. They were reddish on the left side and bluish on the right side of the body.

Baron Reichenbach

Mac Dougall

Later, the American psychologist MacDougall[2] established that the astral body exists and stated: *"The expressions 'astral body' or 'spiritual body' should be preferably used for the unconscious'."*

Dr. Gérard Encausse

His contemporary Dr. Gérard Encausse[3] also explained that he was convinced of the survival of man beyond death.

1 Baron Dr. Karl Ludwig von **Reichenbach** (1788 – 1869) discovered in 1830 paraffin and in 1832 creosote, an antiseptic mixture of phenols. He was a pioneer in psychological research, and he coined the term "Od."

2 Dr. Duncan **MacDougall** (1866 – 1920) was a medical doctor and a psychologist.

3 The physician Gérard **Encausse** (1865 – 1916), also known as "Papus", was the director of the Charité in Paris and author of books on hypnosis and occultism such as Le Tarnt des Bohemiens. He was born in 1865 in Spain, studied surgery and had many different scientific interests, as well as in the world of the extrasensory and the occult. He was also a member of the Theosophical Society in Paris. He died in 1916 in Paris from an infection.

Dr. H.B. James

In the year 1923, the English physician Dr. H.B. James conducted experiments to measure the weight of the body of dead people. It was thereby established that 90 minutes after death occurs, a spontaneous weight loss of 15-19 percent of a milligram takes place.

André Maurois

These experiments were also observed by his friend André Maurois[1] Under a bell jar, Dr. James discovered that, at the time of the weight loss, matter wafted away, which could be seen by means of ultraviolet light in darkness. It was a glowing, milky smoke column, which was neither consistent nor homogeneous, and exhibited flows of clear and dark nature.[2] André Maurois comments on this result: *"It is wondrous, I say, that such important and simple phenomena have remained concealed to humankind up until today."*[3]

Carl Jung

Carl Jung[4] later acknowledged that the autonomous existence of the soul is a fact, and that the latter is completely independent

---

1 André Maurois (Jean-Louis Bigot) (1885 – 1967) was a French writer, literary scholar and historian. He lived from 1940 – 1946 in the USA and wrote biographic novels. He searched for the human basic values in the daily life of work and the fight for existence. Maurois' encouragement consisted of the incitation of free thinking; socialism was to him a means to cover up unnecessary injustice. Maurois developed, primarily in Bernard Quesnay, a model for social progress, based on the mutual trust of employees and employers.

2 **Maurois**, André: Le peseur d'âmes, Paris 1931, p. 102-103.

3 Idem, p. 64.

4 Carl Gustav Jung (1875 – 1961) was a Swiss psychologist, influential thinker and founder of analytical psychology. He studied medicine and worked at the psychiatric clinic of the University of Zurich; he was later a professor for psychology in Basel. He developed, after his separation from Sigmund Freud (1913), the school of analytical psychology. He also explored other fields, including Eastern and Western philosophy, alchemy, astrology, sociology, as well as literature and art.

from all things material.[1]

In order to determine the weight of the astral body, several studies were conducted by different scientists.

Raymont Renat, Van Zelst, Dr. Duncan McDougall

Raymond Renat, Van Zelst, and Dr. Duncan McDougall[2], amongst others, belong to this group.

During these experiments, dying people were weighted shortly before and shortly after death, and they established that, after death, each subject had lost approximately 21 grams of weight. Where these 21 grams went, or where the astral body or the soul went to after death, could not be explained by these scientists through their experiments.

*"And they ask
thee concerning the Soul;
Say:
The Soul is one of the things,
the knowledge of which is only
with my Lord.
And of knowledge,
you (mankind)
have been given only a little."*

The Quran, 17: 85

---

1 cp. **Jung**, C. G.: Modem Man in Search of a Soul, New York 1933, Chapter 9.

2 With the aid of different experimental methods, Dr. MacDougall tried to determine what weight the soul had. He built a bed suspended on a scale, in order to determine the weight, so that he could weigh people before and after the death process. He selected people who were already very exhausted from their disease as his subjects, in order to prevent them from disrupting the balance in the scale during the death struggle. The first subject was laid on the scale one evening at 5:30 p.m. When the subject died almost four hours later, the scale came out of balance. Two dollar coins had to be added in order to bring the scale back to its equilibrium – this corresponds to 21 grams. The New York physician Carrington held MacDougall's discoveries as the most important ones of that time. cp. aforementioned: Soul has weight, physician thinks, New York Times, edition from March 11th 1907.

2.6 Another Path to the Truth

Another Path to the Truth

The scientific studies and experiments mentioned provide us with more indications for the existence of another, enigmatic and invisible world. The information that science has given us about this world is however very limited, since the research methods and instruments known to-date are adapted to a specific world with specific natural laws and measurements. Another world with different standards is hardly comprehensible with our research instruments.

God, who created this enigmatic world, did not leave man in the dark about it, but he sent them a prophet to enlighten them about their eternal future in this coming world.

In order to discover the truth about the afterlife, man needs not to investigate the afterlife with false research instruments, but rather use only his abilities, his senses and, above all, his reason, to recognize God's message and to discern which messages have been composed, altered or falsified by man.

Summary: There is another life and there is another world after this one, and there are many existing facts, the makeup or details of which we currently cannot know. As stars are invisible to us during the day in sunlight, but appear one after another after sunset, many facts become evident to us after the light of our current lives becomes extinguished.

"(It will be said:)
Indeed
you were heedless of this, now
We have removed your covering,
and sharp is your sight this Day!"

The Quran, 50: 22

2.7 What Does the Belief
in an Afterlife Serve?

Max and his friends suffered a plane crash over the desert one day. They were all seriously injured. Max also had two severe injuries. Night came upon them, and he saw each and every one of his friends die one after the other. Max believed that he would surely suffer the same destiny as his friends, being that he had two severe injuries. Suddenly, he heard in the distance the roaring of an approaching lion. According to his map, the injured man had ten days of walking ahead of him before he would reach the nearest town. Hopeless, he held out and pondered how he could save himself, and suddenly a friendly man with a bright face appeared to his right side. He said:

"Do not lose hope. I will give you two spells. If you use them, your wounds will heal and the lion will become a beautiful flying horse that will peacefully take you away from this desert."

Max used both spells given to him, and his wounds began to heal. Shortly after, a second creature appeared to his left side, and offered him all sorts of alluring entertainment, alcohol and sweets. He enticed him:

"Come to me, my friend. Let us enjoy a pleasurable time together. Let us amuse ourselves with my souvenirs, dance to the music and enjoy the delicious wine. But tell me, what was that strange spell you just said?"

Max responded: *"Those are secret magic spells."*

"But what for?", inquired the other.

"To leave this place peacefully and heal my wounds."

The figure replied:

"Get rid of those pessimistic ideas, you are completely healthy! You do not need to leave this beautiful place. Don't waste this chance of enjoyment and entertainment by thinking of the future."

Max felt more and more allured by the ideas of the stranger. But suddenly he shuddered, as though he had experienced a bad dream, came back to his senses and said to the treacherous character:

"If you can save me from this lion and heal my wounds, then show me what you have brought. If not, leave me in peace, for you do not want to save me. And I will not find any salvation here by my self, and I will not survive."

In this story, Max symbolizes man in general, and his friends, who die one after the other, represent those whom man loves in life. The trip through the desert stands for life with all its stages and trials, through to death and Barzakh[1] until the Day of Resurrection and Judgment. Both wounds symbolize human limitations and limitless desires. Both spells are the belief in God, His Prophet, the Afterlife and the power to abandon oneself to God's mercy. The lion symbolizes death, which is transformed by ieman[2] in a servant who frees

---

1 Barzakh is the period between death and the Day of Resurrection.

2 ieman: The belief in God, His prophet and the Afterlife, which deeply rooted in one's heart.

man from the prison of this life and brings him to eternal bliss in Janna.

Thinking solely of this earthly life, material possessions and wealth lead man to enjoy the present moment. But this short joy cannot continue forever, and it does not reveal what will happen after this life has ended. Everything that surrounds us in this life stays back at the gates of the grave.

In life, man makes an effort to protect his possessions with the aid of insurance, and his health is preserved from possible diseases by means of preventive medicine. In order to ensure a future blissful life after death, the acceptance of the Message of God is necessary.

In this life, man feels that he has everything according to his aspirations and needs, and that he does not lack anything. However, man does not possess anything after his death. Some people feel as they become more successful in their lives, that they have achieved and earned everything according to their aspirations and needs, and that they do not need anything else for their upcoming life. However, at the end, defeated on his deathbed, man does not have anything anymore, and he needs everything.

"This life is, compared to the Afterlife, as though one of you dipped his finger in the ocean and then looked at it to see how much he got from it."
Prophet Muhammad

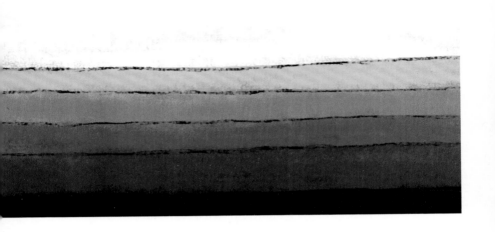

3 WHAT WILL HAPPEN AFTER DEATH?

What will happen after Death?

3.1 Good News for the **Muslim on His Deathbed**

Here, the outline of the human journey after death, as described by Prophet Muhammad in several Hadiths, will be quoted:

The Prophet explained:

God says: *"No decision has been harder for me than to take the soul from a Muslim; he dislikes death, and I equally abhor not following up on his wish."* When the Muslim is leaving this world, God tells the Angel of Death: *"Go to my servant and bring him to me. I will give him serenity."*

The Angel of Death comes, accompanied by a group of angels that have beautiful, bright faces, each one of them with a shroud and scents from *Janna*[1]. They sit in front of this Muslim. At this point, he sees an open door to Janna, and his soul rejoices. The Angel of Death approaches him, sits beside the head of the Muslim and says:

"You good soul, come to Allah's satisfaction and forgiveness."

The Angel of Death is more merciful to him than a mother to her child, for he knows that man is loved by Allah. The soul flows out of the body, like a drop out of a jug.

The Angel of Death takes the soul and gives it to the other angels, who cover it in scented shrouds. At this moment, the soul is invaded by a perfume that smells sweeter than anything one has ever smelt before.[2]

"(Namely)
those who the angels withdraw
while they are in a pious state
(i.e. pure from all evil,
and worshipping none but Allah Alone)
saying (to them):
peace be on you;
enter Paradise, because of (the good)
which you used to do."

The Quran, 16: 32

---

1 Janna is the place of reward, which God created for those who accepted his message. Similar, yet different, versions of this message were sent by God through many prophets. Each prophet (amongst them Noah, Abraham, Moses and Jesus) was sent to specific people in specific times. At the end, God sent the last prophet, Muhammad, with the last version of the Revelation for all people. From the Day of Resurrection until eternity, one leads an unimaginably joyful, beautiful life in Janna, materially, physically and psychically. The sum and beauty of the objects, the rewards, bliss and the degree of luxury found there were once described by the Prophet: *"There are things which no eyes have ever seen, no ears have ever heard, and no man could ever imagine."* A detailed description is also found in the following pages of this book.

2 **IBN HANBAL**, Ahmad: Al-Musnad, Hadith Nº.: 11823, 12965, 17803 and **ABO DAWOOD** As-sunan, Hadith Nº.: 4126.

3.2 Festive Procession **in the Heavens**

The Prophet announced:

the angels ascend to Heaven with the soul. Each time that they encounter another angel, they are asked: *"What is that beautiful scent?"* and they reply *"That is So-and-so"*, and by thus doing they use the favorite name of the person. When they hear it, the other angels pray for him. The soul continues to ascend with its company, until the door of the First Heaven is reached. The angels knock and ask for admission, and it is granted. The favorites amongst the angels of Heaven accompany the soul and all angels of this Heaven pray for it. This repeats itself, until the person has reached the seventh Heaven. There, the angels say *"Oh Allah, this is your servant So-and-so"* and Allah replies *"Bring the registry of his deeds into a higher location in Heaven (Elly-iin) and bring his soul back to the earth, for I have created them (people) out of earth, and they return to the earth, and from the earth I will bring them back."* And thus the soul is brought back to the earth.[1]

3.3 The Last **Trial** *The Last Trial*

The Prophet further describes:

He (the dead Muslim) hears the steps of people, as they leave him after the burial. Then, two angels come to him. Their eyes spew lightning and their voices thunder, and their hewers are like cow horns, their breath is made of flames. They are called Munkar and Nakir. Each one of them holds an enormous hammer in his hands. They say to him: *"Sit."*

---

1 Idem.

He sits with much worry, and they begin the interrogation:

"*Who is your God?*"

"*My God is Allah*", answers the dead.

"*What is your religion?*"

"*My religion is Islam.*"

"*Who is this man that was sent to you (people)?*"

"*He is Muhammad, Allah's messenger.*"

They shout at him as though he had given the wrong answers, and they repeat the questions. And this is the Muslim's last trial.

Here, the Prophet was asked by his companions:

"*Who can, in view of these two angels, as you have described them, answer correctly or even speak?*"

The Prophet answered with a verse from the Quran:
"*Allah strengthens the faithful with the firmly established Word, in this world as well as in the future one; and Allah does not let the sinners go astray; and Allah does as He wishes.*"[1]

3.4 Waiting in Barzakh[2]   *Waiting in Barzakh*

When the Muslim gives the same answers for the second time, a voice calls from Heaven:

"*My servant has spoken the truth, give him clothing and furnishings from Janna, and open for him the door to Janna,*"

and thus he receives scents and other presents. Every morning and every evening he is shown his place in Janna. I swear that from this time on he enjoys a deep bliss, which he will never lose again. And

---

1 Idem.

2 Barzakh is the lapse between death and the Day of Resurrection.

he is shown a place in Jahannam and told:

"This would be your place, had you not accepted the message."

Then, a good looking person comes, who smells particularly good and is beautifully dressed, and tells him:

"Have pleasure with Allah's generosity and eternal good living. Have pleasure with everything that gives you joy. That is what was promised to you."

The Muslim asks:

"Who are you? Your face shows good news."

The person replies:

"I am your good deeds. Truly, you were diligent in pleasing Allah and stayed away from things that do not please Him."

This person keeps him company, so that he is not alone until the Day of Resurrection. When he sees all of this, he says full of joy:

"I want to go to my people and tell them about it."

The answer is:

"Stay calm."

And the Muslim says:

"Please, Allah, let the Day of Resurrection come!"[1]

He visits his friends and relatives who died before him and belong to Janna, and they ask him about their friends who still live. When they ask him about somebody that has already died, he replies:

"He is already dead"

and they say with regret:

"Then he belongs to those who will not come to Janna."[2]

However, those who have not accepted the message will have a completely opposite experience when leaving this world and in Barzakh.

---

1 Idem.

2 cp. **Ibn Al-Qayyim**: Arruh, Beirut 1982, p. 29.

4 OUTLINE OF THE DAY OF RESURRECTION

The dead will continue to enjoy or suffer in Barzakh, until the first gigantic outcry resounds from Heaven, through which all still living creatures on earth die. Almost 40 years without life and in complete silence follow. Afterwards, with the second gigantic outcry, the Day of Resurrection begins. The entire universe quakes impetuously and is destroyed. The bodies of people will be restored to their previous appearance according to divine orders, and they will be rejoined with their souls, as though they were leaves that sprout once more in the spring.

The people will come one after the other from the earth, naked and barefooted, in order to be gathered at one place. There they will be interrogated about their deeds, and there they must account for them before the final evaluation of all their deeds takes place. It is a difficult day for both the body and the soul, which lasts 50,000 years.

Man will believe to have lived only one hour in this world, and Janna and Jahannam will appear.

People will experience this day very differently. Some will feel very comfortable, they will not worry, and they will perceive the day as short. Others will suffer from horrible heat and will be bombarded with enormous flames from Jahannam.

4.1 The Gigantic Outcry

" The Day
when the Trumpet will be sounded
(the second blowing):
that Day,
We shall gather the sinful, Zurqa:
(blue-eyed or blind with black faces),
in whispers will they speak to each other:
'You stayed no longer than ten (Days)';
We know best what they will say,
when the best among them in knowledge and
wisdom will say:
'You stayed no longer than a day!'
And they ask you concerning the mountains;
say:
'My Lord will uproot them and scatter them as dust; He
will leave them as plains smooth and level;
Nothing crooked or curved you will see in their place.'
On that Day will they follow the Caller (straight):
no crookedness will they show him:
all sounds shall humble themselves
for the Most Gracious:
nothing shall you hear but a whisper. "

The Quran, 20: 102-108

" Then, when one Blast is sounded
on the Trumpet (the first one),
And the earth and the mountains
shall be removed from their places,
and crushed to powder
at one stroke,
On that Day shall the (Great) Event befall. "

The Quran, 69: 13-15

"When the sun
(with its spacious light) is folded up;
When the stars fall;
When the mountains vanish (like a mirage);
When pregnant she-camels are left untended;
When the wild beasts are herded together;
When the oceans are ablaze;
And when the souls shall be joined with their bodies;
When the female (infant), Buried alive,
is asked – For what sin was she killed;
And when the written pages of deeds
(good and bad) of every person are laid open;
And when the heavens are stripped off;
And when Hell-fire is kindled to fierce ablaze;
And when Paradise is brought near–
(Then) shall every person knows what
he has brought (of good and evil)."

The Quran, 81: 1-14

"Glorified is He, and High is He
above the Partners they attribute to Him!
The Trumpet will be blown, and all that are in the heavens
and on earth will swoon,
except him whom God wills.
Then it will blow a second time and
behold, they will be standing, looking on!"

The Quran, 39: 67-68

"When the Trumpet is blown,
there will be no kinship among them
that Day,
nor will one ask after another!"

The Quran, 23: 101

"On the Day when He shall gather (resurrect) them together: (it will be) as if they had not stayed (in the life of this world) but an hour of a day:
they will recognize each other:
assuredly those will be lost who denied the meeting with God and refused to receive true guidance."

The Quran, 10: 45

"If you could but see when they will be held over the (Hell) Fire!
They will say:
'Would that we were but sent back!
Then would we not reject the Signs of our Lord, and we would be of the believers!'
Nay, it has become manifest to them what they had been concealing before, but if they were returned, they would certainly revert to that which they were forbidden [...] And they said: 'There is nothing except our life on this earth, and never shall we be resurrected.'
If you could but see when they are confronted with their Lord! He will say: 'Is not this the truth?'
They will say: 'Yea, by our Lord!' [...]
Lost indeed are they who denied their Meeting with God, until all of a sudden, the Hour (of death) is on them, and they say:
'Ah! Alas for us that we gave no thought to it!' "

The Quran, 6: 27-31

"That Day shall a man flee from his own brother.
And from his mother, and his father.
And from his wife and his children.
Each one of them, that Day, will have enough concern (of his own) to make him indifferent to the others."

The Quran, 80: 34-37

4.2 And God Will However Call Man Back to Life

"They say:
'What! When we are reduced to bones and dust,
should we really be resurrected (to be) a new creation?'
Say (O Muhammad): '(Nay!) be you stones or iron,
or created matter which, in your minds,
is hardest (to be resurrected)!' Then will they say:
'Who shall bring us back (to life)?' Say: 'He Who created
you first!' Then will they shake their heads at you, and say:
'When will that be?' Say: 'Maybe it will be quite soon!
It will be on a Day when He will call you,
and you will answer (His call)
with (words of) His praise and Obedience,
and you will think that you have stayed (in this world)
but a little while!' "

The Quran, 17: 49-52

"Be"
and it
is!

"And he makes comparisons for us,
and forgets his own (Origin and) Creation:
he says: 'Who can give life to bones when they have rotted
away and became dust?' Say: 'He will give them life
Who created them for the first time!
For He is the All-Knower of every creation! –
The same Who produces for you fire out of the green tree,
when behold! you kindle therewith.'
Is not He Who created the heavens and the earth able to
create the like of them? – Yea, indeed! For He is the All-
Knowing Supreme Creator! Verily, when He intends a
thing, it is only that He says, 'Be,' and it is! So Glorified is
He in Whose hands is the dominion of all things; and to
Him will you be all brought back."

The Quran, 36: 78-83

" *The* disbelievers pretend
that they will never be resurrected (for Judgment).
Say: 'Yes! By my Lord,
you shall certainly be resurrected,
then you will be informed of all what you did,
and that is easy for God.' "

The Quran, 64: 7

" *They* swear
their strongest oaths by God,
that God will not raise up those who die:
Nay,
(He will raise them up),
a promise (binding) upon Him in truth:
but most among mankind realize it not.
(They must be raised up),
in order that He may manifest to them the truth
of that wherein they differ,
and that those who disbelieved
may realize
that they had indeed (surrendered to)
Falsehood."

The Quran, 16: 38-39

"(remember) *The* Day
that We roll up the heavens
like a scroll rolled up for books –
even as We began the first creation, so shall we repeat it:
a promise binding upon Us.
Truly shall We fulfill it."

The Quran, 21: 104

"even as We began"
"so we repeat it"

5 ACCOUNTABILITY AND THE ENTRANCE INTO JANNA (PARADISE)

In the following section, the description of the Day of Resurrection and Janna (Paradise), as transmitted to us in the Quran and the Hadiths of Prophet Muhammad, will be presented. The following is a collection of different Hadiths on the subject.

5.1 On the Field of the Gathering

On the Field of the Gathering

Prophet Muhammad reports:

Allah will gather all people in one place. They will stand 40 years with their eyes fixed, awaiting the beginning of the judgment. The sun will draw near, so that it will be up to ten times hotter than it is in this world. People will suffer from distress and heat, so that some will say: *"I would leave this place, even if I had to go to Jahannam."* Then, people will say to one another: *"Don't you see how we suffer here? Shall we look for an intercessor to ask Allah to start the judgment for us?"*

Adam

And thus others say: *"Let us go to our father Adam, peace be upon him."* And to Adam they will say: *"You are the father of mankind, Allah lets angels greet you and kneel before you. Ask Allah, for us, to start the judgment, don't you see how much we're suffering?"*

Adam will reply: *"My Lord shows today a wrath that He had never shown and will never show, and I was not obedient when he forbade the tree to me. I can only worry about myself and myself only today. Go to somebody else."* And they will ask: *"Who should we go to?"*

Adam will reply: *"Go to Noah."*

Noah

They will say to Noah: *"O Noah, you are the first of Allah's prophets, and He has called you His grateful servant. Ask Allah for us to start the judgment, don't you see how much we're suffering?"* Noah will reply: *"My Lord shows today a wrath that He had never shown and will never show, and I had the chance to pray for people and I used it against my people. I can only worry about myself and myself only today. Go to somebody else."* And they will ask: *"Who should we go to?"* Noah will reply: "Go to Abraham."

Abraham

They will say to Abraham: *"O Abraham, you are one of Allah's prophets, and you were very close to Him. Ask Allah, for us, to start the judgment, don't you see how much we're suffering?"* Abraham will reply: *"My Lord shows today a wrath that He had never shown and will never show and I can only worry about myself and myself only today. Go to somebody else."* And they will ask: *"Who should we go to?"* Abraham will reply: *"Go to Moses."*

Moses

They will say to Moses: *"O Moses, you are one of Allah's messengers. He spoke to you when He gave you the Message. Ask Allah, for us, to start the judgment, don't you see how much we're suffering?"* Moses will reply: *"My Lord shows today a wrath that He had never shown and will never show, and because of me a person died. I can only worry about myself and myself only today. Go to somebody else."* And they will ask: *"Who should we go to?"* Moses will reply: *"Go to Jesus, Mary's son."*

Jesus

They will say to Jesus: *"O Jesus, you are Allah's servant and one of his messengers. You were created by His word and you could already speak as an infant. Ask Allah, for us, to start the judgment, don't you see*

how much we're suffering?" Jesus will reply: *"My Lord shows today a wrath that He had never shown and will never show and I was worshipped as a god. I can only worry about myself and myself only today. Go to somebody else."* And they will ask: *"Who should we go to?"* Jesus will reply: *"Go to Muhammad, the last prophet, he is the Lord of all people and he is the one who has come today with no sins."*

Muhammad

They will say to Muhammad: *"O Muhammad, you are Allah's messenger and the last prophet. Ask Allah, for us, to start the judgment, don't you see how much we're suffering?"*[1] and Jesus will say to Muhammad: *"The prophets ask you to intercede before Allah, so that he lets the people leave this place, for they are suffering here."*[2]

Prophet Muhammad will stand up, and from his place a particularly beautiful scent will emanate.[3] He will go to Janna (as it is the place of the mercy of God) and knock at the gate. It will be asked: *"Who is there?"* and he will say: *"Muhammad."* The gate will be opened for him, and he will be welcomed. Once he has entered, he will prostrate himself and make Sudjud[4] for God and praise him with such a beautiful supplication that no man has ever prayed before. He will then be called, and to him it will be said:
"O Muhammad, raise your head. Make your intercession and demand what you want, it will be granted to you." He will raise his head and say thrice: *"O my Lord, stand by my people."* And he will be told: *"Muhammad, let those of your Ummah[5] that shall come to Janna*

---

1 **Al-Buchari:** Assahih, Hadith N°.: 3092, **Moslim:** Assahih, Hadith N°.: 287, cp. Attermezi and Musnad Ahmad also.

2 **Ibn Hagar:** Fat-hul-Bari, Riyadh 2005, Vol. 15, p. 84-85, **Ibn Khuzayma:** Attawhid, Riyadh 1988, Vol. 2, p. 616-617.

3 **Ibn Al-Mubarak**, Abdullah: Al-Musnad, Riyadh 1987, 61-63.

4 As-sujud: it is the part of prayer where the forehead is laid on the floor.

5 Each prophet has an "Ummah"; these are people who lived at his times, i.e. the people or tribe to which he was sent. The "Ummah" of Prophet Muhammad are all people who lived during his time and after on the every part of the world.

without being interrogated enter through the right gate. Through the other gates, your Ummah and the other Ummahs destined for Janna will enter." The distance between the two wings of a gate is as large as the distance between Macca and Bosra (140 km away from Damascus)[1]. (The distance is approximately 1700 kilometers).

5.2 The Declaration of the Eternal Fate
The Declaration of the Eternal Fate

So the Youngest Judgment begins, and the books of deeds fly in all directions, each one going to the person concerned. This is the most difficult moment for every person, for the book of deeds determines the last judgment on eternal fate. Janna or Jahannam? At this point, every one worries about himself only; whether they will receive their record in their right hand, like those who will come to Janna, or in their left hand.

> "*Then He
> that will be given his Record
> in his right hand
> will say: 'Ah here! Read my Record!
> I did really believe that my Account
> would (one Day) reach me!'
> And he will be in a life of Bliss,
> in a lofty Paradise,
> the fruits in bunches whereof will be low and near.
> Eat and drink, with full satisfaction;
> because of the (good) that you sent
> before you in the days that are gone!
> And he that will be given his Record*

---

1 **AL-BUCHARI:** Assahih, Hadith N°.: 4343.

in his left hand, will say:
'Ah! Would that my record
had not been given to me!
And that I had never realized
how my account (stood)!
Ah! Would that (Death)
had made an end of me!
Of no profit to me has been my wealth!
My power and arguments (to defend myself)
have perished from me!' (It will be said):
'Seize him, and fetter him! [...]
This was he that would not believe
in God the Most Great,
and would not encourage
the feeding of the indigent!
So no friend has he here this Day.'"

The Quran, 69:19-35

"And the Book (one's Record) will be placed;
and thou wilt see the sinful
fearful of that which is (recorded) therein;
they will say,
'Ah! woe to us!
What a book is this!
It leaves out nothing small or great, but has recorded it!'
They will find all that they did, placed before them:
and not one will your Lord treat with injustice."

The Quran, 18: 49

"The Day when man will see (the Deeds)
which his hands have sent forth,
and the disbeliever will say,
'Woe unto me! Would that I were (mere) dust!' "

The Quran, 78: 40

*" Do they only wait for the Hour –
that it should come on them all of a sudden,
while they perceive not?
Friends on this Day will be foes, one to another,
except the Righteous. My devotees!
No fear shall be on you that Day,
nor shall you grieve,
(You) who believed in Our Signs and were Muslims.
Enter Paradise,
you and your wives, in happiness.
Trays of gold and cups will be passed round to them,
therein all that the one could desire,
all that the eyes could delight in,
and you will abide therein forever.
This is the Paradise
which you have been made to inherit
because of your deeds which you used to do
(in the first life).
Therein for you will be fruits in plenty,
of which you will eat (as you desire).
The Sinners will be
in the punishment of Hell to abide therein forever.
It will not be lightened for them,
and in despair will they be there overwhelmed.
Nowise shall We be unjust to them:
but it is they who have been unjust themselves."*

The Quran, 43: 66-76

5.3 Leaving the **Gathering Field**

Leaving the Gathering Field

Prophet Muhammad says:

Each one of the Ummahs will be called chronologically. Each one with the name of the God they worshipped. They will see appearances of those gods, and they will follow them towards Jahannam. The last remaining ones will be the Muslims of each Ummah.[1] They will be asked: *"What are you waiting for? Why did you not go with the others?"* The Muslims will reply: *"We are still waiting for our God, the one we have worshipped"*[2]. They will be called to Sudjud, and they will do it. Allah will say: *"Raise your heads."* When they do so, each one will receive a light that corresponds to their good deeds

---

1 A Muslim is every person who followed the Prophet of his time. In our times, Muslim is the one who, in addition to his belief in God as the only God, accepts the message of Prophet Muhammad.

2 **AL-BUCHARI:** Assahih, Hadith N⁰.: 764.

and is as large as a mountain, as large as a castle, as large as a house, as large as a tree or even smaller, until the last Muslim only has a small light above his big toe. This light sometimes goes out as well.[1]

5.4 Crossing Jahannam

Prophet Muhammad explained:
a bridge will be stretched over Jahannam. At this moment, all people will stare and remain silent. Only the Prophets will say:
"Please, Allah, save them."
This bridge is slippery and has burning hooks with thorns on their sides. I (Prophet Muhammad) and my Ummah will cross this bridge first. People will cross at different speeds, according to their good deeds. Some will be saved; some will suffer minor wounds but will still be saved; some will be caught by the hooks and fall into the fire of Jahannam.

The deepest point of Jahannam lies approximately two million kilometers deep.

The first group of seventy thousand people, who have successfully crossed the bridge, have faces as bright as the moon. There will be some that will cross the bridge in the blink of an eye, and others as fast as lightning, as clouds, as birds, as galloping horses, as running or walking people. The last one, whose light lies atop of his big toe and has the size of a tea light, will move forward when the light is on, but when it is off, he will remain still. He will crawl on his knees and stomach, one hand holds him, the other one slips; a foot steps right, the other one steps off, and the flames of Jahannam burn him on his sides. He will cry out:
"Why, Allah, did you make me so slow?"

---

1 Ibn Hagar: Al-Matalib Al-Aaliya, Riyadh 1998, Vol. 18, p. 492-493.

The answer will be:

"That was done unto you by your deeds."[1] When he finally crosses the bridge, he will say: *"praised be Allah, He saved me, I was almost lost."*[2]

*"Not one
of you but will pass over it:
this is, with your Lord,
a Decree which must be accomplished.
Then We shall save those who use to fear God
and were dutiful to Him,
and We shall leave the wrongdoers therein,
(humbled) to their knees."*

The Quran, 19: 71-72

5.5 Salvation of **Acquaintances**

Muslims will not find some of their Muslim acquaintances, who prayed, fasted and gave charity to others with them, in Janna. They will ask Allah about them, and He will allow them to save them from Jahannam. There, they will find their acquaintances in different situations, according to their sins. Some of them will be only ankle-deep in the fire, some knee-deep, and some chest-deep or neck-deep. They will take them with them and refresh them in a river in Janna[3].

---

1 **Ibn Rajab:** Gami Al-Ulum Wal-hikam, Cairo 2004, Vol. 3, p. 1028-1029, **Al-Marwazy,** Muhammad Ibn Nasr: Tazim Qadr Assalah, al-Madona al-munawwara 1987, Vol. 1, p. 307-308.

2 **Attabarani:** Al-Mugam Al-Kabier, Hadith Nº.: 9647.

3 **Ibn Hanbal,** Ahmad: Al-Musnad, Hadith Nº.: 10659.

5.6 The Prophet Intercedes for the Salvation of Mankind

The Prophet will bow to Sudjud[1], until Allah tells him:

"O Muhammad, raise your head, make your intercession and demand what you will."

He will raise his head and praise the Lord (Allah) and ask him to save people from Jahannam. Allah will allow him to free people from Jahannam, all within certain conditions. The Prophet will go and save them. When he has come back, he will repeat the Sujud, and he will be given broader conditions, regarding which ones he may save. And so, he will save all of those who said

"La ilaha illa Allah *(There is no God except for Allah)"*[2]

only once in their lives. And only those who will remain forever, will remain[3].

The Quran says about this:

"It will be that your Lord will raise you to a station of Praise and Glory."

The Quran, 17: 79

---

1 Sudjud: the part of prayer where the forehead is laid on the floor

2 **Ibn Hanbal**, Ahmad: Al-Musnad, Hadith Nr.: 11710, **Moslim**: Assahih, Hadith Nr.: 285.

3 **Al-Buchari**: Assahih, Hadith Nr.: 4116, **Moslim**: Assahih, Hadith Nr.: 284.

5.7 Salvation of the Remaining Muslims

Salvation of the Remaining Muslims

People in Jahannam will speak to the Muslims that are there, and will ask them:

"Were you not Muslims?",

and they will say:

"But we were."

And they will ask:

"What did you get from being a Muslim?"

and they will answer:

"We committed many sins, and we are being punished for them."

Allah will order to free all Muslims from Jahannam. And the others will say:

"Oh, had we only been Muslims!"

At this point of the Hadith the Prophet reads this verse:

"It might well be that the infidels wish they had been Muslims.[1]"

 The Prophet said:

"Some people of my Ummah will be sent to Jahannam because of certain sins. And then Allah will order the angels to get them from Jahannam, and they will be sent down below to search for them.

They will recognize the ones they are by looking for the marks that Sudjud leaves on their foreheads, hands, knees and feet, for Allah declared these marks as places that will not burn.[2]"

---

1 **Ibn Abi Aasim**: Assunnah, Riyadh 1988, p. 582-583.

2 **Al-Buchari**: Assahih, Hadith N°.: 764.

5.8 The Last Person Saved from Jahannam

The Last Person Saved from Jahannam.

 The Prophet reported:

A man is brought out, and he is left between Janna and Jahannam, with his face looking in the direction of Jahannam.

He says:

> *"Please, Allah, let my face look in the other direction. The heat and the flames of Jahannam hurt me."*

And God replies:

> *"Will you request anything else, after I save you from Jahannam?"*
> *"Only this; I will not ask you for anything else."*

He makes many promises to God, and he swears an oath. He is turned towards Janna, but there he sees a tree near the gate, and says:

> *"Please, Allah, let me sit beneath the shadow cast by that tree."*
> *"Where are your promises and oaths, O son of Adam?"*

"Please, Allah, this is my last wish. I swear by your Magnificence."
And he continues to swear oaths. When he finally sits beneath the shadow cast by the tree, he sees Janna through the gaps of the gate, and longs for it. The gate is opened, and he sees bliss and joy in Janna. He says:

"Please, Allah, let me in!"
Allah does not get angry at him, but asks:

"Where are your oaths? How disloyal you are, O son of Adam!"
And he says:

"This and then nothing else. If you let me enter Janna, then I won't ask you for anything else."
He is brought to a waterfall in Janna, where he showers. By doing so, he obtains the beautiful skin and the scent of people in Janna. When he is satisfied, an unimaginably beautiful palace appears before him. When he sees the palace, he believes himself to be in a dream. Everything that surrounds him seems worthless in comparison. And he says:

"Please, Allah, give me this palace."
Allah replies:

"Would you ask for anything else if I gave you this palace?"
He says:

"Never, I swear by your Magnificence; there could not be anything more beautiful."
And his wish is granted. When he is inside his palace, an even more beautiful castle appears. When he sees the castle, he believes himself to be in a dream again. He asks for it, and he receives it. He then does not ask for anything more.
God asks:

"Why do you not ask for anything more?"
He replies: *"I have asked for so much, and I have sworn so many oaths, that I am ashamed to ask for anything more."*
Then God says to him:

"Do you remember your previous life?"
He says: *"Yes."*

And God says to him:

> *"Then wish and ask for anything you want."*

The man then asks for everything that comes to his mind, until he cannot think of anything more.

> God gives him everything that he wished for and God says to him:
> *"Would you be satisfied if I gave you all the beautiful things that ever existed on earth?"*

He replies:

> *"All this? Are you mocking me, even though you are the Lord of all Worlds!"* (Here, the Prophet laughed.)

God says:

> *"Still, I will give you that and ten times more, and even everything that you will ever wish for."*

The man says to God:

> *"I am satisfied with it."*

And God says: *"Go to your properties, then."*

Quickly he takes himself among the things there, when something gorgeous and enormous, which he had never seen before, shines before him. He immediately throws himself to the ground to do Sudjud. An angel asks him:

> *"What are you doing?"*

He replies:

> *"I have seen God."*

The angel says:

> *"Oh, that is not but one of your houses."*

He continues to walk, and somebody appears before him, with a beautiful, glowing face. He throws himself to the ground to do Sudjud. He then asks him:

> *"What are you doing?"*

He replies: *"Are angels not greeted like this?"*

But he says:

"I am only one of your servants. I want to show you this castle."

He walks ahead and opens the doors. It is a luxurious building made out of an enormous pearl. His servant also asks him to look out the window. He sees at once all his properties, castles and gardens expanding as far as he can see. He could host all people on earth and make them rich, without he himself lacking anything[1].

> *"They rejoice in the life of the world:*
> *but the life of this world as compared*
> *with the Afterlife is but a brief passing enjoyment."*
>
> The Quran, 13: 26

6 OVERVIEW OF JANNA

The Prophet explains:

"Half a meter in Janna is more precious than everything on earth. There will be no one who comes to Janna and longs for his past life."[2] When people visit each other in Janna, they remember the things that happened in their worldly lives. There is no animosity, no hate, and no envy. Everyone does only good. For here they have everything their hearts could ever desire and everything that had ever graced their eyes. But all descriptions of Janna are only vague sketches, for nothing like it has ever been seen, and there are no words to adequately describe it. At the end of his description, the Prophet said that there are things there that eyes never saw, ears never heard and man never imagined.[3]

---

1 cp. **ADDARAQUTNI**: Arru'ya, Hadith Nº.: 33, **ATTABARANI**: Al-Mugam Al-Kabier, Hadith Nº.: 9647, **IBN HANBAL**, Ahmad: Al-Musnad, Hadith Nº.: 4395.

2 **AL-BUCHARI**: Assahih, Hadith Nº.: 2793, **IBN HANBAL**, Ahmad: Al-Musnad, Hadith Nº.: 10625, 12624

3 **AL-BUCHARI**: Assahih, Hadith Nº.: 5053.

> *"No person knows*
> *what delights the eye are kept hidden (in reserve)*
> *for them – as a reward for their good Deeds."*
>
> The Quran, 32: 17

God created servants in Janna, who resemble man and are the age of children. They are all beautiful. Days in Janna are never cloudy, and a beautiful scent permeates the air. The trees are evergreen and gorgeous birds sing in them. The majority of people in Janna are women. The best women amongst them are Mary, the mother of Jesus, and Khadija, the Prophet's wife. The children who died in their early lives will grow up in Janna. Half of the people there belong to Prophet Muhammad's Ummah, and the other half are Muslims who lived before the times of Prophet Muhammad and followed other prophets.

6.1 The Entrance of People into Janna

The Entrance of People into Janna

They enter in rags. At the gates they see door knobs made out of rubies and adorned with golden bands. And they see a tree, next to whose roots two water sources spring. This water prepares people for Janna. From one source they drink, and the water purifies them. With the water of the other source they wash themselves, and it refreshes their skin and hair. And they will always remain that fresh. Then they continue forward, and they are received by the angels. The angels say:

> *"Peace be upon you!*
> *Well have you done!*
> *Enter you here,*
> *to abide therein."*
>
> The Quran, 39: 73

The first one to enter Janna is Prophet Muhammad; next his companion Abu Bakr, followed by the rest of the Ummah of Prophet Muhammad. Then, several pulpits will be brought for the chosen ones amongst them. Some pulpits are made out of light, some out of pearls, some out of ruby, some out of topaz, gold and silver. Others receive chairs, and others however sit contentedly on the scented sand.

The prophets come, surrounded by light, each one of them escorted by many angels. One of them appears in a procession that surpasses all others, and is surrounded by an even greater light. People in Janna raise their heads and ask:

"Who is that who speaks to Allah?"

And the answer is:

"He is Lord of all people, who prayed for us on the Day of Resurrection; the first one who was called back to life, Muhammad, peace be upon him."

People greet Allah, and Allah greets them back. They say:

"O our Lord, who is pure of all evil and from whom peace comes. You are the God of majesty and generosity."

He answers:

"My servants, peace be upon you. And my mercy and love be with you. Welcome, you were obedient to me, even though you did not see me. You have kept my testament, and you observed my message."

They reply:

"We swear by your Majesty and Grandeur that we never worshipped you adequately. Allow us to do Sudjud for you."

Allah, nonetheless, says:

"Here there is no more mandatory worship. You are here to enjoy Janna and my mercy and to rest yourselves, like I promised. Wish and ask for whatever you want; it will be granted. Today I will not reward you based on your deeds, but according to my mercy, generosity, grace, grandeur and majesty."

They begin to wish until the one who had wished for the least, says:

"O my Lord, in the previous life people on Earth were ostentatious to

one another. I would like to have that which all men have had from beginning to end. I was occupied with your message."

When they are all done with their wishes, Allah says:

"You have achieved very little through your wishes, and you are satisfied with much less than you deserve. I give you that which you have wished for, and that which your wishes did not reach, and the like that you cannot imagine."

People receive precious gifts in Janna every day, and they have never seen anything like them before.

They look around them and find a group of different palaces. Some of them have cupolas made out of a hollow pearl, and towers and gates made out of gold, and beds of ruby, and rugs of thick silk. In the inner courtyards and by the entrances are fountains. Some of these palaces are cut out of a single precious stone. Some of them are made out of a piece of white ruby, and they are embellished with rugs made out of white silk. Or they are made out of red ruby and have red silk rugs, with towers of red gold and white silver. Even the base walls are made out of precious stones. When they see this, they say:

"*Praise be to God,
who has, out of his bounty, settled us in a Home
that will last:
no toil nor sense of weariness shall touch us therein.*"

(The Quran, 35:35)

Each one receives a wagon and takes a tour of his properties. They all possess palaces of gold, silver and precious stones, and palaces where each brick is made out of gold, silver, rubies and chrysolith and peridot. There are servants everywhere.

A man comes to a palace, whose walls are transparent on their inner side. When he enters this castle, he is overwhelmed and astounded. Alongside him there are dunes of scented sand and precious stones, diamonds and pearls, and a green hall, through which a creek flows. Its ground is also made out of diamonds, pearls and precious stones. He asks:

"Who does all this belong to?"

and the answer comes: "You."

In other palaces, angels await him to receive him and congratulate him. A servant approaches his wife, who had already come before him, and announces him. She asks:

"Have you seen him?",

the servant replies: *"Yes."* And she hurries to the entrance and embraces her husband. When he sits, servants come with different jars and carafes that shine like silver but are as clear as glass. Then, the servants say:

"Let us leave the two alone."

6.2 Women in Janna

Women, who were Muslims during their past life, will be rewarded just as men. Every one of their wishes will be granted. They enjoy particular beauty, grace and tactfulness, and they have pleasantly-sounding voices.

Every time their husbands look at them, their hearts are overwhelmed with joy. As time passes, they become more and more beautiful. Women are freed from their monthly period, and their bodies (men's and women's) do not have any other secretions.

They possess only the best personality and body traits, and they only use positive and beautiful words. Their youth never fades. Women perceive that their husbands are elated by them, and hence couples are closer to one another than ever before. Men and women enjoy clean hearts and bodies, they are carefree, strong and never sad, tired or ill; they are never bored. They are all 30 or 33 years old. They never argue and there is not a person who is alone.

"Verily, the dwellers of the Paradise that Day,
will be busy in joyful things.
They and their associates will be in pleasant shade,
reclining on thrones"

The Quran, 36: 55-56

6.3 Promenades in **Janna**   *Promenades in Janna*

People in Janna will marvel at the awe-inspiring sight of the rivers and their dreamlike sweet taste. Next to the rivers of sweet waters there are rivers of pure honey not from bees, wine not from grapes, and milk not from cows, but that spring from Janna itself. This wine neither makes one drunk nor has the unpleasant side effects after drinking.

When one of the wanderers stands by one of the banks of these rivers, he meets other inhabitants of Janna, who are also admiring the river. They become acquainted. The wanderer marvels at the purity of their hearts, the softness of their speech, and the beauty of their behavior. He likes them and desires to become their friend. They reciprocate his feelings and make him very happy.

Later, the single wanderer sits between the trees and tastes their multiple and delicious fruits. He finds a tree with a golden trunk and branches of ruby, chrysolith and mother of pearl. When there is a light breeze, branches touch one another and produce a sound that reminds of wind chimes, which sounds more beautiful than any known melody. As he thus wanders through the trees, sitting here and there, admiring everything, astounded and barely believing his eyes, he sees **"Sidrat-Al-Mun-taha"** – a tree that glows in different colors and its fruits taste of 72 different flavors. The leaves have the size of elephant ears, and around its leaves butterflies flutter, which are sometimes golden and other times made out of other precious materials.

6.4 The Death **of Death**

Death, in shape of a sheep, will stand on the dividing wall between Janna and Jahannam.
It will resound:
> *"O people of Janna!"* They will look. It will then resound:
> *"O people of Jahannam!"*

They too will look. And both will be asked:
> *"Do you recognize this sheep?"*

and they will answer:
> *"Yes, this is Death."*

The sheep will be slaughtered and there will resound:
> *"O people of Janna, eternity without death. O people of Janna, eternity without death!"*

6.5 God's Well-Pleasing **in Janna**

God's Well-Pleasing in Janna

Allah asks: *"Did I keep the promise that I made to you in your past life?"* And they say: *"Yes."*[1] Allah also asks: *"Are you satisfied?"* And they assure him: *"How could we not be satisfied, you gave us something very special! (You made dying easy to us, and you didn't leave us alone in the darkness of the grave. At the second outcry, you preserved us from fear and terror.)"* Allah says: *"Should I give you something better than all of this?"* And they answer once again: *"What could be better than all of this?"* Allah promises: *"I will give you my eternal* **Well-Pleasing***, so that I will never be upset with you."*[2]

It is exclaimed: *"You may live and never die, you may stay and*

---

1 **IBN KATHIER:** Attafseer. n.l. 2002, Vol. 4, p. 459.

2 **AL-BUCHARI:** Assahih, Hadith N°.: 6067, **MOSLIM:** Assahih, Hadith N°.: 5057, **ATTERMEZI:** Assunan, Hadith N°.: 2478.

never leave from here, you may be healthy and never ill, you may be young and never age, you may be blissful and never sad."[1]

"And they will say:
'All the praises and thanks be to God,
Who has guided us to this, never could we have found guidance, were it not that God had guided us! Indeed it was the truth that the Messengers of our Lord did come with.'
And it will be cried out to them:
'This is the Paradise! You have been made its inheritors, for what you used to do'"

The Quran, 7: 43

"And they will say:
'All the praises and thanks be to God, Who has removed from us (all) sorrow.
Verily, our Lord is indeed Oft-Forgiving, Most Ready to appreciate (good deeds).
Who has, out of His bounty, settled us in a Home that will last forever; there, toil will touch us not, nor weariness will touch us.'"

The Quran, 35: 34-35

6.6 The Levels in Janna   *The Levels in Janna*

People live in Janna on different levels; the higher the level, the better were their deeds in their previous life. While the person of a higher level goes for a walk in his gardens of his properties, people in the level below it perceive a pleasant smell and wonder where it

---

1 **ATTERMEZZI**: Assunan, Hadith N°.: 3169.

comes from.

The Prophet described the distance between the levels in Janna in the following manner: *"People in Janna see a higher level as a glowing star in the corner of the sky."* His companions asked him: *"Are these the levels of the prophets and can they not be entered by anybody else?"*

 The Prophet answered:

"No, I swear, these levels are also for those people who believed in Allah and His prophets."[1]

The best place in Janna is called **Al-Firdaus**[2], and it lies in the middle of Janna, on the highest point. It is there where the rivers of Janna spring from.

The parents of those who memorized the Quran by heart in their past lives are brought before God and each one of them receives a crown of light and a robe that is more sumptuous than anything that ever existed on earth. They are astounded and say: *"Why did we receive this?"* And the answer they are given is: *"Because your child (son or daughter) memorized the Quran by heart."* The reward that the child receives eludes all imagination. There, he will recite the Quran in front of God and the people, and with each letter comes his reward. With each verse of the Quran that he recites by heart, he is put on a higher level, until he has reached the highest level of Paradise.[3]

There are special levels for those who loved one another in their first life, and they herald so much bliss that many, who are already in high levels, wish to enter them.

---

1 **AL-BUCHARI:** Assahih, Hadith N°.: 3016, **MOSLIM:** Assahih, Hadith N°.: 5059.

2 The word "Paradise" comes from the Arabic word "Al-Firdaus".

3 **ABO DAWOOD:** Assunan, Hadith N°.: 1252, **ATTERMEZZI:** Assunan, Hadith N°.: 2838, **IBN HANBAL,** Ahmad: Al-Musnad, Hadith N°.: 6508.

7 JAHANNAM (HELL)

Jahannam (Hell)

Jahannam is the place of punishment that God created for those who rejected His message. From the Day of Resurrection until all eternity, they will suffer in the hellfire, completely conscious, unimaginably atrocious tortures to their body and in soul.

As in Janna, there are different levels in Jahannam. Every level is hotter and houses worse pain than the other. Jahannam consists mainly of fire, which feeds off people and rocks. It has a high concentration of poisons and heat. The heat rises in proportion to depth. The main reason for the banishment in Hell lies in the rejection of the Message of God. Other reasons are for instance injustice towards others, pride, envy, treason, black magic, murder, disrespect towards parents, robbery, making up lies about God and His Prophets, or torturing animals. The sinners, in case they did not turn back to God during their lives on Earth in genuine repentance, will be punished. Those who end up in Jahannam for other reasons than rejecting the Message of God will be released after having expiated their punishment. Nothing can buy their way out of this punishment.

" Verily, those who reject faith,
and die rejecting,
never would be accepted from anyone of them
the (whole) earth full of gold,
even if they offered it as a ransom. "

The Quran, 3: 91

↻ Summary of Chapter 2 and Outlook

As a final remark to the topics discussed before about the Day of Resurrection, Janna and Jahannam, the principle of Paradise and Hell, should be clarified once more:

a. In Janna: Body or Soul?

Since God purposely created man with soul and body, and gave him the ability to enjoy with both, man will also live and enjoy physically and spiritually in Janna.

The ability of enjoyment is in itself a grace from God that calls for gratitude. A valuable person to God is the one who controls his impulses and wishes, rightly handles them according to God's regulations, but not the one who ignores his impulses and tries to suppress them.

The idea that man should torture himself, ignore his physical side or perceive his impulses and his ability of enjoyment as "dirty" in order to come closer to God is not in accordance with the Islamic doctrine.

b. Why does Jahannam exist?

Just as there are democratic states in our world that occupy themselves with the preservation of human rights and stand for a world without cruelty and war while also establishing of legal systems, and thus of punishment systems with jails and custody facilities, there is also a place in the Afterlife where people are punished for their bad deeds.

This place is Jahannam (Hell).

The existence of bipolar pairs such as good and evil, happiness and sorrow, light and darkness, beauty and repulsiveness, truth and deceit, rightful guidance and misguidance, as well as Janna and Jahannam entails great wisdom within it. For without evil, good could not be correctly assessed; without sorrow, joy could not be fully experienced; warmth would not be so easily felt without cold; and the many joys of Janna (Paradise) could not so easily exist without Jahannam (Hell).

Janna is the place of all things beautiful; it receives the good, pleasure, light, beauty, truth and rightful guidance. Jahannam is the place of all things ugly, and into it evil, sorrow, darkness, deceit and misguidance flow and remain.

C. To Love God **or to Fear Him?**

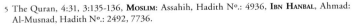

When one hears of "Jahannam (Hell)" in Islam, one wonders: Where is God's mercy? Should I love God and hope for His Jannah (Paradise), or must I now fear Him?

Surely in Islam, God is the most merciful and the most love-worthy one. He loves us and He does not want to hurt us[1]. Moreover, He wants to admit us to Jannah[2] , where we can lead a much more blissful life[3]. He knows our weaknesses[4], and therefore he does not demand from us to be sinless people.[5] He has opened the

---

1 The Quran, 4:28,147, 2:185, 5:6.

2 Idem., 4:174-175, 35:5, 22:14.

3 Idem., 43:68-73.

4 Idem., 4:28, **Attermezzi**: Assunan, Hadith Nº.: 2423, **Ibn Hanbal**, Ahmad: Al-Musnad, Hadith Nº.: 12576.

5 The Quran, 4:31, 3:135-136, **Moslim**: Assahih, Hadith Nº.: 4936, **Ibn Hanbal**, Ahmad: Al-Musnad, Hadith Nº.: 2492, 7736.

Gates of Forgiveness to us, and He has made the path for repentance easy.[1] Every single person has so much value to God[2] that one does not need a mediator to be able to speak to God, or to ask Him for forgiveness. He prepared a place in Paradise for every single person, even the sinners[3], He invited each person to his own place in Paradise through His prophets.[4] Even though all of humanity and the entire earth only represent a small drop in His kingdom, He has nevertheless spoken to mankind, and sent messengers and letters. He who does a good deed receives a reward ten times its size as thank you.[5] But he who performs an evil deed will only be punished once, or not at all.[6] He who comes back to Him will be accepted by God with indescribable joy.[7] He who comes one step closer to God will be hastily met by God.[8] In order to describe the function of His prophet Muhammad, He said: *"I have only sent you as Mercy for all the worlds."*[9] In the Quran, He described, in a summarized fashion, the relationship between Him and those who believe in Him:

"He loves them and they love Him."[10]

When God created the world, He wrote in a noble book:

"Certainly, my Mercy surpasses my Wrath."[11]

On the Day of Resurrection, He will forgive so many people for

1 The Quran, 39:53, 4:110, MOSLIM: Assahih, Hadith N°.: 4852, ATTERMZZI: Assunan, Hadith N°.: 3463.

2 The Quran, 17:70, 2:34, 22:65.

3 IBN MAGAH: Assunan, Hadith N°.: 4332.

4 AL-BUCHARI: Assahih, Hadith N°.: 6738.

5 The Quran: 6:160, 17:19.

6 Idem., 40:40, MOSLIM: Assahih, Hadith N°.: 4852.

7 AL-BUCHARI: Assahih, Hadith N°.: 5833, MOSLIM: Assahih, Hadith N°.: 4927.

8 AL-BUCHARI: Assahih, Hadith N°.: 6856, MOSLIM: Assahih, Hadith N°.: 4832, 4850, ATTERMEZI: Assunan, Hadith N°.: 3527.

9 The Quran, 21:107.

10 Idem., 5:54, 3:31, 9:100, 58:22, 5:119.

11 AL-BUCHARI: Assahih, Hadith N°.: 2955, 6855, 6872, 6999, MOSLIM: Assahih, Hadith N°.: 4939, 4941.

their evil deeds and bring them into Paradise that the Devil will think that he will also be forgiven![1]

This merciful, generous God, however, is not weak! Those who misuse His mercy and mock Him, His messages or His rules, or do not regard them as worthy of observation, will be obliged to know that He is also the most powerful, the most majestic one.[2]

He who commits sins because of his human weaknesses is not like he who rejects God or His message.[3] He who is not interested in God's offer of a place in Paradise, will lose this place! He who belittles the majesty of God, the Lord of all worlds, will be punished according to this majesty. Just like His reward represents His generosity, and is therefore infinite!

The characteristics of the Most Merciful One are different from those of a weakling! He who makes an effort to be good and listens to God is not the same as he who does not do the latter. This justice is in itself a manifestation of God's wholeness.

In this chapter, an attempt was made to derive the existence of the Afterlife with the aid of logic science, situations and events that let us feel the presence of the Afterlife.

Without the instructions provided by God, no clear conceptions of the Afterlife, the events that take place there, and its forms of appearance would be possible, and the way there would not be known either. Lastly, God transmitted His instructions to humans through His Messenger Muhammad. In the following Chapter, it will be discussed how a neutral person can prove if and how Muhammad could really be God's last Prophet.

1 **ATTABARANI:** Al-Mugam Al-Kabier, Hadith No.: 2951, 10362, 5385.
2 The Quran, 16:38-39, 46:34.
3 The Quran, 4:48,116.

Chapter 5

Chapter 3

Prophet Muhammad
Who? What? Why?

1 THE PROPHETS

يَٰبَنِىٓ ءَادَمَ إِمَّا يَأْتِيَنَّكُمْ رُسُلٌ مِّنكُمْ يَقُصُّونَ عَلَيْكُمْ ءَايَٰتِى ۙ فَمَنِ ٱتَّقَىٰ وَأَصْلَحَ
فَلَا خَوْفٌ عَلَيْهِمْ وَلَا هُمْ يَحْزَنُونَ ﴿٣٥﴾

"O you children of Adam!
Whenever there come to you Messengers from amongst you,
reciting to you my Verses,
then whosoever becomes pious and righteous,
on them shall be no fear,
nor shall they grieve."

The Quran, 7: 35

رُسُلًا مُّبَشِّرِينَ وَمُنذِرِينَ لِئَلَّا يَكُونَ لِلنَّاسِ عَلَى ٱللَّهِ حُجَّةٌۢ بَعْدَ ٱلرُّسُلِ ۚ
وَكَانَ ٱللَّهُ عَزِيزًا حَكِيمًا ﴿١٦٥﴾

"Messengers as bearers of good news
as well as of warning in order
that mankind should have no plea against God
after the Messengers.
And God is Ever All-powerful,
All-wise."

The Quran, 4: 165

1.1 Why Did God Send Prophets?

1. Prophets answer the most profound questions of mankind: From Where? To Where? Why?
2. Prophets explain to us the solutions to the riddles of the universe, and they reveal to us the secrets of life.
3. Prophets transmit to men the godly description of life after death and how one can be saved and attain eternal bliss therein.
4. Thus, prophets heal the spiritual sorrows of mankind and take their feeling of restlessness, worry, foreignness, forsakenness and uncertainty.
5. They teach people to overcome obstacles.
6. The message of Prophethood transforms man from a materially limited being into an honored creature of the omnipotent Creator of the Universe.
7. Through His prophets, God expands the horizon of human bliss and existence beyond the limits of this world.

1.2 On Angels and Prophets

Some people may ask themselves why God did not send angels as His messengers.

God's messenger is responsible for the task of leading men to God. The most important thing here is for him to be a person himself. Thus, he shares with other people the same feelings, needs, wishes and drives, and can therefore summon up more understanding and patience for his fellow men.

People, on their side, see in him a living example of the virtues that he preaches to them. Hence, they can follow his example. And as we know from pedagogy, learning from a model is one of the most efficient forms for the building of knowledge and its application.

Angels in Islam, on the other hand, are neither visible nor are they human beings. They are predominantly beings who do not commit any faults, and can barely be comprehended using human characteristics.[1]

Additionally, people would not find tangible and comprehensible beings in angels. The virtues embodied by angels would not become a demonstrative example, but they would remain superhuman, unattainable characteristics. And thus the Message would lose its meaning. Furthermore, by learning from an angel, the trial aspect (on belief) would be lost, for people could not make a choice, but instead, in view of such a powerful being, they would feel forced to believe. However, God wanted His message to be accepted by free will, so that the reward or punishment in the Afterlife could be just.

1.3 The Miracles of the Prophets

The Miracles of the Prophets

God gave each prophet a miracle, so that people could see that he was sharing the truth and thus would pay attention to him. A miracle is something that surpasses human abilities and excludes any possibility of imitation. For instance, Prophet Saleh was given a female camel that was not born naturally, but emerged from the division of a rock. Her milk was enough to nourish an entire city.

---

1 Angels are beings created from light who serve God uninterruptedly and preach His majesty. They are characterized by their obedience to God and their flawlessness. They do not take nourishment, they do not marry, they do not reproduce, and they are neither males nor females . They are countless in their numbers, and they live on earth and in the universe. Their appearance can assume many shapes, all of which are characterized by beauty, and they can be visible to men. In their original form they are invisible to men and of unimaginable size, so that they can move an entire city with a single feather of their seven hundred wings. Every man is accompanied by four angels throughout his entire life. Two of them record his deeds; one of them the good ones, and the other the bad ones. The other two angels protect him from things that do not correspond to God's determination. Some angels are assigned special missions by God. The mission of angel Gabriel was to transmit the messages between God and the prophets. Azrael's mission is to take the soul from living creatures, allowing the body to die.

Prophet Moses received several miracles, amongst them a stick that transformed itself into an enormous snake, and with which he could part the sea.

Prophet Jesus also possessed several miracles, like the ability to immediately heal the ill, to reawaken the dead, and had the ability to speak while still an infant.

2 MUHAMMAD PROPHET OR LIAR? *Prophet or Liar?*

That Muhammad was a Prophet can be recognized in the following facts:

1. The Quran: it was given to Prophet Muhammad as an enduring miracle, not bound by time and place. (See Chapter 4)
2. The other miracles: in addition to the Quran, God also gave the Prophet many other miracles, which are listed in section 2.4.
3. If one studies his life, his deeds and his character and, in addition, takes into consideration his influence on people and history, one reaches the conclusion that truth is to be found in all related aspects, and the latter is addressed in sections 2.1, 2.2 and 2.3.

2.1 Muhammad – Who?

2.1.1 In Macca

Muslims praying around the Kaba in the holy mosque of Macca.

Age	Muhammad in Macca
0	On 20/04/571 CE he was born in Macca, shortly after his father died
6	After his mother's death, he takes shelter with his grandfather

Age	Muhammad in Macca
8	His grandfather dies and his uncle becomes responsible for Muhammad, who is known as **"the truthful and the trust worthy"** in his city
25	Marriage to Khadija, an aristocrat, who bore him four daughters
35	Rescue of the Arabs from the Civil War (during the reconstruction of the Kaaba) through compromise
40	Muhammad became a Prophet, when Angel Gabriel brought him God's first message; the Quran is passed on to him piece-by-piece from this time
43	Beginning of the public calling of the inhabitants of Macca to Islam by Prophet Muhammad and beginning of torturing Muhammad and his followers by the Maccans
From 45	Secret meeting of the Prophet and his followers for Islamic knowledge at the house of Al-Arqam
47	Economic and social isolation of the Prophet, his family and his followers for the duration of three years, to the point that, the leaves of trees were the only nourishment they could find

و ما أوتيتم من العلم إلا قليلا

Age	Muhammad in Macca
50	Death of his uncle who protected him, followed shortly after by the death of the Prophet's wife, who succumbed to the consequences of the isolation; this year was declared the Year of Sadness Highest point of the torture by the Maccans, Muhammad travels to the city of Taif to call the people to Islam, but there he was also brutally tortured; on the return journey he was briefly denied entrance to Macca
51	Invitation of the Arabic tribes to Islam during their peregrination, important tribe leaders from Madina embrace Islam
52	Spread of Islam in Madina Thurs, 12/09/622, meeting of the leaders of Macca and determination of a murder plot against Prophet Muhammad; the Prophet flees to Madina. Signature of a peace treaty between Jews, Muslims and the inhabitants of Madina

2.1.2 In Madina

Year	Muhammad in Madina
624	Fri, 13/03, Battle of Badr: first great armed conflict in the history of Islam; 314 Muslims fight against 950 Maccans and are victorious

Year	Muhammad in Madina
628	11/05, the Prophet addresses letters to the greatest kings and leaders known in his time to invite them to Islam
631	The Year of Delegations: more than 60 delegations of different countries and tribes come to Madina to announce their belief in Islam
632	07/03, Parting Sermon during his first and only pilgrimage
632	Revelation of the last verse of the Quran
632	Approximately 22/05, parting sermon at the cemetery of Madina
632	Beginning of June, death of the Prophet after a three day-long illness

Prophet Muhammad's mosque and grave

2.2 Muhammad's Character – How?

Muhammad's Character - How?

2.2.1 The Prophet's Benevolence and Gentleness

He was a Prophet of mercy and love, although he suffered from grief, sorrow and anguish during his life. He was banished from his city (Macca). Those who believed in him were humiliated and murdered. One day they asked him: *"Oh Messenger of God, won't you curse our enemies?"* He replied, with tears in his eyes: *"I wasn't sent as a curser, but as mercy."* [1]

" Verily, there has come unto you a Messenger from amongst yourselves (i.e. whom you know well). It grieves him that you should receive any injury or difficulty. ardently anxious is he over you: to believers is he most kind and merciful."

The Quran, 9: 128

Every time he saw a child, blissfulness and delight could be seen in his face. Each return of the Prophet to Madina was a very special celebration for children, for he allowed the first two to receive him to ride on his camel. Muhammad kissed and embraced his grandchildren and played with them. Sometimes, he let them ride on his back, carrying them around, crawling on his knees, and exclaiming: *"I am your good camel!"* [2]

---

1 **AL-BUCHARI:** Al-Adab Al-Mufrad, Beirut 1989, p. 119, Similar in **MOSLIM:** Assahih, Hadith No.: 4704, **ATTABARANI:** Al-Mugam Al-Kabier, Hadith No.: 15755, **AL-MAUSILI,** Abo Yala: Al-Musnad, Damascus 1984, Vol. 11, p. 35.

2 **ATTABARANI:** Al-Mugam Al-Kabier, Hadith No.: 2595.

The Prophet's Benevolence and Gentleness

One day, when he was doing Sudjud during his prayers, a child jumped on his back to ride. Muhammad prolonged his Sudjud until the child had had enough and could safely descend from his back.[1]

Once a Bedouin said to the Prophet,: *"We do not kiss our children"*, the Prophet replied *"What can I do if kindness has been taken from your heart?"*[2]

He never let a deserving poor person leave his house without giving him something. Sometimes, when he had nothing to give, he gave the deserving poor person permission to contract debts in his name.[3] He recommended to his companions to always help those who were in debt or in trouble. When the Pharisee, who had accused Muhammad's wife of infidelity and thus created great conflict amongst Muslims, died, he gave him his own shirt as a shroud, so that the Pharisee's children did not have to leave in shame.

When Muhammad conquered Macca, he gathered those who had banished him from his city and tortured him, and asked them: *"What should I do now with you?"* they answered: *"You are our noble brother"*, and he freed them, forgave them, and declared: *"Go wherever you want, you are free."*[4]

Let us hear from the children, the orphans, the ill, the elderly, the mothers, the women, the men and the animals who experienced his mercy and lovingness! Let us hear their words to become acquainted with Prophet Muhammad, for he is the mercy for all worlds.

"We sent you not, but as a mercy for all creatures."

The Quran, 21: 107

---

1 **Ibn Hagar:** Al-Isaba, Calcuta 1856, Vol. 1, p. 676, **Assafadi:** Al-Wafi bil Wafiyyat, Beirut 2000, Vol. 12, p. 67.

2 **Al-Buchari:** Assahih, Hadith N°.: 5539, **Moslim:** Assahih, Hadith N°.: 4281.

3 **Attermezi:** Asch-schamail, Beirut 1996, p. 162.

4 **Ibn Hagar:** Al-Isaba, Egypt 1960 (Attaba Assalafya) Vol. 8, p. 18.

Not only people benefited from his benevolence, but also the animal kingdom. He was merciful to all animals, from the tamest to the wildest. When a cat drank from his jar shortly before his washing, he let her drink until she had quenched her thirst. One day, he also spoke of the mercy of a sinful woman, who had encountered a thirsty dog in the desert. She fetched water from a well in her shoe, and gave it to the dog to drink.

God has forgiven

The Prophet said in her regard: *"God has forgiven the sins of this woman for this deed."*[1]

During his journey with his companions, he was overcome by sadness as he saw how a bird painfully trembled when its hatchling was taken from his nest. He ordered the hatchling to be brought back to his nest.[2] He even protected the smallest animals, such as ants. The Prophet saw a fire next to an ant nest, and consequently he ordered the fire quickly put out.[3] When he was visiting one of his companions, a camel trotted to him, laid its head in his arms and wept. The Prophet caressed it over its nose and back, until it became calm, and reprimanded its owner: *"Don't you have any fear of Allah, that you let this animal go hungry and give it so much work?"*[4]

2.2.2 Muhammad's Honesty

Muhammad's Honesty

Even his enemies attributed him deep honesty. Before he became a Prophet, he was called by the Arabs *"the truthful and the trust worthy"* After he became a Prophet, even his enemies left money in his custody. When he had to flee from Macca, he left the total amount

---

1 **AL-BUCHARI**: Assahih, Hadith N°.: 3208, **MOSLIM**: Assahih, Hadith N°.: 4164.

2 **ABO DAWOOD**: Assunan, Hadith N°.: 2300.

3 **IBN HANBAL**, Ahmad: Al-Musnad, Hadith N°.: 3575.

4 Idem, Hadith N°.: 1654.

Honesty

of money of those who wanted to murder him that night at one of his companions, so that the latter could give it back to them.

2.2.3 No Personal Gain

No Personal Gain

Muhammad lived in poverty, even though he could have had a lot of money at his disposal. When the Arabs offered him lordship and riches, so that he gives up his religion, he said: *"I swear that even if you were to give me the sun on my right hand and the moon on my left hand, I would never stray from this path, until this religion triumphs or I die."*[1] His countrymen tortured him and his companions, and issued a boycott against them. As a consequence, they did not have anything but the leaves of trees to eat. As a result of this famine, Khadija, Muhammad's wife, met her fate.

On the day when his youngest son Ibrahim died, a solar eclipse took place, and people thought that the sun was darkened with grief over him. However, Muhammad said: *"No, the sun and the moon are two of Allah's miracles, and an eclipse has nothing to do with the life or death of anybody."*[2]

2.3 Muhammad's Deeds — What?

Muhammad's Deeds - What?

2.3.1 The Broad and Fast Spread of Islam

With Islam, Prophet Muhammad changed the face of the world in a short time, and thus he deeply influenced history. In the Bible

---

1 **AL-BEIHAQUI:** Dalail Annu-bowwa, Cairo 1988, Vol. 2, p. 187.

2 **AL-BUCHARI:** Assahih, Hadith N°.: 984, Imam **MALIK:** Al-Mu-watta, Hadith N°.: 398.

there is a prophecy that is clearly ascribed to Prophet Muhammad.

There, Prophet Salomon prophesizes the broad expansion of the religion of Prophet Muhammad, and that the tribes of the desert would be his subjects after battling him for a long time:

"He will rule from sea to sea and from the River to the ends of the earth. The desert tribes will bow before him and his enemies will lick the dust."[1]

Salomon further describes: *"All nations will serve him"*[2] and *"May people pray for him and bless him all day long."*[3]

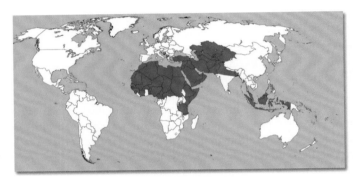

■ *Muslims around the world*

Many people, including Arabs, Egyptians, Turks, Barbarians, Hindus, Persians, Mongolians and Albanians, converted to Islam. Long stretches in the area between the Atlantic and the Indian Ocean thus became part of the Islamic Empire.

Alphonse de Lamartine

Alphonse de Lamartine wrote in this regard: *"Never has a man*

---

1 Psalm 72:8-9 (New International Version).

2 Psalm 72:11.

3 Psalm 72:15.

accomplished in such a short time such an immense and long lasting revolution in the world, in less than two centuries after his predication, Islam, preaching and armed, ruled over three Arabias, and conquered to God's unity Persia, the Khorasan[1], Transoxania[2], Western India, Syria, Egypt, Ethiopia, the known continent of Southern Africa, many islands of the Mediterranean, Spain and part of Gaulle ."[3][4]

"How could one man, single-handedly, weld warring tribes and wandering Bedouins into the most powerful and civilized nation in less than two decades?"[5] Thomas Carlyle

2.3.2 The Swift Abolishment of Bad Habits

When a country's leader wishes to abolish a bad practice that has become a habit, i.e. alcoholism, he makes use of politics as his method, science as the basis of an argument that appeals to health, and mass media to make his campaign widely heard. Other leaders act in an authoritarian and dictatorial fashion to change society. However, noticeable success requires a long time, for, in the end, it is about changing customs that are now deeply rooted in their culture and in all social strata. Perhaps, the country's leader will succeed in prohibiting alcohol consumption in public, but not in the private sphere.[6]

---

1 Khorasan is a historical region in Central Asia, in the area that comprises the modern states of Iran, Afghanistan, Tajikistan, Uzbekistan and Turkmenistan.

2 Transoxania is an ancient name for the region that lies between the rivers Amu Darya and Syr Darya in Central Asia. Politically, the region now belongs primarily to Uzbekistan, Kazakhstan, Tajikistan and Turkmenistan.

3 Gaul basically comprises modern France, Belgium and Northern Italy.

4 DE LAMARTINE, Alphonse: Histoire De La Turquie, Paris 1854, Vol. 2, p. 277.

5 CARLYLE, Thomas: Heroes and Hero Worship and the Heroic in History, Nebraska 2008, p. 42ff.

6 Prohibition in the USA (1919-1932), also known as the "Volstead Act", ended up costing the government approximately 350 million dollars. This law had some negative consequences; firstly, crime experienced a great boost. In Russia, Iceland, Norway and Finland, similar attempts were also undertaken.

The American attempt to prohibit alcohol consumption

Nonetheless, Muhammad managed to peacefully abolish in many countries numerous bad habits, such as alcohol consumption and trafficking in women, as well as the burial of live newborn girls and gambling, without significant resistance or opposition.

2.3.3 Changing the Way of Life of Many Nations

The Cchange in the Way of Life of Many Nations

The deep change elicited by Muhammad in such a short time in the fields of morals, ethics, traditions, and habits of the Arabs and many other peoples could not have been implemented by a common man.

Many peoples who adopted Islam rapidly, such as Egyptians, Algerians and Moroccans, were later colonized by Western countries such as England, France, Spain or Italy. Nonetheless, these world powers could not make their religion and language prevail, in spite of all their efforts given much more time than Muhammad.

2.3.4 Muhammad as Pioneer
for the Renovation of the World
Muhammad as Pioneer for the Renovation of the World

When Muhammad appeared in history, the world was characterized by social injustice and religious tyranny and oppression of the weak by the strong. These widespread and deeply-rooted systems were abolished by Muhammad. His law was one for all. Equality, justice and love for everyone. He created a set of international principles and systems previously unknown to the Arabs, and spread them far and wide. Similar principles and systems were also established in the Western world, but not until many centuries later. For instance, he established a balanced economic system and a consultative political system. He created clear laws and principles based on human rights and international relations in times of peace and in times of war. He ensured freedom of religion and equal rights to all people (regardless of nationality, skin color, gender and religion). His widespread principles are, amongst others: *"All people are equal, like the teeth of a comb."*[1] Is it possible that all of this could have been conceived by an illiterate man who spent his life with tribes in the middle of the Arabian Desert?

2.4 The Miracles of Prophet Muhammad
The Miracles of Prophet Muhammad

These are some of the miracles performed by Muhammad and witnessed by thousands of people:

---

1 **AL-QUDAIE**, Asch-schihab: Al-Musnad, Beirut 1985, Vol. 1, p. 145, **AL-ASBAHANI**, Abo Asch-scheich: Amsaal Al-Hadith, Hadith N°.: 143, 144, 145, **ADDOULABI**: Al-Kuna wal-Asmaa, Hyderabad 1904, Vol. 1, p. 168.

2.4.1 The Multiplication **of Water**

The Multiplication of Water

One day, when Muhammad was en route with his companions through the desert, they did not have water for the evening prayer.[1] The Prophet dipped his fingers in an almost empty jar and water sprung out of it, until all of the three hundred of his fellow travelers had had enough.[2] Throughout his life, many similar cases of water springing from between the fingers of the Prophet were reported.

2.4.2 The Multiplication **of Food**

The Multiplication of Food

When the Prophet, with two thousand of his companions, was excavating a moat, his companion Jaber went secretly to his wife and asked her to prepare a meal for the Prophet, for he had been hungry for a long time and was tired. She replied that she only had a little bit of flour and meat. He asked her to bake bread from it and prepare the meat while he invited the Prophet to his house. He reached the Prophet and said:

"I invite you to a small meal. It is enough for you and six other guests, in case you want to bring someone else with you." The Prophet exclaimed to all those present: *"O people, Jaber has made food for you! All of you, come with me."* Jaber ran to his wife and told her about it. She however said: *"Do not worry, the Prophet knows what he is doing."* In the house, the Prophet served himself and his companions, until all of his companions were all full. Jaber said: *"In the end, the pot was as full as it was in the beginning."*[3]

---

1 Muslims wash their faces, arms, heads and feet before each prayer.

2 **Al-Buchari:** Assahih, Hadith N°.: 3307, **Moslim:** Assahih, Hadith N°.: 44226, **Ibn Hanbal**, Ahmad: Al-Musnad, Hadith N°.: 12281.

3 **Al-Buchari:** Assahih, Hadith N°.: 3793, **Moslim:** Assahih, Hadith N°.: 3800, and other sources.

2.4.3 The Weeping Tree Trunk

The Weeping Tree Trunk

In the Prophet's mosque there was a trunk next to which the Prophet delivered his sermons. One of his companions, who was a carpenter, built him a stable podium with three steps. On the day that the Prophet used this podium and did no longer preach by the trunk, weeping sounds emanated from it. The Prophet descended from the podium and came to it, and he embraced and caressed the trunk. It stopped weeping.[1]

2.4.4 The Speaking Spiny-tailed lizard

The Speaking Spiny-tailed lizard

When the Prophet was at a large meeting with his companions, a Bedouin came to him and swore: *"O Muhammad, no woman ever bore a bigger liar or a more hateful man than you. Would my people not call me 'impatient', I would have killed you at once and made everybody happy."* Some of the Prophet's companions came to hold him back. The Prophet, however, said: *"What brought you to say untrue things and to offend me during my meeting?"* The Bedouin replied: *"And you even dare to speak to me? You affirm that you are a prophet. But I swear not to believe until this animal does."* The Bedouin fetched a spiny-tailed lizard. The Prophet said: *"O, lizard"* and it replied: *"Always and willingly, yes."* The Prophet asked: *"Who do you worship?"* and the lizard replied: *"The one whose throne is up above, who counts earth and sea as His kingdoms, who has His mercy in Janna and his punishment in Jahannam."* And the Prophet asked further: *"Who am I?"* The spiny-tailed lizard replied: *"You are the Messenger of the God of all worlds, and the last Prophet. Those who believe in you will prosper, and*

---

1 **Al-Buchari:** Assahih, Hadith N°.: 3318 , **Attermezi:** Assunan, Hadith N°.: 463.

those who do not believe in you will lose." The Bedouin said: "I attest that there is no God but Allah, and that you truly are His Prophet. When I came here there was no one I hated more than you, but I swear, you just became dearer to me than my own self. I believe in you whole heartedly." The Prophet spoke: "Praise be to Allah, who rightly guided you to this religion."

A company of one thousand soldiers, who had just arrived to murder the Prophet, converted to Islam because of this event. They all kissed the Prophet's head, hands and feet, and attested: "La ilaha illa Allah, Muhammad rasulu Allah."[1] (There is no God but Allah, and Muhammad is Allah's apostle).

2.4.5 The Healing of the Ill

- Qatada, a man whose eye had been pushed out of its socket by an arrow, came with it to Muhammad. The Prophet took it and put it back in its right place. Afterwards, Qatada could see better with this eye than with the other.[2]
- Muhammad Ibn Hatib was a little boy whose arm was burnt by boiling water spilled on it from a metal kettle. When the Prophet touched it, the arm was immediately healed.[3]
- A boy named Mu-au-wath Ibn Afraa came crying to the Prophet, with a cut-off hand. The Prophet took the hand, put it back on his arm, stroked it, and the hand grew back in.[4] There are also several other cases of a similar nature.

---

1 ATTABARANI: Al-Mugam Al-awsat, Cairo 1995, Vol. 6, p. 127, ATTABARANI: Al-Mugam As-sagier, Beirut 1985, Vol. 2, p. 153, AL-BEIHAQI: Dalail Annu-bowwa, Cairo 1988, Vol. 6, p. 36.

2 AL-BEIHAQI: Dalail Annu-bowwa, Cairo 1988, Vol. 3, p. 251.

3 IBN HANBAL, Ahmad: Al-Musnad, Hadith N°.: 26194, 17565, AL-HAKEM: Al-Mustadrak, Hadith N°.: 7010.

4 cp. I-YAD, Al-Qadi: Aschifaa, Beirut 1988, p. 324.

2.4.6 The Acceptance of His Supplication

The Acceptance of His Supplication

- The Prophet performed a supplication for a boy named Anas Ibn
  Malik, by his mother's request, so that he would live long, become rich and have many children.

  He became one of the richest men amongst the Prophet's companions. When he died at the age of 92 in the year 710, the
  number of his children and grandchildren surpassed one hundred. Anas Ibn Malik was the last of the Prophet's companion to
  pass away.[1]

Acceptance

- Abdur-Rahman Ibn Auf was a man who rejected the help of others and always tried to earn his own money.

  The Prophet performed a supplication for him, so that his efforts
  were successful and he received a lot of money. From the day of
  this supplication, all his businesses were successful. He said: *"It
  went so far, that I would find gold or silver when I picked up a rock
  from the ground."*[2]

  One day, Abdur-Rahman Ibn Auf presented poor people with
  one of his caravans, which consisted of seven hundred camels
  and were fully loaded with the most diverse selection of mer-
  chandise.[3] When he died, the gold from his inheritance was
  handed out with shovels.[4]

- As a reward for his beautiful poem, the Prophet made the following supplication for the poet Anna-begah: *"May God always preserve your mouth."* He died at the age of one hundred and twenty,

---

1 **Moslim:** Assahih, Hadith N°.: 4531, **Ibn Hanbal,** Ahmad: Al-Musnad, Hadith N°.: 13104, 26158.

2 **Al-Berti:** Musnad Abdurrahman Ibn Auf, Beirut 1993, p. 42.

3 **Ibn Kathier:** Al-Bedaya Wannehaya, Beirut 1988, Vol. 10, p. 253.

4 idem., p. 256.

of his Supplication

without having even lost a single one of his teeth.[1]

- The Prophet said to Abo-Qatada Al-Ansari: *"May God preserve your skin and your hair."* Until the day of his death at the age of seventy, he looked like a twenty year-old.[2]

2.4.7 Prophecies

When Muhammad secretly fled from Macca to Madina in the year 624, he was followed by an enemy named Suraka. When he had almost caught up to the Prophet, with his sword already in his hand, the hooves of his horse sank into the ground up to its stomach, even though the ground was rock-hard.

He said:

"I know you did this; please, do a supplication for me, so Allah releases my horse. I will not chase you anymore."

He was freed and the Prophet told him:

"I foretell that you will carry the bracelets of Khosrau." Suraka replied: *"Khosrau, the king of Persia?"*

Muhammad replied: *"Yes."*

Sixteen years later, in the year 638, after the Battle of al-Qadisiyya (between Muslims and Persians), the castle of Khosrau was conquered and his bracelets were sent, amongst many other things, as war spoils[3] to the caliph in Madina. Caliph Omar summoned Suraka, gave him the bracelets, and said:

"Praise be to Allah, who took the bracelets of Khosrau, son of Hormizd, and gave them to Suraka, son of Malik, who is only a simple

---

1 **Al-Beihaqi:** Dalail Annu-bowwa, Cairo 1988, Vol. 6, p. 232.

2 **Al-Hakem:** Al-Mustadrak, Hadith N°.: 6067, **Adahabi:** Se-yar Aalam Annobalaa, Beirut 2001, Vol. 2, p. 450.

3 The spoils of war in Islam are divided and, in addition to the army, distributed amongst the following groups: the Islamic state, the Prophet's relatives, the orphans and the deserving poor, and the travelers who have lost their money. Only the belongings of the defeated army, left during the war, are taken . The belongings of the people remain untouched.

Bedouin. "[1]

Khosrau, the king of the Persian Empire, which was a significant world power for many centuries, sent two messengers to arrest Muhammad. They said to him:

"Either you come peacefully with us, or you know that Khosrau could annihilate you and your people."

The next day, Muhammad summoned both messengers. They asked again:

"Are you now ready to come with us?"

Muhammad replied:

"You will never see Khosrau again. God allowed him to be killed at the seventh hour of last night, by his son."

And it had happened exactly as he stated.[2]

He stated that the first member of his family who would die after him would be his daughter Fatima, and it did happen.[3]

2.4.8 Other Miracles

- Safina, one of the Prophet's companions, was on a journey through the forest. A lion started to chase him, but Safina said: *"You lion, I am the servant of the Messenger of Allah."* The lion calmed down, bowed his head and walked away.[4]
- A woman invited the Prophet to eat a grilled lamb. When he wanted to eat of it, he suddenly said to his companions: *"Hands*

---

1 **AL-BUCHARI:** Assahih, Hadith N°. 3616, **MOSLIM:** Assahih, Hadith N°.: 3750, **IBN HANBAL**, Ahmad: Al-Musnad, Hadith N°.: 3, **AL-BEIHAQI:** Dalail Annu-bowwa, Cairo 1988, Vol. 6, p. 325, **IBN KATHIER:** Al-Bedaya Wannehaya, Beirut 1988, Vol. 7, p. 78.

2 **ASSALHI:** Subul Al-Huda War-raschad, Beirut 1993, Vol. 11, p. 362, **IBN KATHIER:** Al-Bedaya Wannehaya, Beirut 1988, Vol. 6, p. 329, **ATTABARI:** Attariech, Leiden 1879, Vol. 2, p. 296.

3 **AL-BUCHARI:** Assahih, Hadith N°.: 5812, **MOSLIM:** Assahih, Hadith N°.: 4488.

4 **ABO NO-EIM:** Marifatus-sahaba, Riyadh 1998, Vol. 3, p. 1392, **AL-BEIHAQI:** Dalail Annu-bowwa, Cairo 1988, Vol. 6, p. 45.

off, the lamb says it is poisoned." One of his companions, who had already eaten of it, died.[1]

- One day, Muhammad was resting alone under a tree. A Bedouin appeared and drew his sword to murder the Prophet, and said: *"Who can protect you from me now?"* The Prophet said: *"Allah!"* The sword fell from his hand, the Prophet picked it up and said: *"Who can protect you from me now?"* The Bedouin replied: *"It is said, you forgive your enemies"* and the Prophet let him go peacefully.[2]

The judge Iyad[3] commented on these events as follows:

"These stories, which took place under masses of people, cannot be doubted. Arabs were always very critical towards these kinds of events, and yet this story was transmitted by numerous Arabs, and it was not denied by any of the affected parties."[4]

2.5 Muhammad, truthful and unique

Reginald Bosworth Smith (1839-1908),
British professor, author and clergyman
"He was Caesar and Pope in one; but he was Pope without Pope's pretensions, Caesar without the legions of Caesar: without a standing

---

1 **Abo Dawood:** Assunan, Hadith N°.: 3912, **Al-Hakem:** Al-Mustadrak, Hadith N°.: 4955.

2 **Al-Hakem:** Al-Mustadrak, Hadith N°.: 4290, Abd **Ibn Humeid:** Al-Musnad, Hadith N°.: 1098.

3 The judge Abo Al-Fadl Iyad Ibn Mousa (1083-1149) is one of the most famous Muslim scholars and judges. He was judge of the city of Ceuta (1121), (1145) and Granada (1136). His works in Islamic Right, Hadith and history have acceptance and authority in the Islamic World, and they are still read and taught.

4 cp. **I-yad**, S. 287.

army, without a bodyguard, without a palace, without a fixed revenue;
if ever any man had the right to say that he ruled by the Divine Right,
it was Mohammed, for he had all the power without its instruments and
without its supports. "[1]

Encyclopaedia Britannica

Encyclopaedia Britannica (1911)
"Of all the religious personalities of the world, Muhammad was the
most successful." (Regarding Muhammad) *"[...] a mass of detail in the*
early sources shows that he was an honest and upright man who had
gained the respect and loyalty of others who were likewise honest and
upright men. "[2]

William Montgomery Watt

William Montgomery Watt (1909-2006)
British professor of Arabic and Islamic Studies at the University of Edinburgh
"His readiness to endure persecution for his beliefs, the high moral
character of the men who believed in him and looked up to him as a
leader, and the greatness of his ultimate achievement - all argue his fun-
damental integrity. To suppose Muhammad an impostor raises more
problems than it solves. "[3]

"Of all the world's greatest men none has been so much maligned as
Muhammad. It is easy to see how this has come about. For centuries Is-
lam was the great enemy of Christendom, for Christendom was in direct
contact with no other organized states comparable in power to the
Muslims. "[4]

---

1 **Bosworth Smith R.**: Mohammed and Mohammedanism, London 1874, p. 235.

2 Encyclopaedia Britannica, Chicago 1921/22, Vol. XII.

3 **Watt**, William Montgomery: Mohammed At Macca, Oxford 1953, p. 52.

4 idem., Oxford 1956, p. 324.

Udo Schaefer

Udo Schaefer (born 1926) *German jurist and Orientalist*
"The accusation that Muhammad was an impostor is no longer ar-gued by any modern scholar. His subjective uprightness and the honesty of his conviction are nowadays generally acknowledged."[1]

Tor Andrae

Tor Andrae (1885-1947)
Swedish religion historian and bishop of Linköping
"That Mohammed acted in good faith can hardly be disputed by anyone who knows the psychology of inspiration."[2]

Washington Irving

Washington Irving (1783-1859)
American writer
"He was sober and abstemious in his diet, and a rigorous observer of fasts. He indulged in no magnificence of apparel, the ostentation of a petty mind, neither was his simplicity in dress affected, but the result of a real disregard to distinction from so trivial a source."[3]

"In his private dealings he was just. He treated friends and strangers, the rich and poor, the powerful and weak, with equity, and was beloved by the common people for the affability with which he received them, and listened to their complaints."[4]

"His military triumphs awakened no pride nor vain glory, as they would have done had they been effected for selfish purposes. In the time

---

1 **Schaefer**, Dr. Udo: Muhammad - ein Lügenprophet? Eine Klarstellung gegenüber des katholischen Glaubens, p. 4. URL: www.udoschaefer.com/pdffiles/muhammad.pdf (Accessed: May 12th 2009).

2 **Andrae**, Tor: Mohammed, Sein Leben und Glaube, New York 2000, p. 47.

3 **Irving**, Washington : Mahomet And His Successors, UK 2007, p.193.

4 Idem, p. 197.

of his greatest power he maintained the same simplicity of manners and appearance as in the days of his adversity. So far from affecting a regal state, he was displeased if, on entering a room, any unusual testimonials of respect were shown to him. "[1]

George Bernhard Shaw

George Bernard Shaw (1856 - 1950)
Irish dramatist, satirist and Nobel laureate of literature in 1925

"*I have always held the religion of Muhammad in high estimation because of its wonderful vitality. It is the only religion which appears to me to possess that assimilating capacity to the changing phase of existence which can make itself appeal to every age. I have studied him - the wonderful man and in my opinion far from being an anti-Christ, he must be called the Savior of Humanity.*

I believe that if a man like him were to assume the helm of the modern world he would succeed in solving its problems in a way that would bring it the much needed peace and happiness: I have prophesied about the faith of Muhammad that it would be acceptable to the Europe of tomorrow as it is beginning to be acceptable to the Europe of today." [2]

Mahatma Gandhi

Mahatma Gandhi (1869-1948)
Indian thinker and leader of the Indian independence movement

"*I wanted to know the best of one who holds today's undisputed sway over the hearts of millions of mankind [...] I became more than convinced that it was not the sword that won a place for Islam in those days in the scheme of life.*

It was the rigid simplicity, the utter self-effacement of the Prophet,

---

1 Idem, p. 203.

2 cp. **ANDREWS**, C. F.: The Genuine Islam, Singapore 1936.

the scrupulous regard for his pledges, his intense devotion to this friends and followers, his intrepidity, his fearlessness, his absolute trust in God and in his own mission.

These and not the sword carried everything before them and surmounted every obstacle. When I closed the 2nd volume of (the Prophet's biography), I was sorry there was not more for me to read of the great life."[1]

Mahatma Gandhi

Annie Besant

Annie Besant (1847-1933)

British theosophist, feminist, journalist, writer and politician

"*It is impossible for anyone who studies the life and character of the great Prophet of Arabia, who knows how he taught and how he lived, to feel anything but reverence for that mighty Prophet, one of the great messengers of the Supreme. And although in what I put to you I shall say many things which may be familiar to many, yet I myself feel whenever I re-read them, a new way of admiration, a new sense of reverence for that mighty Arabian teacher.*"[2]

Michael H. Hart

Michael H. Hart (born 1932)

Professor of astronomy, physics and history of science

"*My choice of Muhammad to lead the list of the world's most influential persons may surprise some readers and may be questioned by others, but he was the only man in history who was supremely successful on both the religious and secular level.*"[3]

---

1 Young India (periodical), 1924, Issue 1, N°. 8.

2 BESANT, Annie: The Life And Teachings Of Mohammed, Madras 1932, p. 4.

3 HART, Michael H.: The 100: A Ranking Of The Most Influential Persons In History, New York 1978, p. 33.

Prof. K. S. Ramakrishna

Prof. K. S. Ramakrishna Rao (born 1932)

Indian professor of philosophy and parapsychologist

"The personality of Muhammad, it is most difficult to get into the whole truth of it. Only a glimpse of it I can catch. What a dramatic succession of picturesque scenes! There is Muhammad, the Prophet. There is Muhammad, the Warrior; Muhammad, the Businessman; Muhammad, the Statesman; Muhammad, the Orator; Muhammad, the Reformer; Muhammad, the Refuge of Orphans; Muhammad, the Protector of Slaves; Muhammad, the Emancipator of Women; Muhammad, the Judge; Muhammad, the Saint. All in all these magnificent roles, in all these departments of human activities, he is alike a hero. [...]

All great religions have preached the same doctrine but the prophet of Islam had put this theory into actual practice and its value will be fully recognized, perhaps centuries hence, when international consciousness being awakened, racial prejudices may disappear and greater brotherhood of humanity come into existence. [...]

An honest man, as the saying goes, is the noblest work of God, Muhammad was more than honest. He was human to the marrow of his bones. Human sympathy, human love was the music of his soul. To serve man, to elevate man, to purify man, to educate man, in a word to humanize man - this was the object of his mission, the be-all and end all of his life. In thought, in word, in action he had the good of humanity as his sole inspiration, his sole guiding principle."[1]

Christian Snouck Hurgronje

Christiaan Snouck Hurgronje (1857 – 1936)

Dutch professor and Islamic scholar

"The league of nations founded by the prophet of Islam put the principle of international unity and human brotherhood on such universal foundations as to show a candle to other nations." He continues: "The fact is that no nation of the world can show a parallel to what Islam has

---

1 cp. **Ramakrishna**, a.a.O.

done towards the realization of the idea of the League of Nations. "[1]

de Lacy O'leary (1872- 1957)
British clergyman, Arabist and semitist

"*History makes it clear however, that the legend of fanatical Muslims, sweeping through the world and forcing Islam at the point of sword upon conquered races is one of the most fantastically absurd myths that historians have ever repeated.* "[2]

Dr. Gustav Weil (1808-1889)
German Orientalist

"*Muhammad was a shining example to his people. His character was pure and stainless. [...] So unpretentious was he that he would receive from his companions no special mark of reverence, nor would he accept any service from his slave which he could do for himself. He was accessible to all and at all times. He visited the sick and was full of sympathy for all. Unlimited was his benevolence and generosity as also was his anxious care for the welfare of the community.* "[3]

Anita Rai (born 1975)
Indian writer

"*For me it is enough that Muhammad is the greatest feminist the world has so far had but has so little come to know of [...]. Personally I am infinitely grateful to Muhammad, who has not only empathized with the crying voice of the despairing and exploited woman but has taken momentous measures blustering all opposition, to alleviate her lot*

---

1 HURGRONJE, C. Snouck: Mohammedanism, n.l. 2007.

2 O'LEARY, De Lacy: Islam At Crossroads, London 1923, p. 8.

3 cp. WEIL, Dr. Gustav in: Brockelmann, Carl (Editor): History of the Islamic Peoples, Cornwell 1947.

and strengthen her in realistic terms. [...] For ages and ages, a woman had found herself begging and groveling in front of her male master, with her heart-wrenching pleas for justice remaining unheard and unaddressed. Muhammad has changed this forever. "[1]

Samuel Parsons Scott (1846-1929)
American author and jurist
  "*The object of religion is the inculcation of morals, the diminution of evil, the promotion of human happiness, the expansion of the human intellect, if the performance of good works will avail in the great day when mankind shall be summoned to its final reckoning it is neither irreverent nor unreasonable to admit that Muhammad was indeed an Apostle of God.*"[2]

Huston Smith (born 1919)
American religious scholar
  "*Muhammad adhered meticulously to the charter he forged for Madina, which - grounded as it was in the Quranic injunction: 'Let there be no compulsion in religion' (2:256) - is arguably the first mandate for religious tolerance in human history.*"[3]

Huston Smith

Raymond Le Rouge
  "*The Arabian Prophet Muhammad is the founder of a revolution unparalleled in history. He founded a political state that will ultimately embrace the entire planet. The law of that Government will rest on justice and kindness. His teachings revolve around human equality, mutual cooperation and universal brotherhood.*"[4]

1 cp. **Rai**, Anita: Muhammad, Uncovering the True Story, o.O. 2007.

2 **Scott**, S. P.: History of Moorish Empire in Europe, Philadelphia 1904. p. 126.

3 cp. **Smith**, Prof. Huston: The Illustrated World's Religions. A Guide to Our Wisdom Traditions, New York 1995, p. 168.

4 **Le Rouge**, Raymond: Vie de Mahomet, Paris 1939.

John Hopkins Denison

John Hopkins Denison (1870-1936)

American sociologist and physiologist

"*Muhammad saved the human civilization from extinction. Ponder! Which person is it who taught mankind the way to establish the greatest society; the society in which blessings descend upon every individual?*"[1]

Dr. Maurice Bucaille

Dr. Maurice Bucaille (1920-1998)

French surgeon and scientist

"*How could a man, from being illiterate, become the most important authors, in terms of literary merits, in the whole of Arabic literature? How could he then pronounce truths of a scientific nature that no other human being could possibly have developed at that time, and all this without once making the slightest error in his pronouncement on the subject?*"[2]

"*A totally objective examination of it [the Quran] in the light of modern knowledge, leads us to recognize the agreement between the two. It makes us deem it quite unthinkable for a man of Mohammed's time to have been the author of such statements on account of the state of knowledge in his day.*"[3]

William James Durant

William James Durant (1885-1981)

American philosopher and writer

"*If we rated the greatness by the influence of the great on people we will say: Muhammad is the greatest of the great in history.*"[4]

1 **Denison**, John Hopkins: Emotion as the Basis of Civilization, New York and London 1928.

2 Bucaille, Dr. Maurice: The Qur'an and Modern Science, Raleigh (North Carolina) 1997, p. 18.

3 **Bucaille**, Dr. Maurice: The Bible, The Qur'an And Science, Paris 1976, p. 125.

4 cp. **Durant**, Will: The Story of Civilization, New York 1935-75.

Geoffrey Parrinder (1910–2005)

Geoffrey Parrinder

Professor of Comparative Religion Studies at the King's College in London

"No great religious leader has been so maligned as Prophet Mohammed. Attacked in the past as a heretic, an impostor, or a sensualist, it is still possible to find him referred to as 'the false prophet'. [...] This man was not married until he was twenty-five years of age, then he and his wife lived in happiness and fidelity for twenty-four years, until her death when he was forty-nine. Only between the age of fifty and his death at sixty-two did Prophet Mohammed take other wives, and most of them were taken for dynastic and political reasons."[1]

Prof. Edward Montet

Prof. Edward Montet

French intellectual during the 19th century

"The teachings of the Prophet and the Quran have invariably kept their place as the fundamental starting point, and the dogma of unity of God has always been proclaimed therein with a grandeur a majesty, an invariable purity and with a note of sure conviction, which it is hard to find surpassed outside the pale of Islam [...] A creed so precise, so stripped of all theological complexities and consequently so accessible to the ordinary understanding might be expected to possess and does indeed possess a marvelous power of winning its way into the consciences of men."[2]

James A. Michener (1907-1997) *American writer*

James A. Michener

"Orphaned at birth, he was always particularly solicitous of the poor and needy, the widow and the orphan, the slave and the downtrodden."[3]

---

1 **Parrinder**, Geoffrey: Mysticism in the World's Religions, New York 1976, p. 121.

2 **Montet**, Edward: La Propaganda Chretienne et Adversaires Musulmans, Paris 1890 in: **Arnold**, Thomas: The Preaching of Islam, Westminster 1896, p. 337.

3 **Michener**, James A.: Islam.The Misunderstood Religion. In: Reader's Digest (The American edition), 05/1955, p. 68-70.

Major Arthur Glyn Leonard

Major Arthur Glyn Leonard (born 1855)

"If ever any man on this earth has found God; if ever any man has devoted his life for the sake of God with a pure and holy zeal then, without doubt, and most certainly that man was the Holy Prophet of Arabia."[1]

Phillip K. Hitti

Phillip K. Hitti (1886-1978)

American professor of Semitic and Oriental literature

"Islam does not set impossible goals. There are no mythological intricacies in this message. No hidden meanings or secrets and absolutely no priesthood."[2]

Thomas Carlyle

Thomas Carlyle[3] (1795-1881)

Scottish essayist and historian

"The lies which well-meaning zeal has heaped round this man (Muhammad), are disgraceful to ourselves only."[4]

"I like Muhammad for his total freedom from cant. He is a rough self-helping son of the wilderness; does not pretend to be what he is not. There is no ostentatious pride in him; but neither does he go much upon humility."[5]

---

1 LEONARD, Major A.: Islam, its Moral and Spiritual Values, London 1909, p. 9.

2 cp. HITTI, Phillip Khuri: History of the Arabs, London 1937.

3 Thomas Carlyle was a Scottish writer and historian. He was born to a Calvinist family and should have become a preacher, but he lost his faith during his studies.

4 Carlyle, Thomas: On Heroes, Hero-Worship and the Heroic in History, California 1993, p. 38.

5 Idem, p. 62.

Edward Gibbon (1737-1794)

Most influential British historian of his time

"His (i.e., Muhammad's) memory was capacious and retentive, his wit easy and social, his imagination sublime, his judgment clear, rapid and decisive. He possessed the courage of both thought and action."

"The good sense of Muhammad despised the pomp of royalty. The Apostle of God submitted to the menial offices of the family; he kindled the fire; swept the floor; milked the ewes; and mended with his own hands his shoes and garments. Disdaining the penance and merit of a hermit, he observed without effort of vanity the abstemious diet of an Arab."[1]

Edward Gibbon and Simon Oakley

"It is not the propagation but the permanency of his religion that deserves our wonder, the same pure and perfect impression which he engraved at Macca and Madina is preserved after the revolutions of twelve centuries by the Indian, the African and the Turkish proselytes of the Quran [...] The Muhammadans have uniformly withstood the temptation of reducing the object of their faith and devotion to a level with the senses and imagination of man. 'I believe in One God and Muhammad the Apostle of God' - is the simple and invariable profession of Islam. The intellectual image of the Deity has never been degraded by any visible idol; the honors of the prophet have never transgressed the measure of human virtue, and his living precepts have restrained the gratitude of his disciples within the bounds of reason and religion."[2]

Benjamin Bosworth Smith (1784-1884)

Bishop in Kentucky

"Here in Islam every thing is different. Instead of the shadowy and

---

1 GIBBON, Edward: The Decline and fall of the Roman Empire, n.l. 1823.

2 GIBBON, E./ OACKLEY,S.: History of the Saracen Empire, London 1870, p. 54.

the mysterious, we have history.[...] We know of the external history of Muhammad....while for his internal history after his mission had been proclaimed, we have a book absolutely unique in its origin, in its preservation. [...] on the Substantial authority of which no one has ever been able to cast a serious doubt."[1]

Alphonse de Lamartine
Alphonse de Lamartine (1790-1869)
French poet, writer and statesman

"*Never has a man undertaken a work so far beyond human power with so feeble means, for he (Muhammad) had in the conception as well as in the execution of such a great design, no other instrument than himself and no other aid except a handful of men living in a corner of the desert.*"[2]

"*If greatness of purpose, smallness of means, and astonishing results are the three criteria of a human genius, who could dare compare any  great man in history with Muhammad? The most famous men created arms, laws, and empires only. They founded, if anything at all, no more than material powers which often crumbled away before their eyes. This man moved not only armies, legislations, empires, peoples, dynasties, but millions of men in one-third of the then inhabited world; and more than that, he moved the altars, the gods, the religions, the ideas, the beliefs and the souls.*"[3]

"*On the basis of a Book, every*

---

1 cp. **Bosworth Smith R.**: Mohammed and Mohammedanism, London 1874.

2 **Lamartine**, Alphonse de: Histoire De La Turquie, Paris 1854, Vol. II, p. 277.

3 Idem, p. 277f.

letter which has become law, he created a spiritual nationality which blends together peoples of every tongue and race. He has left the indelible characteristic of this Muslim nationality the hatred of false gods and the passion for the One and Immaterial God. This avenging patriotism against the profanation of Heaven formed the virtue of the followers of Muhammad; the conquest of one-third the earth to the dogma was his miracle; or rather it was not the miracle of man but that of reason."[1]

"His life, his meditations, his heroic revelings against the superstitions of his country, and his boldness in defying the furies of idolatry, his firmness in enduring them for fifteen years in Macca, his acceptance of the role of public scorn and almost of being a victim of his fellow countrymen: all these and finally, his flight and his incessant preaching, his wars against odds, his faith in his success and his superhuman security in misfortune, his forbearance in victory, [...], his endless prayers, his mystic conversations with God, his death and his triumph after death; all these attest not to an impostor.

[...] Philosopher, orator, apostle, legislator, warrior, conqueror of ideas, restorer of rational dogmas, of a cult without images; the founder of twenty terrestrial empires and of one spiritual empire, that is Muhammad. As regards all standards by which human greatness may be measured, we may well ask, is there any man greater than he?"[2]

---

1 Idem, p. 278.
2 Idem, p. 280.

Chapter 4

The Quran, The Last Letter From God

Muhammad (570-632) was the last Prophet. His Message is valid to all people on earth.

The miracle given by God to him is not bound by place and time, so that future generations also have the opportunity to perceive it. This enduring miracle is the Quran.

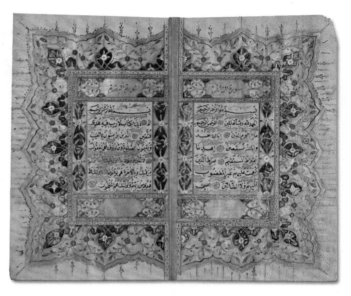

Mushaf by Hafiz Mustafa (1796)

The Quran is the only divine book that has been preserved unchanged in each and every one of its exemplars, down to the very last letter, up until today – more than 1400 years later. With great care, it has been preserved both verbally and in written form.

Its transmission by the Prophet took place piecewise over 23 years, and each word was recorded by scribes.

Each newly transmitted part was copied four times by the companions of the Prophet, and it was learnt by heart by many believers. In this manner, nothing could have been lost.

After the Quran was fully revealed, the Prophet taught his companions the order of the verses. At the end of his life, hundreds of his companions could recite the entire Quran from memory.

The Quranic written pieces, which had been dictated by the Prophet, were collected shortly after by a committee in the Mushaf[(1)]. This committee was composed of companions known for being able to flawlessly recite the Quran by heart. In spite of their in-depth knowledge of the Quran and as a security measure, they did write a verse into the Mushaf without observing two conditions:

1. The Prophet's original dictation (the Quranic written piece) had to be available for comparison. A piece was only original when two witnesses, who were with the Prophet at the time of its record, were present.

2. In addition to this committee, the other companions that had learned the Quran by heart had to corroborate that there were no discrepancies at all between what was written and what they knew.

The committee also completed nother six copies of the Mushaf.

The preserved copy of the first Mushafs

---

1   It is the book that contains the whole text of the Quran.

The most famous copy of these seven, which is preserved until today, is in the manuscripts library of the Auqaf Ministry in Cairo.

Nowadays, the Quran is the only book that has been learned by heart by many thousands of people at all times since its revelation. The largest number of people in one country who can nowadays recite the Quran by heart without a model is seven million people in a non-Arab country, where yearly one hundred thousand people are added to this number.

And so, Allah promised in the Quran:

"Verily We have sent down the Quran;
and We will assuredly guard it (from corruption)."
The Quran, 15: 9

Muslims are not only concerned with the preservation of the Quran to the last letter from generation to generation, but also with the pronunciation of every single letter and every single word following the example of the intonation and the form of expression of Prophet Muhammad. For this purpose, there is a special kind of phonetic studies called Tajwid.

In spite of the many translations, the Quran is only seen as "the" Quran in Arabic – its original language, for a translation is always subject to the interpretation of its translator, and this human influence on God's word cannot do the original justice.

The Quran discusses different topics, such as belief, worship, life philosophy, relations between people, daily life, manners, overviews of the Afterlife and the Day of Resurrection, descriptions of Janna and Jahannam as well as social, commercial, civil and criminal law, and combines them in a harmonic fashion. It contains different scientific facts of geology, oceanography, astronomy, psychology and even embryology, which could be determined in their exactitude only recently with the aid of modern science.

1 THE LINGUISTIC MIRACLES OF THE QURAN

1.1 No Imitation Possible *No Imitation Possible*

Rhetoric, literature and poetry played a very important role in the pre-Islamic Arabic society. They served to transmit news, record historical events, preserve and glorify the honor and position of the tribe, and diffuse laments for the dead and satires on the enemies. The Arabic tribes always attempted to improve their literature and their poetry, in order to raise their cultural status. When a tribe produced a talented poet, a festival was held in celebration. Yearly they held poetry competitions, whereby there were committees that evaluated the works based on carefully defined standards. At this time, when the Arabs had reached their peak in literature and the poetic arts, Muhammad appeared. He was neither literate nor had he any knowledge of the poetic arts. This man, called to be a Prophet, was now suddenly challenging them with his recitation of the Quran.

> "*Say:*
> '*If the mankind and the Jinn*[1] *were to gather together to produce the like of this Quran, they could not produce the like thereof, even if they backed up each other with help and support.*' "
>
> The Quran, 17: 88

Even though the best poets of the time, as well as his opponents, did not leave anything untried to prove that the Quran was the work

---

1 The clanship of Satan. The human prophets were also sent to them; some of them became Muslims, some of them rejected the Message.

of Muhammad himself and that it had nothing to do with God, they remained without a similarly fantastic work. God then challenged the Arabs to compose ten chapters (surahs) equal to the Quran (114 Surahs). They also failed to do this.

"Or they may say,
'He forged it (the Quran).'
Say: 'Bring you then ten forged Surahs (chapters)
like unto it, and call (to your help) whomsoever you can,
other than God! – if you speak the truth!'
If then they answer not your (call),
know then that this Revelation (the Quran) is sent down
with the knowledge of God,
and that there is no god but He!
Will you even then submit to Islam?"

The Quran, 11: 13-14

Finally, God challenged them to compose just one equal chapter (surah), and they also failed.

"And if you are in doubt concerning
that which We have sent down (i.e. the Quran)
to Our servant,
then produce a Surah (chapter) of the like thereof and call
your witnesses (supporters and helpers) besides God,
if you are truthful.
But if you do it not, and you will never can, then fear the
fire whose fuel is Men and Stones,
which is prepared for those who reject Faith."

The Quran, 2: 23-24

1.2 The Quran's Rhetoric and Inimitable Style

The rhetoric of the Quran is shown in its special style, in the magnificence of its descriptions and the precision of its word choice, and in the fact that several meanings are united in such a few words in the Quran, without rendering them complicated or leaving them unclear.

The fluency and the sublime nature of its verses widely surpass the linguistic arts of even the most eloquent speaker; and, in addition to the verses themselves, there is a unique musical melody that accentuates the meaning of each verse.

The Quran's alluring beauty and its own charm present themselves through sentences which are rich in meaning, and are expressed in a majestic style and short, concise manner.

Its rhymes possess an expressive power and an explosive energy, which cannot be transmitted in a literary translation.

The style of the Quran, which was revealed to the Prophet over a period of twenty three years, clearly differentiates itself from the rhetoric of the Prophet himself.

However, to maintain two different rhetoric styles for so long is even unimaginable for a professional writer.

The French Orientalist Régis Blachère (1900-1973) says in this regard:

"The literary wonder of the Quran is the proof of its mission. The Prophet did not achieve the rhetoric level of the Quran in his speech." [1]

---

1 **BLACHERE**, Régis: Introduction au Coran, Paris 1959

1.3 The Quran's **Particular Influence**
The Particular Influence

Convinced by the daily growing influence of the Quran on the hearts and minds, and by the increase of believers, the infidels forbade their countrymen to listen to the Quran or Muhammad.

"And those who disbelieve said:
'Listen not to this Quran, and make noise in the midst of
its (recitation) that you may overcome!'"

The Quran, 41: 26

1.3.1 In **Private** *In Private*

In spite of this public aversion, the biggest enemies of Muhammad, the leaders of Macca, snuck to his house at night to listen to his recitation of the Quran. Amongst them were Abo Gahl, Al-Akhnas ibn Shu-raeiq and Abo Sofian. They did not see each other when doing this; it was not until dawn, when they were sneaking out of Muhammad's house, that they encountered each other. The leaders cursed one another and promised each other never to come back to Muhammad's house and listen to the Quran. The following night, the event repeated itself, and on the third night they all met each other unintentionally. This time, however, they swore an oath to never listen to Muhammad again. [1]

---

1 **AL-BEIHAQI:** Dalail Annu-bowwa, Cairo 1988, Vol. 2, p. 206.

1.3.2 Warning the **Guests**

Attofail Addausi was a prominent leader of his tribe Daus and a renowned poet. When he came to visit Macca, the city's leaders welcomed him and warned him about Muhammad and the Quran. Their explanation was that the Quran acted as witchcraft, through which a person left his father, his wife and his tribe to follow Muhammad. *"Out of concern for you, we advise you to avoid a meeting with him at any cost, and never pay heed to him."* Attofail was so worried that he decided to follow the Maccan's advice. Shortly thereafter, he went to the Kaaba to worship his idols. He had pressed cotton in his ears, so that, in case he encountered Muhammad, none of his words could reach his ears. However, much to his dismay, he encountered the Prophet praying alone at the Kaaba. Slowly, Attofail Addausi approached him, compelled by an unspecific curiosity, and attracted by Muhammad's strange prayer. In spite of the cotton in his ears, he heard single verses of the Quran. He was overcome by a deep spiritual peace and asked himself: *"What are you doing? You are yourself a poet and a man of reason, and you can determine yourself what is good and what is bad. I will listen to Muhammad."* He spoke to the Prophet and asked him: *"Can you recite something of this Quran to me?"* After a few words from it, Attofail said: *"No, I have not heard anything as beautiful and just before this,"* he converted to Islam and spoke to the Prophet: *"I will go back to my tribe and teach them about Islam."*[1]

1.3.3 The Tempting **Offers**

With the intention of putting an end to Islam, the leaders of Macca gathered and looked for the one who was the best-versed in the arts of magic, poetry and soothsaying, in order to send him to negotiate with the Prophet. The decision was made, and Otba Ibn Rabia was chosen, who was also a smart leader. He went to the Prophet with tempting offers, and declared:

"Muhammad, I submit some offers to you, so listen and think about them. Maybe you will accept some of them, and thus we will be again united." *"Speak, I am listening,"* said the Prophet, and Otba continued: *"O son of my brother, if your goal were to amass money through religion, then we would give you so much money, that you would be the richest amongst us, and your children and grandchildren would live in richness. If you want to attain leadership, then we will make you our king, and nothing will be decided without your order. If you were possessed by a devil who forces you to stray from our religion, then we would look for doctors who could heal you. But please, renounce your religion."* *"Are you done with your offers?"* the Prophet finally asked. Otba

---

1 **IBN KATHIER:** Assyra, Beirut 1971, Vol. 2, p. 72-73 and **ASSALHI:** Subul Al-Huda Warraschad, Beirut 1993, Vol. 2, p. 417.

replied: *"Yes,"* and the Prophet said: *"Then listen to my answer."* The Prophet began to recite a Surah from the Quran (Surah 41, verse 1-38); Otba reclined and listened attentively to him.

At the end, the Prophet asked him:

"Did you hear, Otba?" – "Yes." – "Then do what you please."

Otba returned to his people and they received him with the words: *"You have come back with a different face than the one you left us with."* Otba said: *"I swear I have never heard anything like that which I heard from that man. It is not, I swear, a poem, magic or soothsaying. My people, obey me just this time! Leave this man and his religion in peace. The words that I heard from him will have a powerful future."* They dissented: *"He has hexed you with his tongue."* But Otba only said: *"This is my opinion. Do as you wish now."* [1]

1.3.4 Another Attempt to Stop the Message

The leaders of Macca attempted to convince Muhammad to renounce the Quran yet another time. This time, they sent Al-Walid Ibn Al-Mughira to Prophet Muhammad. The Prophet recited to him a couple of verses from the Quran. Al-Walid returned and displayed his astonishment about it. The leaders of Macca were disappointed and asked him to report something negative about the Quran: "We will be angry with you until you come to your senses and say something reasonable about the Quran!" He replied: "I swear, there is not one amongst you who is more versed in the poetic arts than me. I swear what this man recites does not resemble any poem. It is so sweet, so beautiful, so smooth; it surpasses all forms of rhetoric. No human created these words."[2]

---

1 **Al-Beihaqui:** Dalail Annu-bowwa, Cairo 1988, Vol. 2, p. 204-205, **Ibn Kathier:** Assyra, Beirut 1971, Vol. 7, p. 161-163.

2 **Al-Hakem:** Al-Mustadrak, Hadith N°.: 3831.

2 THE SCIENTIFIC WONDERS OF THE QURAN

The following section will be dedicated to some of the scientific facts contained in the Quran, which were attainable and realized by humankind only after the discovery of modern research. At the times of Prophet Muhammad – fourteen centuries earlier – no scientist possessed such knowledge. In the Islamic world, this represents yet another proof for the superhuman source of the Quran.

2.1 The "Roots" of the Mountains

While previously it was assumed that mountains were only elevations of the surface of the earth, scientists more recently established that mountains are not only elevations of the surface of the earth, but that they expand over fifteen times of their visible height underground (Mount Everest, with its peak at 8848 meters, expands subterraneously more than 125 kilometers towards the center of the earth). The Quran alluded that mountains have "roots" in the following verse:

"Have We not made the earth as a wide expanse, and the mountains as pegs?"

The Quran, 78: 6-7

2.2 The Primitive Phase of Galaxies

The Primitive Phase of Galaxies

Astronomers and physicist hypothesize that galaxies existed as gaseous masses in their original state. To describe this state of the universe, the word "smoke" is more accurate than "mist". While mist is composed of a cold, evaporated water mass, smoke is usually the product of burning processes.

The Quran also makes this difference:

" Moreover
He Comprehended in His design the sky,
and it had been smoke:
He said to it and to the earth:
'Come you together,
willingly or unwillingly.'
They said: '
We do come (together),
in willing obedience.' "

The Quran, 41: 11

The Arabs did not know about galaxies and the Big Bang at the times of Prophet Muhammad.

Formation of a star. This is how stars look in their original state: as a gaseous mass. The entire universe once looked like this. At the times of Muhammad, it was impossible to obtain these kinds of photos.

Position of our Sun in the Milky Way.

2.3 The Existence of Individual Orbits of Planets

> *"It is not permitted to the Sun to catch up the Moon, nor can the Night outstrip the Day. They all swim, each in an orbit."*
>
> The Quran, 36:40

This verse of the Quran already mentions the astronomic fact of the existence of individual orbits for the sun and the moon for their journey through space. To describe the movement of the sun and the moon, the Quran used the word **"Falak"**, which means **"orbit"** in Arabic[1]. Today we know that the Moon makes a complete orbit around the Earth every 27.3 days. It is also known that the sun orbits around the Galaxy. Astronomers have calculated that it takes the Sun approximately 226 million years to completely orbit around the center of the Milky Way.[2]

2.4 The Size of the Universe

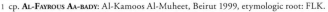

> *"And indeed We have adorned the nearest heaven with lamps."*
>
> The Quran, 67: 5

---

1 cp. **AL-FAYROUS AA-BADY:** Al-Kamoos Al-Muheet, Beirut 1999, etymologic root: FLK.

2 Cain, Fraser: Sun Orbit. URL: www.universetoday.com/guide-to-space/the-sun/sun-orbit (Accessed: Feb. 18th 2010).
We use "approximately" 226 million years because there are different opinions regarding it between astronomers. For example: Patrick Moore and Robin Kerrod calculated 225 million years, while Ken Croswell 230, Frances Hess 240 and Mark Morris 250 million years. Sources:
  1 Moore, Patrick: *The International Encyclopedia of Astronomy,* New York 1981, P. 45.
  2 Kerrod, Robin: *Encyclopedia of Science Heavens 2,* New York 1997, P. 35.
  3 Croswell, Ken: *The Alchemy of the Heavens Searching for the meaning of the Milky Way,* New York 1995, P. 2.
  4 Hess, Frances: Earth Science, New York 2002, P. 348.
  5 Morris, Mark: "The Milky Way."
     The World Book Encyclopedia, Chicago 2002, Vol. 13: 551.

Not until modern science could we confirm what we long knew from the Quran: namely, that the stars we see in the sky at night only represent a small part of the Universe.

2.5 The Description of the Developmental Phases of the Embryo

"*Indeed*
We created man (Adam)
out of an extract of clay;
thereafter
We made him (the offspring of Adam)
as a drop in a safe lodging (womb of the woman);
then We made the drop into a clot of congealed blood;
then We made the clot into a little chewed lump,
then We made out of that little chewed lump bones,
then We clothed the bones with flesh,
and then
We brought it forth as another creation.
So blessed be God, the Best to create!"

The Quran, 23: 12-14

The Arabic word 'alagah' has three meanings: (1) leech, (2) suspended thing and (3) blood clot.

If we compare a leech with an embryo in the 'alagah stage', we will find resemblances[1] between the both, as evinced in Figure 1. The embryo also receives nourishment from the blood of the mother in this phase, just like the leach needs the blood of others.[2]

---

1 **MOORE, K.L./ PERSAUD**, T.V.N.: The Developing Human. Clinically Oriented Embryology, 1993, p. 8.

2 **MOORE, K.L.** et al: Human Development as Described in the Quran and Sunnah, p.36.

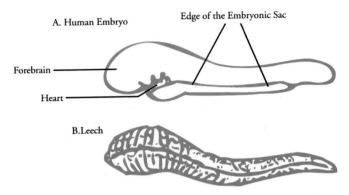

A. Human Embryo

Edge of the Embryonic Sac

Forebrain

Heart

B. Leech

Figure that represents the external resemblance between a leech and the human embryo in the alagah phase

Not until recently did we know about the developmental phases of the embryo. Hamm and Leeuwenhoek were the first scientists to observe human sperm cells (spermatocytes) by using an improved microscope in 1677 (over 1000 years after Muhammad). However, they believed that the sperm cells contained a complete miniature person that grew when it reached the female genital tract.[1]

Drawing of the 17th century by Hartsöker, which represents a miniature person within the sperm cell

---

1 MOORE, K.L./ PERSAUD, T.V.N.: The Developing Human. Clinically Oriented Embryology, 1993, p. 9.

Professor Keith L. Moore

Professor Keith L. Moore[1] comments in this regard:

"It is clear to me that these statements must have come to Muhammad from God because most of this knowledge was not discovered until many centuries later."[2]

Embryo – partially formed and partially unformed

If the embryo of the *chewed lump* stage was dissected, we would see inner organs that are partially formed and partially un developed.

If we then declared the embryo as a complete creation, we would disregard the unformed part; but if we called it an incomplete creation, we would exclusively describe the unformed part.

Hence, the Quran already speaks of the embryo as "partially formed and partially unformed."

" Verily!
We have created you (i.e. Adam)
from dust,
then from drop,
then from clot of congealed blood,
then from a little chewed lump,
partly formed
and partly unformed"

The Quran, 22: 5

---

1 Dr. Emeritus Keith L. MOORE, professor of anatomy and cell biology at the University of Toronto, Canada and dean of the anatomy department. He is the author of the book "The Developing Human", which was translated into eight languages and chosen in the United States as the best book for understanding human development. In 1984 he was awarded the most coveted prize in the field of anatomy in Canada, the J.C.B Grant Award. He has also presided over many international associations, such as the Canadian and American Association of Anatomists and the Association for Biosciences.

2 MOORE, Keith L.: Video 1,
   at: www.dies-ist-die-wahrheit.de/video/index.htm (Accessed: April 25th 2009).

2.6 "Haman" and ancient Egyptian Inscriptions

*"Pharaoh said: 'Oh Haman! Build me a tower,
that I may attain the ways and means –
The ways and means of (reaching) the heavens,
and that I may mount up to the God of Moses;
but as far as I am concerned,
I think he (Moses) is a liar!' "*

The Quran, 40: 36-37

In the Quran, a man named Haman is mentioned in relation to Moses and the Pharaoh. He is described as one of the men who stood the closest to the pharaoh and was responsible for the execution of construction projects under the Pharaoh's orders. The name *"Haman"* appears in six different parts of the Quran. In the Bible, *"Haman"* is not mentioned in relation to Moses, the Pharaoh or Egypt. In the field of Egyptology, the name Haman remained unknown until the 19th century, when the Egyptian inscriptions (the

demotic, the hieratic and the hieroglyphs) were decoded by the French scientist Champollion with the help of the Rosetta Stone in the year 1822. It was established that Haman was indeed an important man in the Pharaoh's court, namely *"the head of the stone quarry workers."* According to discoveries in Egyptology, this knowledge was impossible in times of the Prophet, for the inscriptions of ancient Egypt could not be read by anyone many centuries before Muhammad.[1] Therefore, it is impossible for the Quran to come from a human source.

---

1 cp. **RYBKA**, T.: Hieroglyphen. URL: www.siltry.de/artikel.htm (Accessed: May 25th 2009) and cp. **KURTH**, Dieter: Das Ältere Ägypten, Nürnberg 2000, p. 16.

3 THE QURAN FROM THE PERSPECTIVE OF INTELLECTUALS AND SCIENTISTS

In order to further support the phenomena of the Quran and its scientific information, as described in items 1 and 2, some scholars, scientists and philosophers who have commented on them will now be quoted.

Hamilton Gibb (1895-1971)   *Hamilton Gibb (1895-1971)*
Scottish Professor of Islamic Studies and Middle East Expert
"As a literary monument the Quran thus stands by itself, a production unique to the Arabic literature, having neither forerunners nor successors in its own idiom."[1] *"The influence of the Quran on the development of ArabicLiterature has been incalculable, and exerted in*

---

1 **GIBB**, H. A. R.: Arabic Literature – An Introduction, Oxford 1963, p. 36.

many directions. Its ideas, its language, its rhymes pervade all subsequent literary works in greater or lesser measure. Its specific linguistic features were not emulated, either in the chancery prose of the next century or in later prose writings, but it was at least partly due to the flexibility imparted by the Quran to the High Arabic idiom that the former could be so rapidly developed and adjusted to the new needs of the imperial government and an expanding society. "[1]

Harry Gaylord Dorman (born 1906)

Harry Gaylord Dorman (born 1906) *American Writer*

"Its miraculous quality resides partly in its style, so perfect and lofty that neither men nor Jinn could produce a single chapter to compare with its briefest chapter, and partly in its content of teachings, prophecies about the future, and amazingly accurate information that Muhammad could never have gathered of his own accord." [2]

George Sale (1697-1736)

George Sale (1697-1736) *Orientalist and Lawyer*

"The style of the Quran is generally beautiful and fluent, [...] and in many places, specifically where the majesty and attributes of God are described, sublime and magnificent. [...] He succeeded so well, and so strangely captivated the minds of his audience, that several of his opponents thought it the effect of witchcraft and enchantment." [3]

Laura Veccia Vaglieri (1893-1989)

Laura Veccia Vaglieri (1893-1989) *Italian Orientalist*

"On the whole we find in it a collection of wisdom which can be adopted by the most intelligent of men, the greatest of philosophers and the most skilful of politicians [...] But there is another proof of the

---

1 IDEM.

2 DORMAN, HARRY G.: Towards Understanding Islam, New York 1948, p. 3.

3 SALE, George: The Koran. The Preliminary Discourse, London and New York 1891, p. 47-48.

Divinity of the Quran; it is the fact that it has been preserved intact through the ages since the time of its Revelation till the present day [...] Read and reread by the Muslim world, this book does not rouse in the faithful any weariness, it rather, through repetition, is more loved every day. It gives rise to a profound feeling of awe and respect in the one who reads it or listens to it [...] Therefore, above all, what caused the great and rapid diffusion of Islam was through the fact that this Book was the book of Allah."[1]

John William Draper (1811-1882)

John William Draper (1811-1882)
Anglo-Saxon Natural Scientist and Historian

"This fragmentary construction yields texts, and mottoes, and rules complete in themselves, suitable for common men in any of the incidents of life."[2]

Arthur J. Arberry (1905-1969)

Arthur J. Arberry (1905-1969) *English Orientalist*

"This very characteristic feature – "that inimitable symphony," as the believing Pickthall described his Holy Book (The Quran) – has been almost totally ignored by previous translators; it is therefore not surprising that what they have wrought sounds dull and flat indeed in comparison with the splendidly decorated original."[3]

Dr. Maurice Bucaille (1920-1998)

Dr. Maurice Bucaille (1920-1998) *French surgeon and scientist*

"A totally objective examination of it (the Quran) in the light of modern knowledge, leads us to recognize the agreement between the two, as has been already noted on repeated occasions. It makes us deem it

---

1 **VECCIA VAGLIERI**, Laura: Apologie de I'Islamisme. o.O. 2002, p. 57-59.

2 **DRAPER**, John William: A History of the Intellectual Development of Europe, London 1875, Vol. I, p. 343-344.

3 **ARBERRY**, Arthur J.: The Koran Interpreted, London 1964, p. x.

quite unthinkable for a man of Muhammad's time to have been the author of such statements on account of the state of knowledge in his day. Such considerations are part of what gives the Quranic Revelation its unique place, and forces the impartial scientist to admit his inability to provide an explanation which calls solely upon materialistic reasoning.[1]

Sarojini Naidu (1879-1949)
Sarojini Naidu (1879-1949) *Indian Poet*

"The sense of justice is one of the most wonderful ideals of Islam, because as I read in the Quran I find those dynamic principles of life, not mystic but practical ethics for the daily conduct of life suited to the whole world."[2]

Prof. Keith. L. Moore
Prof. Keith. L. Moore *Canadian Professor of Anatomy*

"It is clear to me that these statements must have come to Muhammad from God because most of this knowledge was not discovered until many centuries later. [...] Because the staging of human embryos is complex, owing to the continuous process of change during development, it is proposed that a new system of classification could be developed using the terms mentioned in the Quran and Sunnah. The proposed system is simple, comprehensive, and conforms with present embryological knowledge."[3]

1 BUCAILLE, Dr. Maurice: The Qur'an and Modern Science, Raleigh (North Carolina) 1997, p. 18.

2 NAIDU, Sarojini: Speeches and Writings of Sarojini Naidu, Madras 1918, p. 167.

3 MOORE, Keith L.: Video 1, at URL: www.dies-ist-die-wahrheit.de/video/index.htm (Accessed: April 25th 2009).

Prof. Alfred Kroner (born 1939)

Professor of Geo-Sciences at the University of Mainz

"I think it is almost impossible that he (Muhammad) could have known about things like the common origin of the universe, because scientists have only found out within the last few years with very complicated and advanced technological methods that this is the case."[1]

Prof. Yushidi Kusan *Director of the Tokyo Observatory, Japan*

"Say, I am very much impressed by finding true astronomical facts in the Quran, for us modern astronomers have been studying a very small piece of the universe. Because, by using telescopes, we can only see very few parts of the sky, without thinking about the whole universe. So by reading the Quran and by answering to the questions, I think I can find my future way of investigation of the universe."[2]

Prof. Durja Rao *Professor of Marine Geology*

"It is difficult to imagine that this type of knowledge was existing at that time, around 1400 years ago. Maybe they had a simple idea about some of the things, but to describe those things in great detail is very difficult. So this is definitely not simple human knowledge. A normal human being cannot explain this phenomenon in so much detail."[3]

Dirk Walter Mosig *USA*

"I have read sacred Scriptures of every found what I encountered in Islam: perfection.

The Noble Quran, compared to any other Scripture I have read, is like the light of the sun compared to that of a match."[4]

---

1 Idem.

2 Idem.

3 I dem.

4 Search term: "Walter Mosig" at URL: www.islaam.ca (Accessed: December 21st 2009).

Dr. Udo Schaefer (born 1926)

Dr. Udo Schaefer (born 1926) *German Islamic scholar*

"The speed of the spread of this religion, which stings in the eyes and was not observed in any of the historic religions before, relies on the external and inner attractiveness of the new religion, the creative impulse of the new Divine Word and the convincing new model of an in itself ordered and united community, where people of all races and high religions lived together in peace; on a force of attraction that had nothing to subtend to the then divided, almost in agony lying Eastern Christendom."[(1)]

Johann Wolfgang von Goethe (1749-1832)

Johann Wolfgang von Goethe (1749-1832) *German poet*

To him, the Quran was a *"holy book, which, no matter how often we approach it, always cloys us anew, then attracts us, staggered in awe, and, in the end, enforces our reverence. [...] The style of the Quran is, in accordance to its contents and purpose, stern, great, formidable, and in places truly sublime."*[(2)]

1 SCHAEFER, Dr. Udo: Muhammad - ein Lügenprophet? Eine Klarstellung gegenüber des katholischen Glaubens, p. 6. URL: www.udoschaefer.com/pdffiles/muhammad.pdf (Accessed: May 12th 2009).

2 J. G. Cotta'schen Buchhandlung (Publisher): Goethe's Werke, Stuttgart and Tübingen 1828, Vol. 6, p. 34-35.

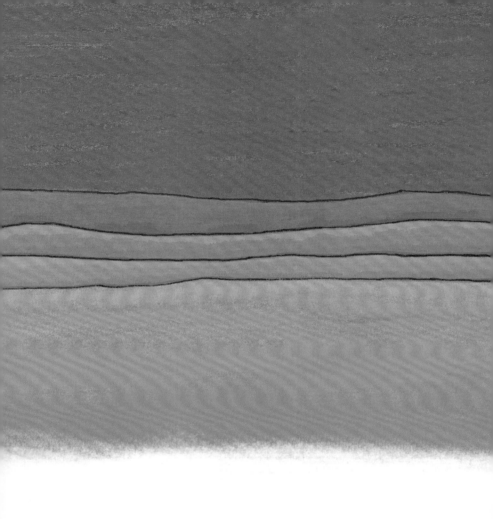

Chapter 5
Why?

Sense and Meaning
of Life and Worship
in Islam

1 THE VALUE OF MAN IN ISLAM

The Value of Man in Islam

"Indeed We have honored the Children of Adam, and We have carried them on land and sea, and have provided for them sustenance with good things, and have preferred them above a great part of Our Creation."

The Quran, 17: 70

The Quran emphasizes that man is not a conventional creature, but a unique one. To manifest his honor to him, God let all angels do the symbolic Sudjud (prostration) before the father of all men, Adam. Man is the only living creature on Earth that can become aware of the universe and the Wonder of Creation. God created him in the best form, and He prepared a place in Janna for every person, to which He invites them through the Prophet:

"But God does call to the Home of Peace (i.e. Paradise)"

The Quran, 10: 25

The latter reveals the love of God for man. One of the biggest sins in Islam is to murder someone. One of the greatest Hasanat (virtues) is, therefore, to save a person.

The Prophet said: *"Man is the work of God, he who destroys it; is cursed."* Muslims are obliged to save others. In Islam it is forbidden, out of respect for man, to harm the human body, in life as in death. The Prophet said: *"To break the bones of a dead man is just as bad as to break the bones of a living man."*[1]

---

1 **Abo Dawood**: Assunan, Hadith N°.: 2792, **Ibn Hanbal**, Ahmad: Al-Musnad, Hadith N°.: 23596, **Ibn Magah**: Assunan, Hadith N°.: 1605.

2 THE MEANING OF OUR EXISTENCE IN ISLAM

The Meaning of our Existence in Islam.

If we ask why we exist, the answer is to come from outside ourselves; from Him, the independent Creator that gave us our existence.

With the intention of highlighting the question of *"Why?"*, the meaning of our existence, we will use the following symbolic story, which was passed from an angel to Prophet Muhammad[1] and representatively illustrates this subject matter.

---

1 It is to be noted that the story, as found in the Hadiths, is much shorter and simpler. The author added some details here for illustration purposes.

2.1 The Story about the King and His Palace

There was once a rich king who possessed many enormous treasure chambers, which contained all kinds of gold and jewels. He was very educated in all sciences. He was talented, skilful, competent and proficient in all trades and practiced them himself. Out of his successes, he built an extraordinary, inimitable palace. The many different parts of the palace were each furnished in their own style, and the roofs were adorned with elaborately crafted ornaments, which reflected his talents. When the palace was finished, he invited his subjects to his palace. On the different tables his guests were offered unimaginable delicacies of the finest ingredients, all of which he had prepared himself.

The king commissioned his ambassador to reveal to his guests all the secrets of the palace, to explain the reason for the construction of the palace, where the meaning of all symbols and treasures distributed all over the palace lied, and also to convey his instructions regarding protocol and etiquette.

His ambassador stood in the middle of the largest hall, and his assistants were distributed in the rest of the palace. He began his speech:

"O people, truly our king, the lord of this palace, wishes to introduce himself to you through all you see here, and he expects from you that you become eager to know him.

He wants to manifest his attention to you through all these ornaments. He invited you here out of his hospitality, grace and generosity, and gave you all of this.

The king loves you, and he wants you to love him as well, to be grateful and to follow his instructions. So, at the end of the celebration, he will grant you your wishes, shower you with his grace, and show you further benefaction."

There were two kinds of guests.

One type wandered around the palace, observed its wonders, astounded, and said to one another: *"A mighty king must stand behind this palace, who surely pursues determined goals. Why did he invite us and honor us so? Why did he craft all these things?"*

As they conversed, they heard the voice of the ambassador, as he began his speech, and hurried to hear him. They listened to him attentively and respectfully, and they conscientiously followed his instructions. At the end of the celebration, the king invited those guests to live in another, even more beautiful palace. They were rewarded according to the majesty of the king.

The other type of guests, as soon as they entered the palace, were only concerned about their own pleasure. They enjoyed themselves everywhere in the palace and did not ask who had prepared all of it for them, and why they had been invited. They missed the speech of the ambassador, and they did not show any interest in him. They did not observe his instructions at all, and at the end of the celebration they were punished by the king according to his magnificence.

Hence, this palace symbolizes our Earth, which is embellished by plants and animals, and the sky, adorned with stars. The assistants of the ambassador are the other prophets, who were distributed on Earth at different times.

The angels once said that he who obeys Muhammad is also obedient to God and will come to Janna. The fate of man is decided through Muhammad.[1]

In order to summarize the meaning of life in Islam, one can say that man should benefit from this life without forgetting the Afterlife. The latter means that man should accept the Message of God and not ignore the Word of God.

1 cp. **Ibn Hagar:** Fat-hul-Bari, Riyadh 2005, Vol. 17, p. 129-130.

3 MAN AND SIN IN ISLAM

Man and Sin in Islam

Man is born free of sin and in the course of his life he commits good and bad deeds, for which he receives either a positive point (Hasana)[1] or a sin point (Sayye-ah)[2]. A person is held accountable only for his own deeds. However, in Islam, the system takes into consideration human weaknesses and flaws. It is not expected that man lives free of sin like an angel, but that different impulses to the bad and the good, which reign within man, can stand in conflict to one another.

"Verily,
We created Man from a drop of mixed semen,
in order to try him,
so We gave him (the gifts)
of Hearing and Sight."

The Quran, 76: 2

"And We have shown him
the two ways
(good and evil)"

The Quran, 90: 10

God wants man to develop his good sides by practicing them in life, and He promises him a great reward for it. In return, man

---

1 Hasana (pl. Hasanat) is a positive point that one receives with each good deed, i.e. for each letter that one recites from the Quran, for helping someone, or for giving alms. The Hasana is immediately recorded by an angel, and enumerated on the Day of Resurrection. According to them, the level in Janna is determined.

2 In contrast to Hasanat, there are the sin points (Sayye-aat, singular Sayye-ah). A Sayye-ah is only recorded and not multiplied.

must fight his bad impulses, which is perceived by God as a sort of Jihad.[1]

"*And by the Soul,*
and Him Who perfected it in proportion;
Then He showed him what is wrong for him
and what is right for him;
Truly he succeeds who purifies it,
And he fails that corrupts it!"

The Quran, 91: 7-10

However, when man commits sins, whether purposely or unknowingly, his evil impulses triumph, and he seeks to fulfill his wishes in a sinful manner. Regardless of willingly or not, Islam requires man to end sinful practices and return to God in both cases.

"*And whoever*
does evil or wrongs himself,
but afterwards seeks God's forgiveness,
he will find God Oft-Forgiving,
Most Merciful."

The Quran, 4: 110

"*And those who*
when they commit an indecency
or do injustice to their souls remember Allah
and ask forgiveness for their faults;
- And do not persist in what (wrong) they have done,
while they know.
For such the reward is forgiveness from their Lord,
and gardens with rivers flowing underneath,
an eternal dwelling"

The Quran, 3: 135-136

---

1 cp. **AL-BAEIHAQI:** Azzuhd Al-Kabier, Beirut 1987, p. 165.

Every person has two angels that record his Hasanat and his sins. The angel to the right is responsible for the Hasanat, and the one on the left for the sins. Prophet Muhammad said: *"The writer that records the Hasanat is the boss of the writer that records the sins. When a person commits a sin, the angel to the right says to the other:*

'Give him seven hours, maybe he will ask God for forgiveness, or praise God.'"[1]

The Prophet also said:

"God said: 'He who commits a Hasana receives ten times the reward or more. He who commits a sin receives only one punishment or I will forgive him. He who comes closer to me by the length of a hand, I approach him by the length of an arm.'"[2]

Allah looks forward to the return of a man to Him from his sin more than to the return of one who was in the desert and lost his camel with food and drink – one that had lost hope of finding his camel again and lay down by the shade of a palm tree. Suddenly, he stood up and found the camel standing before him.

He took the reins and said out of mere confusion and happiness:

"Thank you God, truly You are my slave and I am Your Lord."[3]

The Prophet said:

"Allah is more merciful with his servants (mankind) than a sparrow to its chicks."[4]

---

1 **ARRUYANI: AL-MUSNAD**, Cairo 1995, Vol. 2, p. 286, **AL-BAEIHAQI:** Schu-ab Al-Ieman, Beirut 2000, Vol. 5, p. 390-391, **ABO NOEIM:** Hilyatul-Awli-yaa, Beirut 1988, Vol. 6, p. 124, **AL-QURTUBI:** Attafsier, Beirut 1985, Vol. 17, p. 10.

2 **MOSLIM:** Assahih, Hadith N°.: 4852.

3 Idem, Hadith N°.: 4932.

4 **IBN ABI OSAMA**, Al-Harith: Bughyat Al-Bahith, Cairo, Bughyat Al-Bahith, Cairo, n.d., p. 280.

4 SEX IN ISLAM

Sex in Islam

Islam handles human impulses and needs in a practical fashion and it recognizes that the human longing for love and sex was created with the intention of God. In order to preserve the benefits of sex, its practice was only allowed within a specific framework: marriage.

For in marriage:

1. Family cohesion is preserved, the gradual shrinkage of population is prevented, and further negative influential factors of society on family are reduced.
2. Women are preserved from sexual exploitation.
3. Children are protected and they grow up in a largely stable family atmosphere.

> "*And among His Signs is this,
> that He created for you
> mates from among yourselves,
> that you may dwell in tranquility with them,
> and He has put between you
> affection and mercy.
> Verily in that are indeed Signs
> for those who reflect.*"
>
> The Quran, 30: 21

Islam encourages all Muslims to marry, and the Prophet said:

"*He who loves my manners and ways should accept my Sunnah (living practices), and marriage belongs to them.*"[1]

---

1 **AL-BAEIHAQI:** Assunan Al-Kubra, Hyderabad 1925, Vol. 7, p. 78, **ABDURRAZZAQ:** Al-Musannaf, Hadith No.: 10378.

Furthermore, he depicted marital sex, next to the profession of faith, as something one is rewarded for.

 The Prophet said:

"For each 'Alhamdulillah' (Praise to God), 'Allahu-akbar' and 'La ilaha illallah', and for making love, one receives a Hasana (positive point)."

He was asked:
"How can it be that one is rewarded for one's lust?"

 The Prophet replied:

"If man was to enjoy it in a prohibited way (extramarital), would he not receive sin points on his record of deeds? Therefore, he would receive positive points if he was to do it in an allowed fashion (marriage)."[1]

Since marriage in Islam is the only legitimate way to have sexual intercourse, it is handled in a flexible and practical manner, as follows:

1. Islam accepts a marriage even if it is done not for the wish to have children, but for the lust for physical contact or togetherness.

2. In order to marry someone, only a specific oral contract in the presence of two witnesses and mutual agreement are required.

3. The relationship between the spouses is seen practically in Islam. Since not all relationships are successful and some couples do not work together, or do not find love and happiness in marriage, divorce is allowed in Islam. Therefore, everybody has another chance to have a new and successful relationship.

---

1 **Moslim**: Assahih, Hadith Nº.: 1674, **Ibn Hanbal**, Ahmad: Al-Musnad, Hadith Nº.: 20508, **Al-Baeihaqi**: Assunan Al-Kubra, Hyderabad 1925, Vol. 4, p. 4.

> *"But if they separate (by divorce),*
> *God will provide abundance for all*
> *from His all-reaching bounty:*
> *for God is Ever All-Sufficient for His creatures' need,*
> *All-Wise."*

The Quran 4: 130

At the same time, however, Islam considers divorce an unwanted decision. The Prophet said in this regard: *"Of the things that are allowed, divorce is the most disliked by God."*[1]

Islam appeals to Muslims that they should not give up on a marriage lightly or precipitously, for in every relationship there are misunderstandings, times and situations where it seems that there is no future.

5 MORALITY IN ISLAM

Prophet Muhammad said:
"I was sent to accomplish good morality."[2]

To comprehensively explain Islamic morality is not possible here, for it is a complex subject of much significance in Islam, and several books could be written about it. But since it is such an important topic, the most relevant aspects of it will be presented here:

To forgive others, truthfulness in word and action, the act of charity, to salute others, humility, no Ghibah (not to speak bad about someone when they are not there to defend themselves), no

---

1 **Abo Dawood:** Assunan, Hadith N°.: 1863, **Ibn Magah:** Assunan, Hadith N°.: 2008, **Al-Baeihaqi:** Assunan Al-Kubra, Hyderabad 1925, Vol. 7, p. 322.

2 **Al-Baeihaqi:** Assunan Al-Kubra, Hyderabad 1925, Vol. 10, p. 192, **Al-Qudaie,** Asch-schihab: Al-Musnad, Beirut 1985, Vol. 2, p. 192-93.

Namiima (not to tell anyone the bad things another person has said about them), generosity, and to be able to bear pain.

Respect for parents assumes an important place in the Islamic moral system. Muslims are reminded that their parents are the reason why they were given life.

"*And your Lord has decreed*
that you worship none but Him,
and that you be kind to your parents.
Whether one or both of them attain old age in your life,
say not to them a word of disrespect,
nor shout at them,
but address them in terms of honor.
And, out of kindness,
lower to them the wing of humility, and say:
'My Lord!
Bestow on them your Mercy
as they did bring me up when I was small.' "
The Quran, 17: 23-24

"*And we have enjoined on man*
(to be dutiful and good) to his parents:
his mother bore him in weakness and hardship upon
weakness and hardship,
and in two years was his weaning:
Show gratitude to me and to your parents,
unto Me is the final destination."
The Quran, 31: 14

6 THE RELIANCE ON GOD (TAWAKKUL)

Reliance on God (Tawakkul)

A Muslim has the task, amongst others, to work for his life and subsistence, to act foresightedly and responsibly, and to observe God's Commands in thus doing.

Simultaneously, a Muslim, who was given Tawakkul, relies on God in regard to the results of his efforts. He puts his heavy burdens and his future in the merciful hands of God,

and says:

"Tawakkaltu Ala-llah" –

as long as God exists and as long as He is the Lord of the entire Universe, as long as He holds the key to well-being and bliss, and as long as He knows my situation, He will not let me become lost.

> *"And if whosoever puts his trust in God,
> then He will suffice him"*
>
> The Quran, 65: 3

This conviction, perceived as fatalistic, is related in some cultures to a certain pessimism.

However, it is the contrary; this belief in predestination ensures the Muslim a certain inner peace, calmness and confidence, and, in addition, it protects him from desolation and forlornness.

It does not comprise, in any case, the task of free will and an own idea of happiness and the shaping of one's life.

The importance of the pursuit of an occupation in life can be traced to different parts of the Quran:

Reliance on God

He will not let me become lost.

"Work (righteousness):
soon God will observe your work,
and (so will) His Messenger,
and the believers:
soon will you be brought back to the All-Knower
of what is hidden and what is open:
then He will inform you of what you used to do."

The Quran 9: 105

"That man can have nothing but what he does;
And that his deeds will be seen;
Then he will be recompensed with a full and the best
recompense"

The Quran 53: 39-41

To prevent his camel from getting lost, a Bedouin asked the Prophet:

"Should I bind my camel, or should I not leash it and rely on God?"[1]

 The Prophet replied:
"Tie your camel and rely on God."[1]

This hadith, very well known in Islamic circles, is to Muslims an important indication that relying on God does not imply not to work anymore and not to plan one's life, but to trust God for the success of one's activities.

The Prophet also said:

"The truly trustworthy businessman will be in Paradise with the Prophet, the saints and the martyrs."[2]

---

1 **ATTERMEZI**: Assunan, Hadith N°.: 2441.

2 Idem, Hadith N°.: 1130.

And he added:

"Nobody has ever eaten better food than the one he earned through his own work."[1]

In all the events of his life, the Prophet always remarked that a Muslim should try his hardest and, in addition, rely on God.

This is also shown in his journey to Madina, planned to the very last detail, his battles, and in the fact that he sometimes stored enough food for his family to last an entire year.

When some Muslims wanted to travel to Macca for pilgrimage without sufficient provisions and said:

"We are those who rely on God", the Quran issued the order that they should bring enough food.[2]

A saying of the second caliph Omar goes:

"Nobody may sit without working for his earnings and say:
'God, give me!'
for you know that neither gold nor silver rain from the sky."[3]

Nobody may sit without working for his earnings and say: 'God give me!'

---

1 **AL-BUCHARI:** Assahih, Hadith N°.: 1930.

2 Idem, Hadith N°.: 1426.

3 **AL-KASEMI**, Gamaluddin: Mau-esat Al-Mumneen, Beirut 1995, p. 111.

7 WHAT DO WE NEED ISLAM FOR?

What do we need Islam for?

Some people ask: "*What do I get from believing in the Prophet, the Afterlife and the Last Testament of God? I enjoy my life without the limitations of a religion, in the end I will die and my body will decompose in the grave.*"

On the one hand: the true answer about death and the Afterlife could only be given by the Revelation of God. The missing notion of a life after death does not have an influence on the fact that there is an eternal life that begins with death, even though the body decomposes.

On the other hand: without God and Janna, the entire capital and the happiness of man would consist only of a limited life full of unlimited wishes that cannot find their fulfillment in this life.

In this life, man is surrounded by people and things that are bound to his heart through strong love bonds, even though they are not lasting for him, nor is he lasting for them. Man is distressed when he loses one of them, and finally he has to enter his grave alone.

Many non-believers do not experience a lack without religion, or they do not fear to have missed on something. It is with age that concern about illnesses and the fear of death grow in most of them, until they are finally confronted, at the time of their death, with the eternal life that follows.

A slipping mountain climber who can still hold on for a few moments will accept the rope that his friend throws to save him. Since, otherwise, his fall would be inevitable, he will take the rope even if it is not strong enough to hold his entire body weight.

The only rope available to man for his salvation, which guarantees him eternal life, is unfortunately rejected by many. It is the secure rope of God. Our life is, compared to the Afterlife, only a few moments long.

> "*Nor sell the Covenant of Allah*
> *for a miserable price:*
> *for verily,*
> *what is with God is far better for*
> *you if you only knew:*
> *Whatever is with you,*
> *will be exhausted,*
> *and whatever with God will remain.*
> *And we will certainly bestow,*
> *on those who patiently persevere,*
> *their reward to the best of*
> *what they used to do.*"
>
> The Quran, 16: 95-96

But even the most ingenious philosophers cannot help the non-believing person deal with this question, or accompany him through the grave until the Day of Resurrection, or even give him eternal bliss.

Only the Message of God can guarantee us that there will not be anything bad for us in the grave. He who embarks on a long journey better relies on the travel plan of the one who knows the way best.

But naturally, God has not forbidden us – Muslims – to also enjoy this life on Earth:

"*Say:*
Who hath forbidden
the beautiful (gifts) of God,
which He has produced for his slaves,
and the good things
(which He hath provided)
for sustenance?
Say:
they are, in the life of this world,
for those who believe,
(and) purely for them
on the Day of Judgment."

The Quran, 7: 32

When Islam pronounces a prohibition to Muslims then it is to prevent the detriment of personal health and mankind in general, or the harming of other people.

Thus, it applies: a Muslim enjoys as many things as every non-Muslim, and the difference lies in an eternity in Paradise.

8 SPIRITUAL BLISS THROUGH ISLAM

Spiritual Bliss Through Islam

Many people do not experience happiness, even though they do not lack anything material; some are even pushed to suicide by the futile search for meaning in their lives. But God preserved the Muslim from such sorrow, for the true belief in God and His Prophet lightens the soul, calms and fulfills the heart, and creates in the Muslim a state of bliss.

"O mankind!
There has come to you a direction
from your Lord
and a healing for the (needs) in your hearts
– a guidance and a mercy for the believers.
Say: 'In the Bounty of God, and in His Mercy
– in that let them rejoice':
that is better than the (wealth) they amass."

The Quran, 10: 57-58

"Those who believe,
and whose hearts find satisfaction
in the remembrance of God:
Verily, in the remembrance of God
do hearts find satisfaction.
For those who believe and work righteousness,
is (every) blessedness,
and a beautiful place of (final) return."

The Quran, 13: 28-29

A Conversation with the Heart

True belief closes all dark doors, does not let the Muslim feel lonely in this existence, and speaks to his heart as follows:

"*O man, do not be sad that your life is limited and short, for an eternal life awaits you.*

Do not be sad and do not worry if you cannot realize your wishes and goals in this life, for you will have them realized in Janna."

And further: "*You possess neither yourself nor the universe nor the future, but you are rather a creature of the Most Merciful, who has made you here an honored guest. He has planned the schedule of your future journey and he promised you eternal bliss. He expects from you only that which you are capable of doing. Do not worry about the things around you, you are not responsible for them, but the One who created them is.*"

And finally: "*Even though this life is temporary, it produces an eternal fruit, for one prepares for Janna through it."*

"*And this life of the world is only amusement and play! But verily the Home in the Afterlife, that is life indeed, if they but knew."*

The Quran, 29: 64

"*On the other hand, for those who fear their Lord, are gardens, with rivers flowing beneath, therein are they to dwell (for ever), a gift from the presence of God, and that which is in the presence of God is the best (bliss) for the righteous."*

The Quran, 3: 198

A Divine Light

The spiritual peace that belief and worship produce in the Muslim is a fact that can be experienced. It is difficult to convey this to non-Muslims, for it is not something easily grasped or worldly, or an idea, but a light from God, which penetrates the soul and the heart.

Ibrahim Ibn Ad-ham, a Sufi and Muslim scholar (died 779) said: *"If the kings and the sons of kings knew what joy and blissfulness we have, they would try to wrench it from us with swords."* His friend Abo Yusuf Al-Ghasuli said in this regard: *"They sought this joy, but they missed the right path."*[1]

Let us try to describe the effects of spiritual peace:

- In spite of valuable material or personal achievements, the soul cannot be adequately satisfied and it longs for more, for the soul is more valuable than the material world. A limited world like

---

1 IBN AL-GAWZI: Sefat Assafwa, Alexandria, Egypt, n.d. Vol. 2, p. 788.

ours cannot fulfill the endless human needs.

As soon as heart and reason find the way to Allah and the truth of His Message, the soul is overwhelmed by a certain light. Man instantly experiences a feeling of spiritual peace, contentment and blissfulness. With each prayer that man does for Allah, the feeling of inner peace grows.

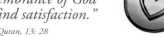
those who have chosen His path a good life

The Prophet said:

"The highpoint of my contentment lies in prayer."[1]

He wished never to stop praying, because of the calmness and the peace that he experienced in thus doing, and the light that he received. He longed for prayer and told his caller to prayer Bilal:

"O Bilal, call for the prayer, calm us with it."[2]

> " *Verily,*
> *in the remembrance of God*
> *do hearts find satisfaction.*"
>
> The Quran, 13: 28

- Even if one tries to embellish the untruth and thus convince the mind of it, it is not possible to deceive the soul as well, for it has a certain sensitivity for the truth. The untruth does not fulfill the needs of the soul. So, the soul remains restless and unfulfilled. Every new fact of belief that the Prophet explains is received by the soul as light, which fills a void perceived in the soul, and consequently eliminates the corresponding feeling of restlessness and confusion. The elements of belief have this effect on the

---

1 **ANNASAII:** Assunan, Hadith N°.: 3878, **IBN HANBAL**, Ahmad: Al-Musnad, Hadith N°.: 11845, **AL-BAEIHAQI:** Assunan Al-Kubra, Hyderabad 1925, Vol. 7, p. 78, **AL-HAKEM:** Al-Mustadrak, Hadith N°.: 2627.

2 **ABO DAWOOD:** Assunan, Hadith N°.: 4333, **ATTABARANI:** Al-Mugam Al-Kabier, Hadith N°.: 6090, 6091.

soul, for they both come from God. God created the soul; He knows all of its needs and secrets the best. The Quran points to this fact several times, amongst others in the following verses:

"Verily, His is the Creation and Commandment. Blessed be God, the cherisher and sustainer of the worlds!"

The Quran, 7: 54

"(God) Most Gracious! It is He Who has taught the Quran. He has created man."

The Quran, 55: 1-3

"Read! In the Name of your Lord, Who has created (all that exists)"

The Quran, 96: 1

And thus the soul receives one fact of belief after the other, until man reaches complete calmness and blissfulness. During this time, man longs for his Creator and is confident that He will not abandon him in this life and will later bring him to Janna. This longing will be fulfilled for the dying Muslim through Allah's words:

"O (you) soul, the one in (complete) rest and satisfaction! Come back thou to thy Lord – well pleased (yourself), and well-pleasing unto Him! Enter you, then, among my Devotees! Yea, enter you my Paradise!"

The Quran, 89: 27-30

And so God promises those who have chosen His path a good (peaceful) life in this life and in the Afterlife:

"For those who believe and work righteousness, is (every) blessedness, and a beautiful place of (final) return."

The Quran, 13: 29

9 AGING FROM THE ISLAMIC PERSPECTIVE

Aging from the Islamic Perspective

In advanced age, God lets a tire of life and a yearning for quiet grow within man. This spiritual state helps those who have the ieman[1] to part and "*move*" to Janna.

In this chapter of life, God allows man to feel the transient nature of this carnal life, and enhances the pursuit of eternal joy in the Afterlife.

This spiritual state "*translates*" for human the meanings of this

---

1 ieman: The belief in God, His prophet and the Afterlife, which deeply rooted in one's heart.

Life in this world which is as a divine book. This book, with its letters and words, points to the characteristics of its Creator and "*tells*" man:

- "*I (this life) am the soil for the Afterlife. Occupy yourself with cultivation and do not pick the blossoms, for you will harvest their fruit in the Afterlife.*"
- "*What you see here are mirrors that reflect the name and characteristics of God. Become acquainted with Him through them and focus on Him, for mirrors are fragile.*"
- "*You are an honored guest in this house, enjoy the hospitality, behave properly, observe the house rules and do not look behind you when you take your leave.*"

"*And the life of this world is nothing
but play and amusement.
But far better is the house in the Afterlife
for those who are pious.*"

The Quran, 6: 32

"*Verily!
We have made that
which is on Earth
as an adornment for it,
in order that We may test them
(mankind)
– as to which of them are best in deeds.
And verily!
We shall make all that is on it (the Earth)
a bare dry soil
(without growth or foliage).*"

The Quran, 18: 7-8

10 DEATH FROM THE ISLAMIC PERSPECTIVE

Death from Islamic Perspective

After living creatures complete the lifetime that God has established for them and fulfill their mission, the time comes when they are released from their tasks in life.

10.1 The Gate **to an Illuminated World**

The Gate to an Illuminated World

For the Muslim, death, which represents for many the final ending, is only a change of location, a gateway to the illuminated world of the eternal bliss and mercy of God.

There is no fear, no worry or sorrow, as one rests from the noise of this world.

The Quran says about the last moments of this life:

" Verily,
those who say:
'Our Lord is Allah,'
and,
further, stand straight and steadfast,
on them the angels will descend
(at the time of their death)
(saying):
'Fear not, nor grieve!
But receive the Glad Tidings of the Paradise
which you have been promised!
We have been your friends
in the life of this world
and are (so) in the Therein
you shall have (all)
that your inner-selves desire,
and therein you shall have (all)
for which you ask for!
— A hospitable gift from
One Oft-Forgiving,
Most Merciful!"

The Quran, 41: 30-32

10.2 **Release** *Release*

The ieman[1] teaches the Muslim that this life, in spite of all its joys, can only seem like a narrow space in comparison to the Afterlife with all its beauty.

 The Prophet said:

"This life is a cage to the Muslim and paradise of the non – Muslim."[2]

---

1 ieman: The belief in God, His prophet and the Afterlife, which deeply rooted in one's heart.

2 **MOSLIM**: Assahih, Hadith N°.: 5256, **ATTERMEZI**: Assunan, Hadith N°.: 2246 and **IBN HANBAL**, Ahmad: Al-Musnad in different parts.

10.3 Reunion

The time of death is not the time of parting with all that we love, but the time of meeting all we had wished for. In that world there, man does not live anonymously and lonely, but he reunites with his acquaintances, relatives and his loved ones. He will meet new people with the purest hearts. Amongst them, there are the Prophets and their descendants.

10.4 Unbearable Difficulties

Through age and illness, which burden life and make it difficult, death sometimes appears as a great favor. Imagine that your grandparents, their parents and grandparents and twenty generations back, all lived and suffered still, with all their weaknesses and illnesses, and if death did not exist, you would have had to take care of them all.

10.5 The Return of Youth

The Return of the Youth

 The Prophet said:

"Those who have died old or young will be thirty-three years old in Janna, and not older, just like the people from Jahannam." [1]

For the people of the wrong path – the Disbelievers and sinners –, however, death is the beginning of true pain and sorrow.

" Do those
who earn evil deeds
think that We shall hold them
equal with those who believe
and do righteous good deeds,
in their present life and after their death?!"

The Quran, 45: 21

---

1 **ATTERMEZI:** Assunan, Hadith Nº.: 2486.

11 PRADER

Only the direct relation between God and man is accepted in Islam, for everything and everyone was created by God alone, and only God Himself has endless capabilities and knowledge. Consequently, there is no pope and no priest or rabbi as a representative of God in Islam, as there is in other major world religions.

Prayer in Islam is one of the most important methods to establish this direct relationship to God. It gives man the possiblity to talk to God directly. Therefore, prayer is one of the five pillars of Islam.

A Muslim does not perceive prayer as an obligation, but as an honor. It emphasizes that man belongs to the Creator of all Worlds.

The denial of God would break the honorable connection and the belonging to God. This allows for the non-believing person to become an adherent and servant of temporary relations and things.

He only lives for them and he only yearns for them as long as they last, or until he leaves everything behind through death. Thus, the value of this person becomes limited to his material and earthly existence.

During prayer, the believer praises his God and asks Him for His support; for this purpose, he begins each prayer with the words:

بِسْمِ ٱللَّهِ ٱلرَّحْمَٰنِ ٱلرَّحِيمِ ۝ ٱلْحَمْدُ لِلَّهِ رَبِّ ٱلْعَٰلَمِينَ ۝ ٱلرَّحْمَٰنِ ٱلرَّحِيمِ

۝ مَٰلِكِ يَوْمِ ٱلدِّينِ ۝ إِيَّاكَ نَعْبُدُ وَإِيَّاكَ نَسْتَعِينُ ۝

ٱهْدِنَا ٱلصِّرَٰطَ ٱلْمُسْتَقِيمَ ۝ صِرَٰطَ ٱلَّذِينَ أَنْعَمْتَ عَلَيْهِمْ

غَيْرِ ٱلْمَغْضُوبِ عَلَيْهِمْ وَلَا ٱلضَّآلِّينَ ۝

1. *In the Name of Allah,
the Most Beneficent,
the Most Merciful.*

2. *The praises and thanks
be to Allah,
the Cherisher and Sustainer of the Worlds;*

3. *Most Gracious, Most Merciful.*

4. *Master of the Day of Recompense.*

5. *You (Alone) we worship,
and You (Alone) we ask for help
(for each and everything).*

6. *Guide us to the Straight Way.*

7. *The way of those on whom you have bestowed
Your Grace,
not (the way) of those
who earned Your Anger,
nor of those who went astray.*

The Quran, 1: 1-7

When Muslims do their prayer in congregation, they arrange themselves in rows behind the imam and pray from all continents towards Macca.

This benevolent dynamic is also found in Macca, when Muslims circle around the Kaaba in uniform movements seven times counterclockwise.

If we look beyond the simple movements, this ritual evokes once more the movement of the planets on their orbits, or the power of a swarm of birds, which points to the unity of man, nature, universe and religion in Islam.

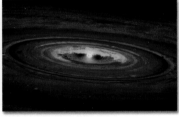

The following will address the reasons for the different prayer times, which are not subject to a set temporal rhythm (i.e. every 4,5 hours distributed over day and night), but are adapted to a natural rhythm.

11.1 The Dawn **Prayer**

The Dawn Prayer

In Islam, sleep is regarded as a *"small death"*, for the contact between soul and body is weaker.

When the first morning rays of the sun break through the horizon of the night sky, the time for this prayer has come. After the long quiet of the night, the birds fly away from their nests and start their singing, people take themselves to their workplaces, and daily life begins.

This moment of the day evokes the time of the Resurrection after death. Just like the day inevitably follows the night, and the spring follows the winter time and time again, death is followed by the Resurrection.

 In this consciousness, the Prophet always said after waking up:

"Praise be to Allah, who awoke us after letting us die, and to Him we shall resurrect."[1]

And he used to say: *"You will die like you slept, and you will resurrect like you awoke, and there will only be Janna (Paradise) forever or Jahannam (Hell) forever."*[2]

At the time of this prayer, the human soul has the need to knock at the door of God, the Merciful, the Majestic, the Almighty, to ask for his help and right guidance to master the difficulties, obstacles and tasks of the day. Man also prays to be preserved from the horror of the Day of Resurrection and to be protected in the future.

The prayer ends with the words:

"O God, I ask You for Your help and forgiveness and right guidance. I have come back to You and I believe in You and I rely on You. I praise You with all things beautiful, I am grateful to You and I do not deny

---

1 **Al-Buchari:** Assahih, Hadith Nº.: 5837, **Moslim:** Assahih, Hadith Nº.: 4886, **Ibn Hanbal,** Ahmad: Al-Musnad, Hadith Nº.: 17938.

2 **Assalhi:** Subul Al-Huda War-raschad, Beirut 1993, Vol. 2, p. 322.

You, and I claim myself free of those who deny You. I worship You and pray and do Sudjud for You. I make an effort and rush to You. I hope for Your Mercy and fear Your punishment, etc."[1]

11.2 The Noon Prayer *The Noon Prayer*

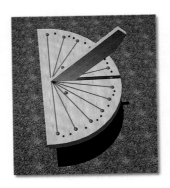

In the middle of the day, when the sun has just abandoned its zenith and man has reached the highpoint of his daily activities, the Noon Prayer creates a reprieve and time for reflection for both the soul and the mind. Thereby, man stands in motionless humility in front of God and thanks Him for His favor, seeks His forgiveness and asks for His support for the rest of the day. Through Rukua[2] and Sudjud he manifests his love and devotion for God. The Noon Prayer is not only the time of the zenith of the sun and the middle of the day, but it also symbolizes the midpoint of the season and the time of the complete blooming of life.

---

1 cp. **Ibn Abi Schei-ba**: Al-Musannaf, Beirut 1988, Vol. 2, p. 200-201, **Al-Baeihaqi**: Assunan Al-Kubra, Hyderabad 1925, Vol. 2, p. 210, **Abdurrazzaq**: Al-Musannaf, Hadith No.: 4968-4970, 4983, 4989, 4997.

2 Rukua is a phase of the prayer during which Muslims bend over at the waist at a right angle.

11.3 late-afternoon **Prayer**

The late-afternoon Prayer

During the last phase of the day, approximately halfway between the zenith and the sunset, when the shadows have doubled since the Noon Prayer, the third prayer takes place.

The first fruits of the daily activities and efforts can be harvested. Man slowly experiences weariness from the day, the luminous glow of the sun diminishes, and a gentle gold color appears in the world. This time evokes associations to the autumn months, when the leaves lose their lively green color and are blown in their warm red-yellow tones from the trees. When the fields are harvested, man is reminded of old age, the final phase of life, when he leaves his young days behind and harvests the fruits of his life. At this point, man increasingly feels that he is a guest in this life, and that, in the end, everything on Earth is temporary.

> *"All that is on Earth will perish;*
> *but will abide forever*
> *the Face of you Lord,*
> *full of Majesty,*
> *Bounty and Honor."*
>
> *The Quran, 55: 26-27*

The human soul, created for an eternity, stands at this point in front of the gate of God, and calls wholeheartedly:

"Please accept my good deeds and forgive my bad ones, and rightly guide me for the rest of my days. Enlighten the end of my life in this world, like you enlightened my life in the past."

Through the latter, it finds true solace and peace.

11.4 The Sunset **Prayer**

After the long journey of the sun from East to West, it finally sets, its rays begin to fade and the sky begins to darken. The singing of the birds ebbs away, and they return to their nests. The plants react to the lacking sunlight by closing their blooms. The muazzin now calls for the fourth prayer.

Man reflects on the events of the day. And just like the sun now glides behind the horizon and into the dark earth, so does the life of man go under in the end. He will take leave of all who love him and whom he loves on earth, where he will wait for the Day of Resurrection in Barzakh.[1]

Through this association of ideas of death and sunset, the soul awakens from the possible unconsciousness and longs for the Sudjud before the One that is eternal, to ask Him to be accompanied by His mercy during her journey to the Afterlife. For this prayer, man stands before God, leaving all the temporary creatures of the day that left him behind, and praises: *"Allahu Akbar"* (Allah is greater), and further:

" *The praises and thanks be to Allah,*
the Cherisher and Sustainer of the Worlds,"
"You (Alone) we worship,
and You (Alone) we ask for help
(for each and everything)."

---

1 Barzakh is the lapse between death and the Day of Resurrection.

Man recognizes the finiteness of the existence and capabilities of all living creatures of this world – his own as well – and he manifests his helplessness through Rukua.

Thereby, he attests:

"Praised be my God, the Magnificent."

Then he bows to Sudjud and says:

"Praised be my God, the Highest."

At the end, he sits down and salutes all of God's righteous servants, and renews his bond to the Prophet, the right guide to God: *"Assalamu Aleika"* (Peace be upon you).

Thus, the Muslim has, in the company of God and the Prophet, washed away sorrow and pain from his soul, and he is reminded to only do good the next day and follow God's word, for, with the coming of death, the time of trial has finally ended. There is no more possibility of redemption or intercession.

11.5 The Night Prayer *The Night Prayer*

When it is completely dark and the last light and the last vestige of the day have disappeared, the time for the Night Prayer has come.

Like the last vestige of the day has disappeared shortly after the sunset, the last vestiges of man and the memories of him will soon disappear after his death. The last ones to know him and cry for him will follow him one day, and the veil of oblivion will be cast upon him.

The time of the Night Prayer reminds man of the final closing of this life's doors after the relocation of all its inhabitants to the Afterlife, and the opening of the Afterlife's vastness.

The stars, not visible during the day, now appear gradually, for before they were hidden by the daylight. The same also happens to man after death. He will discover many new facts and things, which had remained hidden to him before by the light of his earthly life.

> *"Indeed you were heedless of this;*
> *now have We removed your veil,*
> *and sharp is your sight this Day!"*
>
> The Quran, 50: 22

To illuminate this hidden future, the soul knocks at the gates of God at this time. Through prayer and conversation, God heals the spiritual wounds caused by the parting of the loved ones, and he forgets those who have long forgotten him. Now, one leaves everything behind which had long left one behind. Before man falls in a sleep that resembles death, he bows in Sudjud before God to ask for His company. With the night Prayer, man puts a bright end to his record of deeds of the day.

In summary, we can say that prayer in Islam is harmonically integrated in the daily life of man, and that it creates moments of reflection and peace. It binds the soul, the heart and the mind with the events of the universe and the future. The prayers of the day symbolize the entire life with all its phases, and they produce in the Muslim a consciousness of this present life. These prayers are also characterized by their proximity and immediacy to man and God.[1]

12 SUPPLICATION (DO'A)
Supplication

Through supplication, man turns directly to God in a very personal conversation. This is a private moment, which offers a place for grievance, the expression of wishes, or the presentation of needs.

However, the question arises of why we sometimes seem to vainly

---

1 One of the people who wrote very beautifully about the sense and meanings of these five times is the Turkish scholar and philosopher Bediüzzaman Said Nursi in his work "Rasael Annour." (several volumes).

await the fulfillment of our wishes by God.

Supplication

The Prophet explained the influence of supplication as follows: *"There is no Muslim that asks God for something and does not receive one of the following three things: he either has his supplication fulfilled, or it is stored for the Hereafter, or he is preserved from harm of equal value."*

His companions responded: *"Then we will make many supplications"* and the Prophet replied: *"God can give you more than what you could ever wish for."*[1]

God always answers your supplications, but at a time and manner that are in accordance with His wisdom. The events of the universe are decided upon certain wise criteria, even if they seem serendipitous or irrational.

Sometimes, pain and sorrow preserve man from an even larger future tragedy, even if man does never find out about it because God averted it. On the other hand, the Muslim suffers in this life in replacement of the punishment in the Hereafter.

The Prophet said about this:

"Every weariness, illness, worry, sorrow, harm or bitterness, down to the smallest bit, is deducted from the Muslim's sins."[2]

"Muslims will receive trials from themselves, their children and their possessions, until they stand before God free of sin."[3]

"When God wants good for his servant, he lets him receive his punishment in this life, for otherwise He would keep his sin for him and let him receive it on the Day of Resurrection."[4]

---

1 **ATTERMEZI:** Assunan, Hadith N°.: 3497, **IBN HANBAL**, Ahmad: Al-Musnad, Hadith N°.:10709 and **AL-HAKEM:** Al-Mustadrak, Hadith N°.:1770.

2 **AL-BUCHARI:** Assahih, Hadith N°.: 5210.

3 **ATTERMEZI:** Assunan, Hadith Nr.: 2323 and **IBN HANBAL**, Ahmad: Al-Musnad, Hadith Nr.: 7521, 9435.

4 **ATTERMEZI:** Assunan, Hadith Nr.: 2319.

13 THE MEANING OF THE PILGRIMAGE IN ISLAM

The Meaning of the Pilgrimage in Islam

One of the pillars of Islam is to undertake the hajj (pilgrimage) to Macca.

The Muslim spends a few days there in different places, and at the same time lives through this experience and shares it with over two million Muslims from all over the world representing all kinds of cultures and who speak the most diverse languages.

They all move into Macca dressed in simple white clothes, and their occupation, age, and social status do not matter, least of all nationality or skin color.

During the pilgrimage, man divests himself of all worldly superficialities, and he is thrown back to his roots as a human being and a creature of God.

Control over oneself plays an important role during the pilgrimage, and man is directed towards the friendly and peaceful interaction with others – which, taking into consideration the millions of pilgrims in a small area, and the efforts to prepare for the journey itself, can represent a major challenge.

The conscious interaction with the environment is also part of the pilgrimage.

In Macca, no Muslim may harm any animal or plant, regardless of whether they are large or small. Thus, man is reminded that he is not lord over everything, but only a creature of the same God.

The experiences of this peaceful gathering and of the collective praising of God in Macca represent a turning point in the life of a Muslim, for it leaves the impression of an unforgettable closeness to God and fraternity with other Muslims.

One of these decisive experiences is documented in history in great detail: the pilgrimage of the American civil rights activist

Malcolm X[1] in 1964, which made an actively racist nationalist into a peaceful man, in the company of all ethnicities.

Malcolm X describes his experiences during the pilgrimage as follows:

Malcolm X
(1925-1965)

> *"Never have I witnessed such sincere hospitality and overwhelming spirit of true brotherhood as is practiced by people of all colors and races here [...] For the past week, I have been utterly speechless and spellbound by the graciousness I see displayed all around me by people of all colors. [...] There were tens of thousands of pilgrims, from all over the world. They were of all colors, from blue-eyed blondes to black-skinned Africans. But we were all participating in the same ritual, displaying a spirit of unity and brotherhood that my experiences in America had led me to believe never could exist between the white and non-white.*
>
> *America needs to understand Islam, because this is the one religion that erases from its society the race problem. [...] I have never before seen sincere and true brotherhood practiced by all colors together, irrespective of their color.*
>
> *You may be shocked by these words coming from me. But on this pilgrimage, what I have seen, and experienced, has forced me to re-arrange much of my thought-patterns previously held, and to toss aside some of my previous conclusions.*
>
> *[...] We were truly all the same (brothers)--because their belief in one God had removed the white from their minds, the white from their behavior, and the white from their attitude."*[2]

---

1 Malcolm X (born in 1925 as Malcolm Little in Omaha, Nebraska) was an American leader of the Civil Rights Movement. The majority of his family was brutally murdered by white nationalists. In 1949 he joined the "Nation of Islam", a sect based on Islam but that represents black racism. Numerous violations against the code of the "Nation of Islam" finally led to his expulsion of the organization in 1963. During his pilgrimage to Macca, he experienced the beauty of true brotherhood and the equality amongst people of all ethnicities. He accepted true Islam. During his public speech in New York in 1965, he was shot by his opponents for this reason.

2 cp. **HALEY**, Alex: The Autobiography of Malcolm X., as well as URL: www.malcolm-x.org/docs/let_Macca.htm

14 WHY DOES GOD LET ALL OF THIS HAPPEN?

Why does God let all of this happen

If God exists, is just, knows all and is capable of everything, then why does he allow for devastating things such as war, genocide or illness to happen around us? Why does he let innocent people die, without punishing their murderers? Why does he let children simply die when they have not ever committed sin?

To answer this, one must firstly remember that this life is not a place for accountability, reward or punishment, but that it is a place of trials.

"And surely We shall try you
until We test those among you
who strive their utmost and persevere in patience;
and
We shall test your facts."

The Quran, 47: 31

"And certainly,
We shall test you with something of fear,
hunger, some loss in wealth, lives and fruits,
but give glad tidings to those who patiently persevere.
Who say, when afflicted with calamity:
'To God we belong,
and to Him is our return.'
They are those on whom (descend) blessings from God,
and Mercy,
and it is they who are the
guided-ones."

The Quran, 2: 155-157

> *"Think not
> that God is unaware
> of that which the wrong-doers do.
> He but gives them respite up to a Day
> when the eyes will stare in horror."*
>
> The Quran, 14: 42

Someone who only sees this life and believes that it does not continue afterwards is overwhelmed by loss in times of grief or pain, catastrophes or long illnesses.

The Muslim undoubtedly feels sadness and pain as well, but he lives with the certainty that this life is only a very small chapter of his existence.

He lives with the certainty that the Day of Judgment will soon come, although *"soon"* is a vague term, which can last from five minutes (*"I'll come home soon from work"*) to even decades (*"Soon, the little one will be all grown up"*), depending on the situation and perception.

Surely, in relation to man's life on Earth, which has existed for numerous tens of thousands of years, the life of an individual of approximately 80 years seems relatively short.

Following the latter, reward or punishment occur for the length of eternity.

14.1 Behind Every Event Is a Meaning

Behind every Event is a Meaning

The Muslim believes that nothing happens by chance and meaninglessly, but that everything that occurs in this world follows a specific sense and wisdom known to Allah – even if we cannot discover the meaning behind everything.

"No calamity befalls on the earth or in yourselves
but is inscribed in the Book of Decrees,
before We bring it into existence.
Verily, that is easy for God.
In order that you may not be sad
over matters that you fail to get,
nor rejoice because of that which has been given to you.
And god likes not prideful boasters."

The Quran, 57: 22-23

Through storms, earthquakes, natural disasters and death, man repeatedly sees that not all world incidents can be predicted or controlled by politics and science.

Catastrophes also show the true value of this life, and that it is not a place to settle down, but is passing and represents a trial phase.

Pain and misfortunes awaken those who have forgotten God and prompt them to think about their paths in life and their behavior towards others, and to seize the opportunity of their lives to save their place in Janna.

"And verily,
We will make them taste of the Penalty of this (life)
prior to the supreme Penalty,
in order that they may (repent and) return."

The Quran, 32: 21

The Prophet says: *"Muslims will receive trials from themselves, their children and their possessions, until they stand before God free of sin."*[1]

This life has no value to God in comparison to the Afterlife.

---

1 **ATTERMEZI:** Assunan, Hadith Nº.: 2323.

Happiness and pain are different variables of the trial; they are not proof of the love or the punishment of God for man, even though man may assume this:

"*As for man,*
when his Lord tries him by giving him honour and gifts,
then he says (puffed up):
'My Lord has honoured me.'
But when He tries him,
restricting his subsistence for him,
then he says: (in despair),
'My Lord hath humiliated me!' "

The Quran, 89: 15-16

The Prophet said:

"If this life was worth a midge wing to God, he would not even have given a swallow of water to a single Kafir. [1] *"*[2]

When the companions of the Prophet saw him, as he slept on a hard straw mat that left marks on his skin, they said:

"If you had let us know, we would have gotten you something soft to sleep on."

The Prophet replied:

"I don't have anything to do with this life. I am like a traveler, who briefly rests beneath the shadow of a tree and then continues on his journey."[3]

---

1 A Kafir is, according to Islamic belief, a person that has heard from God and his Prophet Muhammad, and still refuses to believe in them. But he must be treated justly and mercifully by the Muslim, just like every other person.

2 **Attrmezi**: Assunan, Hadith N°.: 2242.

3 Idem, Hadith N°.: 299, **Ibn Magah**: Assunan, Hadith N°.: 4099.

14.2 Injustice In This Life

Injustice In This Life

God gave man the freedom to choose his path and to determine the kind of life and behavior he wants for himself.[1] He has enabled him – not forced – to be a righteous man, for he is in a trial, based on which his eternal fate will be decided. There is not a true test for behavior without the existing freedom to freely choose and determine one's actions. Only then the true face of man is shown, and only then can the reward or the punishment be fair. Without this freedom, man would act like a marionette that does not abstain from bad deeds out of love for God, but only because its behavior repertoire only contains good deeds.

Moreover, what person could say about himself that he has never committed any bad deeds? If God would only leave those who have solely committed good deeds on earth, the earth would be swept empty. However, God is merciful, and He gave us the chance to come back to Him and improve our behavior.

> *"If God*
> *were to punish men for their wrongdoing,*
> *He would not leave,*
> *on it (the earth) a single living creature:*
> *but He gives them respite for a stated term:*
> *when their term expires,*
> *neither can they delay*
> *nor can they advance it an hour."*
>
> The Quran, 16: 61

This world we currently live in is like a stage, and our life is a play whose scenes are recorded down to their very last detail, so that, in the end, everything can be evaluated based on those recordings.

---

1 cp. the Quran, 41:46, 17:18-20, 76:2-3, 18:29, 11:15-16, 17: 18-19, 42: 20.

14.3 Generous **Redemption**

This life will not remain forever. We will leave it in our own, pre-established way. God will not leave a man who died as a toddler without a generous replacement for the life he lost. It is the same for those who were unjustly murdered.

> *"But if it had been God's Will,*
> *He could certainly have exacted*
> *retribution from them (Himself);*
> *but (He lets you fight) in order to test you,*
> *some with others.*
> *But those who are killed in the way of God,*
> *He will never let their deeds be lost."*
>
> The Quran, 47:4.

The worldly trial of a dead child will always be regarded as "passed" in the Hereafter, and thus the child comes protected into Janna, without fear of punishment or accountability, for it is only with sexual maturity that sins are assumed.

A Muslim who dies from a crime comes to the level of Shahid (martyr) in Janna as a reward. The sins of a Shahid are forgiven, and thus he will come into Janna without being held accountable.

In Janna it is said: *"When those who were tried in this life receive their reward on the Day of Resurrection, those who did not suffer as much in this life will wish their skin had been peeled off."*[1]

---

1 **ATTERMEZI**: Assunan, Hadith N°.: 2326.

14.4 Where Things March To the Beat of a Different Drum

Our life is a trial; we play a minor part in a theater play, even though it feels like the main role. If we take into consideration that millions of people already lived before us tens of thousands of years ago, and that many more will follow, we then realize that we are only a little drop in the ocean of time and humanity. Compared to the eternity of the Afterlife, the trial phase on earth is only of minor duration. On the Day of Resurrection, people will know to measure time with different parameters.

"He will say: '
What number of years did you stay on earth?'
They will say:
'We stayed a day or part of a day.
Ask of those who keep account.'
He will say:
'You stayed not but a little
— if you had only known!
Did you then think that We had created you in play,
and that you would not be brought back to Us
(for account)?' "

The Quran, 23: 112-115

"And to God belongs
the unseen of the heavens and the earth.
And the matter of the Hour (of Judgment)
is not but as a twinkling of the eye,
or even nearer. Truly!
God is Able to do all things."

The Quran, 16: 77

15 THE GENERAL CHARACTERISTICS OF ISLAM

The character of Islam can be described by the following reference points:

- There is only one God; and He created everything.
- Islam is a simple dogma that agrees with the heart and reason of man.
- Man is responsible for himself. No intermediaries (i.e. priests in Christianity) or expiatory sacrifices can help him.

> "*Then guard yourselves against a day (of Judgement) when no person shall avail another, nor shall compensation be accepted from him, nor shall intercession be of use to him, nor shall they be helped.*"
>
> *The Quran 2:123*

- All people are equal before the Justice of God. Neither nationality nor skin color, nor gender, occupation or religion matter.
- Islam prompts people to believe in all prophets and follow the last one, Muhammad.
- Islam can be practiced in every society, every nation and every era without any problems, and nothing that surpasses one's abilities is being expected from anyone.

> "*On no soul does God place a burden greater than it can bear.*"
>
> *The Quran 2:286*

- Islam provides a religious, economic, social, political and military order, valid for each individual, each family, and society. It balances this life and the Hereafter, and it is concerned with the fulfillment of the needs of the body and the soul.
- There is no monasticism in Islam. For the Muslim, life is a big mosque, and his daily work is a form of worship.
- The goal of Islam in this life is for man to live happily and enjoy the beauty of this life. Only that which could harm the health, others or society is prohibited.
- To violate the rights of others, injustice, deceit and dictatorship are in Islam great sins.
- In Islam, science and religion work together.

" Those truly fear God,
among His Servants,
who have knowledge"

The Quran 35:28

- The religious texts in Islam – the Quran and the Sunnah – were noted and copied with highest precision, and then they were preserved with utmost care. For this purpose, Muslims developed disciplines to order and test the Quran and the Hadiths systematically, according to strict transmission rules and methods.

Here we will attempt to clarify the position of Islam to topics such as the use of headscarves, polygamy, the role of women, genital mutilation, Islam as state system, the interaction with people of different faiths, and the Jihad. The question of why Islam is understood as the only way to paradise represents another important aspect, which will be elaborated on.

Thereby, we will clarify some mistakes that have been sustained, again and again, by selective, biased media coverage. Here, the differentiation between Islam and the practices of a culture, with its rites and traditions, as well as their undisputed interpretations of the holy sources of Islam (the Quran and the Sunnah), which are sometimes very removed from Islam, is necessary.

Chapter 6

Critical Questions

1 ISLAM AS THE ONLY WAY TO PARADISE

Islam as the Only Way to Paradise

On the way to Paradise, one cannot ignore God. God invites man to accept His message and not to ignore His messengers:

> "*Say: 'If you (really) love God,*
> *follow me: God will love you, and forgive your sins,*
> *for God is Oft-Forgiving, Most Merciful.'*
> *Say: 'Obey God and His Messenger;'*
> *but if they turn back,*
> *God loves not those who reject Faith.*"
>
> The Quran, 3: 31-32

God also declares that He will only accept Islam:

> "*And whoever seeks a religion other than Islam,*
> *never will it be accepted of Him,*
> *and in the Afterlife*
> *he will be one of the losers.*"
>
> The Quran, 3: 85

> "*The (accepted) Religion before God is Islam*"
>
> The Quran, 3: 19

The Prophet clearly says in this regard:

"*I swear by the One who holds my soul in His hand: Everyone that hears of me and still does not accept my Message will belong to the people of Jahannam.*"[1]

---

1 MOSLIM: Assahih, Hadith N°.: 218, IBN HANBAL, Ahmad: Al-Musnad, Hadith N°.: 7856.

The question is, why does God only accept Islam as the way to Janna? Why must we accept the message of Prophet Muhammad?

There is only one God, and He gave man only one religion. This religion was transmitted to man by different Prophets in different eras and in different places. They all taught: *There is only one God, He the Almighty, the Merciful, who is above all, for he created everything. He does not resemble any man, anything, and does not have any Partner or any kindred. This life is a trial. Afterwards, there is only Janna or Jahannam for all eternity. Janna is for everyone who accepted the Message of God. Jahannam is for everyone who denied the Message of God.*

This religion is **"Islam"**, which was not named after a specific person, or a nation, or a country or a tribe, for all people and all countries are equal before God.

The word **"Islam"** derives from the Arabic root "slm" (pronounced "sa-la-ma"), from which three different meanings can be derived:

a) *"to submit oneself"*
b) *"purity"*
c) *"peace."*

"Islam" comprises these three meanings, because: a person that devotes himself to God and worships Him purely (i.e. solely Him) will live in peace and tranquility in this life and in the Hereafter. Therefore, he or she is a *"Muslim"*.

Every Prophet was given a specific version of this religion. The difference between the versions lies only in the details of their respective prohibitions and commandments. Prophet Muhammad was sent with the last version. He is the new bearer of the same flag that all the other prophets before him defended their entire lives, and under which they served.

1.1 The Caravan of Humanity

The Caravan of Humanity

The caravan of humanity on the way to Janna was led by hundreds of Prophets from all nations throughout history. Amongst them was Prophet Abraham, who guided the caravan at a specific time according to a specific map. Afterwards, Prophet Moses took over the leadership with a new version of the map, and this is also how we perceive the role of Jesus. Finally, God sent Prophet Muhammad as the last leader with the *"newest"* version:

> *"Muhammad is not the father of any of your men,*
> *but (he is) the Messenger of God,*
> *and the last (end) of the Prophets"*
>
> The Quran 33:40

*"And We have sent
down to you
(O Muhammad)
the Book (this Quran) in truth,
confirming the scripture that came before it,
and guarding it in safety"*

The Quran, 5:48

*"Say (O Muhammad):
O mankind!
Verily, I am sent to you all
as the Messenger of God
- to Whom belongs the dominion
of the heavens and the earth.
There is no god but He:
it is He
that gives both life and death.
So believe in God
and His Messenger,
the Prophet who can neither read nor write,
who believed in God and His words:
follow him that (so) you may be guided."*

The Quran, 7: 158

I was sent to all Mankind, and I was made the last Prophet

The Prophet said: *"I was sent to all Mankind, and I was made the last Prophet."*[1]

---

1 **MOSLIM:** Assahih, Hadith Nº.: 812, **ATTERMEZI:** Assunan, Hadith Nº.:1474, **IBN HANBAL,** Ahmad: Al-Musnad, Hadith Nº.: 8969.

All prophets, the leaders of the caravan, where chosen by God. He is the Lord that all Prophets serve and have devoted their lives to. Their mission was to transmit His instructions to mankind, and to show them the way to Janna.

Someone who loves the prophets Abraham, Moses and Jesus and wants to reach the final destination of the caravan will also love Prophet Muhammad and follow him, for he is the caravan leader with the new Instructions of God for the last stage into Paradise.

The final destination of the caravan becomes unreachable to those who ignore or consciously deny the last leader (Muhammad) and follow the map of a previous prophet.

The Message of Prophet Muhammad stresses that all the previous Prophets were loyal to the Lord, transmitted the truth, and completely fulfilled their task. Therefore, as a Muslim, one must recognize all Prophets and follow the last one. Islam is the only religion that recognizes all Prophets. Instead of saying: "*I am Christian*" or "*I am Mohammedan*", one simply says: "*I am Muslim*".

The Prophets are brothers they are from the same God

The Prophet stresses:

"*The Prophets are brothers, who belong to the same Father but to different mothers (i.e. they are from the same God and different eras), and out of all people I am the next one to Jesus. Between him and I there were no other Prophets.*"[1]

---

1 IBN HANBAL, Ahmad: Al-Musnad, Hadith Nr.: 8902, IBN-HIBBAN: Assahih, Hadith Nr.: 6940.

Janna is the final destination of the caravan, and only God knows the right way there. Our love to Him and our respect for Him was tested by God through the different Prophets.

Some people prefer to worship God in their own way, and they refuse the instructions of the Prophet that was sent to them. Unfortunately, even if they lead their lives as pious believers and thought of themselves as close to Paradise, they will never be able to get there without acknowledging Muhammad as a prophet.

> "*As for those who disbelieve,*
> *their deeds are like a mirage in a desert.*
> *The thirsty one thinks it to be water,*
> *until he comes up to it, he finds it to be nothing,*
> *but he finds God with him,*
> *Who will pay him his due (Hell).*
> *And God is swift in taking account.*"
>
> The Quran, 24: 39

Janna is not a product of human thought, and therefore the way to it cannot be decided by human thought.

2 THE TRUE TEACHING OF JESUS, ACCORDING TO THE QURAN AND THE BIBLE

On the Day of Resurrection, Jesus will tell those who strayed from the path of the caravan after him that they are not right, and the following discussion will be held:

"*And* (remember)
when Allah will say (on the Day of Resurrection):
O Jesus the son of Mary!
Did you say unto men,
'worship me and my mother as two gods besides Allah?'
He will say:
'Glory be to You!
Never could I say what I had no right (to say).
Had I said such a thing, You would indeed have known it.
You know what is in my inner-self though
I do not know what is in Yours.
Truly, You, only You, are the All-Knower
of all that is hidden and unseen.
Never did I say to them
aught except what You (Allah) did command me to say:
Worship Allah, my
Lord and your Lord.;
and I was a witness over them
whilst I dwelt amongst them;
but when You took me up,
You were the Watcher over them,
and you are a Witness to all things.' "

The Quran, 5: 116-117

2.1 What Did Jesus Invite Us To?

What Did Jesus Invite Us To?

There is not a place, neither in the Quran nor in the Bible, where Jesus proclaimed: *"I am a god"* or *"Worship me"*, and he never appealed for the Trinity.

If we read the New Testament bearing in mind the question of what it was that Jesus announced in his conversations and preaches during his visits in many cities and towns, and with what mission he sent his twelve apostles, then we discover that Jesus never demanded to be seen and worshipped as a god, or to believe in the Trinity.

He rather appealed for such practical topics as *"to desire other women is adultery; divorce, malediction and vengeance are prohibited; love your enemies; do not pray on the street corners, but rather in secrecy; do not amass riches on this earth; etc."*

Jesus thereby emphasizes that he was sent to continue the mission of the Prophets before him:

"Do not think that I have come to do away with the Law of Moses and the teachings of the Prophets. I have not come to do away with them, but to make their teachings come true."[1]

- *"(He) taught in the synagogues, announced the Message of the Kingdom of God, and healed all the ill and sufferers."*[2]
- He said to his apostles: *"Do not go among the Gentiles or enter any town of the Samaritans. Go rather to the lost sheep of Israel. As you go, preach this message: 'The kingdom of heaven is near.' Heal the sick, raise the dead, cleanse those who have leprosy, drive out demons. Freely you have received, freely give."* (NET, Matthew, 10:5-8).

---

1 The Bible, Today's English Version (hereafter referred to as TEV), Matthew, 5:17.

2 The Bible, Neue evangelistische Übersetzung (hereafter referred to as NET), Mt 9:35, 4:23, Lu 4:44, Mk 1:39.

It is clear that Jesus sent his apostles exclusively to the Jews, for he was only sent for them, which he repeatedly underlined:

- *"I was sent only to the lost sheep of Israel."* (NET, Matthew, 15:24).
- He even refused the title of *"Good Master"*:

"And, behold, one came and said unto him, Good Master, what good thing shall I do, that I may have eternal life? And he said unto him, Why callest thou me good? there is none good but one, that is, God." [1]

If *"Good Master"* was not acceptable to him, it seems unthinkable that he would accept the title of *"God"*.

"No pupil is greater than his teacher; no slave is greater than his master." (TEV, Matthew, 10:24).

Jesus transmitted to us his complete Message, he left no secrets or open points to be completed by his apostles after him:

"What I have taught is known everywhere. For I have preached in public, in the synagogues and temples, where everyone could hear it. I never taught anything different in secret." [2]

"On the Day of Judgement many will call me their Lord. They will say, "We preached in your name, and in your name we forced out demons and worked many miracles. But I will tell them, 'I will have nothing to do with you! Get out of my sight, you evil people!'" [3]

---

1   The Bible, King James Version (hereafter referred to as KJV), Matthew, 19:16-17.

2   The Bible, Hoffnung für Alle, John, 18:20.

3   The Bible, Contemporary English Version (hereafter referred to as CEV), Matthew, 7:22-23.

2.2 Jesus Says: "I Am a Messenger of God"

Jesus declared many times that God had sent him to divulge His message, and that he himself did not have any power.

- *"whoever receives me, doesn't receive me, but him who sent me."* [1]
- *"Most assuredly I tell you, he who hears my message, and believes him who sent me, has eternal life."* [2]
- *"I can do nothing on my own authority; I judge only as God tells me, so my judgment is right, because I am not trying to do what I want, but only what he who sent me wants."* (TEV, John, 5:30).
- *"Jesus answered, 'What I teach is not my own teaching, but it comes from God, who sent me.'"* (TEV, John, 7:16).
- *"I have not come on my own authority. **He who sent me, however, is truthful.**"* (TEV, John, 7:28).
- *"But the one who sent me is truthful"* (CEV, John, 8:26).
- *"Jesus cried out and said, 'Whoever believes in me, believes not in me, but in him who sent me.'"* (WEB, John, 12:44).
- *"And eternal life means to know you, **the only true God,** and to know Jesus Christ, whom you sent."* (TEV, John, 17:3).
- Jesus thus says: *"I cannot do anything by myself"* and he calls God *"the only true God"*.

The statements of Jesus about his mission are logical because:

> *"It is not (possible) for any human being to whom God has given the Book and Wisdom and Prophethood to say to the people: Be my worshippers rather than God's. On the contrary (he would say): Be you worshippers, because you are teaching the Book, and you are studying it."*
>
> The Quran, 3:79

---

1 The Bible, World English Bible (hereafter referred to as WEB), Mark, 9: 37.

2 The Bible, WEB and CEV, John, 5:24.

2.3 Jesus, the Man

"*Not a man is God, that he lies, nor a Son of Man, that he regrets.*"
(Numbers, 23:19)[1]

- "*But now you seek to kill me, a man who has told you the truth, which I heard from God.*" (WEB, John, 8:40).
- "*This man was a prophet and was considered by God and by all the people to be powerful in everything he said and did.*" (TEV, Luke, 24:19)
- In numerous parts of the New Testament, Jesus is called the Son of Man, for instance: "*The Son of Man came eating and drinking [...]*" (WEB, Matthew, 11:19)

2.4 In the Bible It Is Said: God Cannot Be Seen

1. "*No one has ever seen God.*"
   (TEV, John, 1:18 and 1 John, 4:12)

2. "*His appearing will be brought about at the right time by God, the blessed and only Ruler, the King of kings and the Lord of lords. He alone is immortal; he lives in the light that no one can approach. No one has ever seen him; no one can ever see him. To him be honor and eternal power!*" (TEV, 1 Timothy, 6:15-16).

3. When Moses wished to see God, the latter answered him: "*Thou canst not see my face: for there shall no man see me, and live.*" (KJV, Exodus, 33:20).

---

1 The Bibel, Elberfeld Bible 1905 (hereafter referred to as EB), cp. also: The Bible, WEB.

2.5 To Worship the Same God as Jesus

To Worship the Same God as Jesus

"*While Jesus was on earth, he begged God with loud crying and tears to save him. He truly worshiped God, and God listened to his prayers. […] he had to suffer before he could learn what it really means to obey God.*"[1] (CEV, Hebrews, 5:7-8). Jesus said: "[…] *The true worshippers will worship the Father in spirit and truth, for the Father seeks such to be his worshippers.*" (WEB, John, 4:23).

The only Biblical basis for the Trinity is found in this verse of the King James Version (KJV):
"*For there are three that bear record in heaven, the Father, the Word, and the Holy Ghost: and these three are one.*" (KJV, 1 John, 5:7).

This text has been removed from most of the modern versions of the Bible, such as the American Standard Version, Good News Bible (Today's English Version), World English Bible, Contemporary English Version and Phillips Modern English Bible and has been also removed from the Revised Standard Version which is based on the oldest preserved manuscripts.

The scholars of Christianity say this verse was interpolated into the text around the late 4th century. Dr. C.I. Schofield and 32 other scholars, backed by a committee of representatives of fifty co-operative denominations, came to the conclusion about this verse that

---

1 Islam unequivocally explains that God did not forsake his honored Prophet Jesus, but rather answered his prayers and saved him by ascending him in body and soul and thus saving him from death on the cross. The one who truly died on the cross was Judas Iscariot, the traitor. After Jesus' ascent, God gave him (Judas) the appearance of Jesus, so that Judas was arrested and killed on the cross.

"That they said (in boast): We killed Christ Jesus the son of Mary, the Messenger of God; but they killed him not, nor crucified him, but the resemblance of Jesus was put over another man (and they killed that man), and those who differ therein are full of doubts, with no (certain) knowledge, but only conjecture to follow. For surely; they killed him not. Nay, God raised him up unto Himself. And God is Ever All-Powerful, All-Wise."
The Quran, 4: 157-158.

"It is generally agreed that this verse has no manuscript authority and has been inserted."

Jesus explains why only one God is to be worshipped:
"No one can serve two masters, for either he will hate the one and love the other; or else he will be devoted to one and despise the other."
(WEB, Matthew 6:24)

2.6 Jesus' Explanation of Salvation

Jesus' Explanation of Salvation

When Jesus was asked
"What good thing shall I do, that I may have eternal life?" he answered:
"keep the commandments."
(WEB, Matthew, 19:17)

The Quran Makes an Appeal to Mankind

2.7 The Quran Makes an Appeal to Mankind

"O mankind!
Verily, there has come to you the Messenger (Muhammad)
with the truth from your Lord,
so believe in him, it is best for you.
But if you disbelieve,
to God belong all that is in the heavens and the earth.
And God is Ever All-Knowing, All-Wise.
O People of the Book!
Commit no excesses in your religion,
nor say of God aught but the truth.

Christ Jesus the son of Mary is not but a Messenger of God,
and His Word, which He bestowed on Mary,
and a Spirit created by Him;
so believe in God and His Messengers.
Say not 'Trinity': desist: it will be better for you.
For God is only One God, Glory be to Him:
(for Exalted is He) above having a son.
To Him belong all that is in the heavens
and all that is in the earth.
And All-Sufficient is God as a Disposer of affairs.
The Christ will never be proud
to reject to serve and worship God, nor do the angels,
those nearest (to God).
And whosoever rejects His worship and the arrogant ones,
He will gather them all together unto himself.
So, as for those who believed and did deeds of righteousness,
He will give their (due) rewards, and more,
out of His bounty.
But as for those who refuse His worship and were arrogant,
He will punish with a grievous penalty;
nor will they find, besides God,
any to protect or help them."

The Quran, 4: 170-173

"Surely, disbelievers are those who said:
'God is the third of the three (in a Trinity).'
But there is no god except One God.
And if they cease not from what they say, verily, a painful
penalty will befall the disbelievers among them.
Will they not repent to God and ask His Forgiveness?
For God is Oft-Forgiving,
Most Merciful.
Christ the son of Mary was no more than a Messenger;
many were the Messengers that passed away before him.

His mother was a woman of faith.
They both used to eat food (as any other human being).
Look how God doth makes His Signs clear to them;
yet look in how they are deluded away!"

The Quran, 5: 73-75

2.8 The Love of Muslims for Jesus

The Love of Muslims for Jesus

In Islam, Jesus is one of the closest people to God, and one of the five greatest Prophets.

Additionally, Muslims regard the depiction of the Prophets or God as a lack of respect, for no human form of depiction, be it drawing, painting, photomontage or caricature, could do their completeness justice. This "*sensitivity*" can also be comprehended with the aid of the following example:

Many Englishmen were surprised about the wrathful reaction of British Muslims over a Jesus rubber doll, which appeared in a TV show called "*Spitting Image*". The UK Action Committee for Islamic Affairs considered the doll of Christ, whom they honor as a Prophet, as a lack of respect. The doll was consequently withdrawn.[1]

This example makes it also clear that the love of Muslims is not limited to Prophet Muhammad, but that it comprises all the Prophets.

---

1 cp. The Sunday Telegraph, 10/18/1992.

3 WOMEN

3.1 The Status of Women in Pre-Islamic Cultures *The Status of Women*

The magnitude of the change experienced by the position of women through Islam can only be evaluated if one also takes a look at the role of women in other cultures. Like we will see, we are confronted with times of oppression, exploitation and defenselessness of women in a world dominated by men. This disparity between both genders is mostly rooted in the texts of the Holy Scriptures, or in the centuries-old culture of a nation, which push(ed) women into such a situation.

3.1.1 Women in Ancient Greece (approx. 750 BC – 30 BC)

Women in Ancient Greece

"All women in Athens had a *kyrios* - a guardian – who was usually her husband or, if she was unmarried, her closest male relative. The kyrios had a huge amount of control over the woman.

Athenian men saw women as weaker than them in all spheres of life – physically, morally, socially and intellectually. They did not give women rights and considered them corruptible, cunning and untrustworthy."[1]

A girl is beaten with a sandal - Ancient Greece.

"If a family had a daughter it needed to raise a substantial sum to pay the dowry to her husband. If there was no son, the daughter passed her father's inheritance to her spouse, for which reason she would be married to a close male relative: cousin or uncle. Normally, she was married a few years after puberty to a man much older than herself."[2]

---

1 cp. **BBC:** Women in Ancient Athens, URL: www.bbc.co.uk/dna/h2g2/A23428659 (Accessed: May 30th 2009).

2 **GILL, N.S.:** Evidence about Greek women in the archaic age, URL: http://ancienthistory. about.com/od/greekwomen/p/022900ArchGkwom.htmAbout.com (Accessed: May 29th 2009).

Dr. Gustave Le Bon says about the status of women in ancient Greece: *"The Greeks generally saw women as inferior creatures, solely useful to take care of the household and guarantee the survival of the species. If a woman gave birth to a deformed child, they would dispose of her. 'In Sparta,' writes M. Troplong, 'those sad creatures who could not promise the State any brave soldiers were killed.'"*[1]

When Socrates saw a sick woman, he said that the evil (the sickness) rests and dwells with the evil (the woman).[2]

3.1.2 Women in Ancient Rome *Women in Ancient Rome* (approx. 750 BC – 500 AD)

In early Roman times *"unwanted children in Rome, especially girls, were abandoned at birth: many were picked up by passers-by and sold as slaves."*[3]

"Equality was a foreign concept to the Roman mind."[4]

1 LE BON, Gustave: La civilisation des Arabes, Paris 1884, Book IV, p. 86.

2 CAXTON, William: Famous Prefaces. The Harvard Classics 1909–14, Epilogue to Dictes and Sayings of the Philosophers, First Edition (1477), URL: www.bartleby.com/39/4.html (Accessed: March 1st 2009).

3 THOMPSON, James B.: Women and Slavery in Ancient Rome, URL: www.womenintheancientworld.com (Accessed: July 05th 2010).

4 THOMPSON, James B.: Legal status of women in ancient Rome, URL: www.womenintheancientworld.com (Accessed: July 05th 2010).

"As was formerly the custom, a wife could be put to death, for having tasted wine, a treacherous kiss from her husband upon his return home or betraying him, and her infant daughter could be exposed or murdered at the pleasure of her husband who, as unrelenting master, was frequently wont to refuse her pleadings for the life of her babe, calling her prayers naught but the scruples of a foolish woman."[1]

A bequeathed example is the murder of the wife of the Roman Egnatius Metellus (at the time of Romulus); he *"took a club and beat his wife to death because she had drunk some wine. Not only did no one charge him with a crime, but no one even blamed him. Everyone considered this an excellent example of one who had justly paid the penalty for violating the laws of sobriety.*

Quintus Antistius Vetus felt no differently when he divorced his wife because he had seen her in public having a private conversation with a common freedwoman."[2]

Later, in the mid-Roman period, a form of marriage known as "usus" finally became the basis of the Roman judicial concept of marriage. Thanks to this more just concept, women were allowed to keep their family names and inheritance.[3] But all of this changed as soon as Christianity gained control. Under the Christian forms of marriage, the wife had to submit herself, her possessions, her consciousness and her name to the unchallengeable control of her husband[4], like a slave who was given to a new master.[5]

1 GAGE, Matilda J.: Woman, Chruch and State, New York 1893, p. 298.

2 LEFKOWITZ, Mary R./ FANT, Maureen B.: Women Life in the in Greece & Rome, Husbands' punishment of wives in early Rome, URL: www.stoa.org (Accessed: April 12th 2009).

3 GAGE, l.c., p. 299.

4 GAGE, l.c., p. 297.

5 GAGE, l.c., p. 299.

3.1.3 Women in Hinduism *Hinduism*

In Hinduism, the law code of the god Manu is followed, which says the following: "*The bed and the armchair, like lust, wrath, dishonesty, maliciousness and bad behavior – thus is the nature of women.*"
(Chapter 2, Verse 213 and 9:17).

Manu dictates that a woman may not act nor decide autonomously, not even in her own house; she is not able to do so at all. She should live, as a child, under the control of her father; as a spouse, under the control of her husband, and, after his death, under the control of her sons. (5: 147ff and 9: 2f).

Within the caste system, Manu positions women in all religious issues at the level of the Shudras, i.e. the servants and laborers who represent the fourth and lowest of castes. Accordingly, women, like Shudras, may not read the holy scriptures, namely the Vedas, and they may not offer any ritual sacrifices, unless they are accompanied by their spouses (5: 155).[1]

Even the murder of a woman is simply regarded as a "*venial misdemeanor*"[2] (11:67).

In Brahmanical literature, women are described like dogs, Sudras and black birds as "*oddity, sin and darkness*" Satapatha Brahmana), and excluded from spiritual ceremonies: "*Neither a girl nor a woman,*

---

1 cp. Neue Zürcher Zeitung (publisher): Indiens Frauen und der Hinduismus, Nº. 100, p. 9, (2001).

2 cp. SCHREFLER, Harald: Das traditionelle Frauenbild gemäß den brahmanischen Gesetzgebern, University of Vienna 2003, URL: www.pensis.net/documente/22schriftlichearbeiten_Rel/Frauenbild.Altindien-Referat-041203.pdf (Accessed: August 25th 2009).

[...], nor a fool, nor a sick person, nor an unhallowed one may be by the priest of the Fire Sacrifice." (Manu 11:36f)[1]

The Burning of Widows in India:

The Burning of Widows in India

The so-called Sati, a thousands year old, atrocious tradition, obligates a widow to immolate herself in the crematory of her deceased husband. Today, these burnings of widows are still practiced in the north-Indian state of Rajasthan.[2]

Sati, a burning of a widow

3.1.4 The Abortion of Girls in India

The Abortion of Girls in India

As an Indian-Canadian study[3] from 1997 shows, the systematic abortion of girls in India over the past 20 years has led to a deficiency of approximately ten million women.

The Indian police yearly register around 7000 girls (the

---

1 **Winternitz**, Moriz: Die Frau in den indischen Religionen, in: Hirsch, M (Editor): Archiv für Frauenkunde und Eugenetik (1915-1916), Berlin 1916. p 207.

2 **Groll**, Tina: Ohne Ehemann kein Recht auf Leben. Frauenseiten Bremen, URL: www.bremen.de/sixcms/detail.php?id=3860580 (Accessed: June 1st 2009).

3 Anonymous: Zehn Millionen Mädchen in Indien gezielt abgetrieben, URL: www.3sat.de/dynamic/sitegen/bin/sitegen.php?tab=2&source=/nano/news/87449/index.html (Accessed: May 31st 2009).

Babies' bodies found in abandoned well

▶ Grim find raises fears of female infanticide

▶ Managers at local clinic being questioned

Jeremy Page Delhi

The remains of dozens of foetuses and newborn babies have been found in an abandoned well in India, apparently aborted or discarded after birth because they were female.

Police are investigating whether a clinic in the state of Orissa identified the infants' sex before birth, which is illegal yet widespread in India, and then discarded them at their parents' request.

A 12-year-old boy raised the alarm after finding the remains of seven baby girls stuffed into bloody polythene bags in a disused well near the Krishna clinic in the district of Nayagarh on July 14. Police told The Times yesterday that they had found the skulls and body parts of 23 more infants over the weekend. Some reports now put the body count at as high as 37.

The find is the latest illustration of how widespread female foeticide and infanticide remain in India, despite repeated government attempts to eradicate the practices. Many Indian families still regard a daughter as a financial burden because tradition dictates that when she is married they must pay her husband's family a large dowry. Sons are also preferred because they are considered stronger workers and because daughters traditionally look after their in-laws in old age, rather than their own parents.

The Government outlawed ultrasound gender tests for unborn babies in 1994, but prosecutions are rare and many families bribe doctors to get past the ban and then choose to abort if the child is a girl.

Estimates of the number of girls aborted annually vary widely. Last year an international team of researchers claimed that over the past two decades half a million female foetuses had been aborted each year in India, which has a population of 1.1 billion. The Indian Medical Association believes that the figure could be ten times higher.

The result is an increasingly severe gender imbalance, with 927 women for every 1,000 men, according to the 2001 census — down from 945 women per 1,000 men a decade earlier. That compares with a global average of 1,050 women for every 1,000 men.

The imbalance in Nayagarh, a poor rural area, is even more extreme, with an estimated 901 females for every 1,000 males — the worst ratio in all of Orissa's 30 districts.

Yogesh Bahadur Khurania, a local police official, said that investigators had yet to establish the precise number and genders of the corpses found in the well.

But he confirmed that Sabita Sahu,

the Krishna clinic's owner, and Shyam Sahu, its manager, had been detained for questioning.

Tapasi Praharaj, a women's rights activist, said that the Krishna clinic was one of 11 unlicensed clinics allegedly involved in an illegal abortion racket with local police and health officials. "They're all in this nexus and they should all be punished," she said, calling for the health minister of Orissa to resign.

"The Government is totally careless and doesn't take any action. What we really need is for attitudes to change at every level of society."

While female infanticide is still

largely a rural problem, some studies show that female foeticide is most prevalent among the urban middle classes, which have ready access to ultrasound technology.

Last month police arrested a man posing as a doctor in a wealthy suburb of Delhi, the Indian capital, after remains of aborted babies were found in a septic tank at his clinic.

In February police found the remains of at least 14 infants buried in the backyard of a hospital in the central state of Madhya Pradesh.

Last year police recovered 25 foetuses from a well in the northern state of Punjab.

Gender gap

● India's gender deficit has increased more than tenfold since the 1901 census, when the country had 3.2 million fewer women than men, a century later the gap had grown to 35 million.

● Among the 0-6 age group, the number of girls per 1,000 boys plummeted from 1,010 in 1941 to 927 in 2001. 80 per cent of Indian districts underwent an increase in the gender imbalance between the 1991 and 2001 censuses. Only Pondicherry, Lakshadweep and Kerala improved.

● The disparity is larger and increasing at a faster rate in urban areas than rural ones.

● In 14 of India's richest districts, around Haryana and Punjab, there are fewer than 800 girls per 1,000 boys.

● Despite a law banning foetal sex determination being passed in 1994, it was 12 years before there was a conviction. In 2006 a doctor was fined 5,000 rupees (£60) and imprisoned for two years.

● In Salem, Tamil Nadu, researchers found a mobile ultrasound scanning unit being advertised with the slogan: "Pay 500 rupees and save 50,000 rupees later". Girls often require a large dowry to get married

Source: Unicef; UN Population Fund; Oxfam; overpopulation.org

Many families still regard a daughter as a liability, and some choose abortions after paying for illegal gender tests

estimated number of unreported cases speaks of 20,000 to 30,000 cases) who, in order to avoid paying the mandatory dowry, are killed.

The abortion statistics in Bombay clearly speak to this regard, for each year approximately 100 male embryos are aborted – compared to 6900 aborted female embryos.[1]

---

1 **Alt**, Franz: Kampf gegen Mädchenmorde, Fokus, N°. 9/2001.

3.1.5 Women in the Middle Ages (approx. 500 AD – 1500 AD)

Women in the Middle Ages

The inequality between man and woman is also established in medieval society. Women were regarded as unable creatures and were also excluded from education.[1]

"At this period, the soldiers of Christian Europe found pleasure in torture for its own sake, chiefly selecting women as their victims.

In medieval England, the condition of women was one of deep degradation. For many hundred years after the introduction of Christianity, wives were bought and the daughter was held as a portion of the father's property to be sold to the highest bidder."[2]

---

1 **SHULAMITH**, Shahar: Die Frau im Mittelalter, Königstein 1981, p. 15-25.

2 **SPENCER**, Herbert: Descriptive Sociology of England, in: Gage, Matilda J.: Woman, Church And State, New York 1893, p. 301.

Even though 4th century England was Christianized, it required another six hundred years for a Christian woman to have the right to eat at the table with her spouse, and for the daughter to receive the right to reject a spouse chosen by her father.

"No closeness of relationship was security for either a married or a single woman. Husbands frequently set a price upon his wife's virtue, and trafficked in the honor of their wives, fathers sold their daughters, yet if under temptation, a woman fell, outside of such sale, her punishment was most severe." [1]

"A husband, attracted by a new face, more wealth, greater political influence, or for any reason desiring to be rid of his wife, was regarded as justifiable in hiring an assassin to strangle her, or if walking by a river-bank, himself pushing her into the water where her cries for help were disregarded.

Those in whose hearts pity rose were prevented from giving aid, by such remarks as, 'It is nothing, only a woman being drowned.'

A horse or other domestic animal received more consideration than the women of a household and this condition constituted the domestic life of England from the 12 th century to the first civil war (ca. 1642)." [2]

---

1 **GAGE**, Matilda J.: Woman, Church And State, New York 1893, p. 202f.
2 **GAGE**, l.c., p. 204f.

3.1.6 The Bible and the Status of Women

The Bible and the Status of Women

In the prison   Preparing to burn a witch   The Holy Inquisition

The fear of gender and the despise of women were entered into Christianity with the apostle Paul.[1] Paul called woman the "*vessel*" of man[2], and for him she was – in contrast to Jesus – "*a person of second class.*"[3] "*[…] Man is the image and glory of God, but woman is the glory of man.*"[4] Man was not created for woman, but woman was created for man.[5] Therefore, women should keep silent in the churches, and veil their heads as a sign of their inferiority.[6] The seal of confession in church lists special female sins, partially

---

1 1 Cor. 11:3.

2 1 Thes. 4:4.

3 **Leipoldt**, J.: Jesus und die Frauen, 1921, p. 109.

4 1. Cor. 11:7.

5 1. Cor. 11:9.

6   1. Cor. 11:3 and 1. Cor. 14:34.

differentiated into subgroups.[1] Woman is bitterer than death[2], and one finds, amongst thousands, one righteous man, but not a single woman.[3]

"*To woman He said [God], 'I will surely multiply your pain in childbearing; in pain you shall bring forth children. Your desire shall be for your husband, and he shall rule over you.'*"[4]

If a woman seizes her husband by his private parts during a fight, then her hand should be cut off.[5] The church father Tertullian wanted women only to matter if they were virgins, and he referred to them as the "*gate of incursion*" to Satan.[6] The same position was held by the extremely prudish church fathers Hieronymus and Ambrosius.

Augustine, to whom even birth was a dirty process ("*inter faces et urinam nascimur*" – "*we are born amongst feces and urine*"), shared this disdain for women without any reservation. The moral and spiritual praising of women was first brought about by the troubadours and minnesingers of the 11th and 12th centuries.[7]

St. Peter's in Vatican
1505

Dr. Udo Schaefer comments in this regard:
"*And where does the minnesong come from? It has an Arabic-Islamic origin.*"[8]

---

1 **Shulamith**, Shahar: Die Frau im Mittelalter. Königstein 1981, p. 10-15.

2 Bible, Ecclesiastes: 7:26.

3 Bible, Ecclesiastes: 7:28-29.

4 Genesis, 3:16.

5 Deuteronomy, 25:11.

6 1 Tert. coutu fem. X1.

7 cp. **Erckmann**, Rudolf: Der Einfluß der arabischspanischen Kultur auf die Entwicklung des Minnesangs, Darmstadt 1933.

8 **Schaefer**, Dr. Udo: Muhammad - ein Lügenprophet? Eine Klarstellung gegenüber des katholischen Glaubens, p. 16. URL: www.udoschaefer.com/pdffiles/muhammad.pdf (Accesed: May 12th 2009).

3.2 Women in Islam

Women in Islam

3.2.1 Rules and Measures to Improve their Position

With the appearance of Islam, the rights and the position of women in society were established, even though the oppression of women still dominated the world. Many new laws were issued; and measures and codes were introduced in order to systematically protect women, such as:

Equality between men and women.
They both have the same rights and obligations, both in this life and in relation to their accountability before God and their admission into Janna.

> "*And women shall have rights similar to the rights against them, according to what is equitable.*"
>
> *The Quran, 2: 228*

> "*Whoever works righteousness, whether man or woman, while he (or she) is a believer, verily, to him will We give a good life, and We will bestow on such their reward in proportion the best of their deeds.*"
>
> *The Quran, 16: 97*

"Never will I allow
to be lost the work of any of you,
be he male or female;
you are members, one of another."

The Quran, 3: 195

"For Muslim men and women –
for believing men and women,
for devout men and women,
for true men and women,
for men and women who are patient and constant,
for men and women who who are humble,
for men and women who give in charity
for men and women who fast (and deny themselves),
for men and women who guard their chastity,
and for men and women who remember God
much with their hearts and tongues –
for them has God prepared forgiveness and great reward
(i.e. Paradise)."

The Quran, 33: 35

The differentiation made in certain obligations conforms to aptitude. It is asked in which fields women and in which fields men have more aptitudes to assume responsibility.

The Prophet said:

"Women are men's other half."[1] And thus, men and women complement each other in their shared responsibility for family and society in Islam. Both of them are obliged to reprimand one

---

1 ABO DAWOOD: Assunan, Hadith No.: 204, ATTERMEZZI: Assunan, Hadith No.: 105, IBN HANBAL, Ahmad: Al-Musnad, Hadith No.: 24999, AL-BAEIHAQUI: Assunan Al-Kubra, Hyderabad 1925, Vol. 1, p. 168.

another for religious breaches and misconducts. Within a marriage, the woman must not serve her husband; she can demand money for every service rendered. The contribution of the wife to the family budget is a voluntary act worthy of gratitude in Islam.

Women and men are absolutely equal in their humanity in Islam. The differentiation made regarding certain obligations is only based on their aptitude.

In Islam, the woman is not responsible for the expulsion from Janna.
Instead, Adam and Eve ate from the tree at the same time, seduced by the Devil's words, and thus they are both responsible.

Islam gives women the right of ownership and the right to dispose of their own finances. The husband has the obligation to pay for her sustenance, in spite of her own possessions, and in case of divorce he has to pay compensation.

Islam guarantees her the right of inheritance:

*"There
is a share for men
and a share for women
from what is left by parents
and those nearest related,
whether,
the property be small or large -
a determinate share."*

The Quran, 4: 7

Man and woman have an equal right to education in Islam.
A large amount of female scientists, poets and scholars that have appeared in Islamic history do not leave any doubt about this.

In Islam it is prohibited to force a woman into marriage. A young girl came to the Prophet and complained: "*My father forces me to marry a man that I don't like.*" Then, the Prophet called the father and gave the girl the choice. The girl said: "*O Messenger of Allah, I want to marry the man; I only wanted women to know that their fathers do not have the right to choose in their stead.*"[1]

Women were no longer abandoned to the capricious whim of men, and were given a secured legal position through their marriage contract. Man's whims were restricted by limiting his right of repudiation, by arranging alimony for the divorced woman, and by introducing the right for women to divorce their husbands. (over a judicial action).

In Islam, women have the right to a dowry, which is considered a gift that has to be brought by the groom at or before the marriage ceremony. This dowry is underlined as the bride's right several times in the Quran. In case of divorce, the man may not demand to have any part from the dowry back.

"*But if you decide*
to take one wife in place of another,
even if you had given the latter a whole treasure for dower,
take not the least bit of it back:
would you take it by slander and a manifest wrong?
And how could you take it
when you have gone in unto each other,
and they have taken from you a solemn covenant?"
The Quran, 4: 20-21

Islam explicitly prompts men to treat their women justly.

---

1 IBN HANBAL, Ahmad: Al-Musnad, Hadith N°.: 23892.

The Prophet said:

"The best man amongst you is the one who is best to his wife."[1] There is no justification for bad treatment:

"And live with them on a footing of kindness and equity.
If you dislike them,
it may be that you dislike a thing,
and God brings through it a great deal of good."

The Quran, 4: 19

In Islam, the mother assumes a special position;

she is honored, provided for in old age, and in every case her word is respected. According to the Prophet, Janna lies at the feet of the mother[2], i.e. the honoring of the mother is a secure path to Paradise. A hadith reports the following: one day, a man came to the Prophet and asked him: *"Who has the right to be treated the best by me?"* The Prophet answered: *"Your mother"* and the man asked again: *"And then?"* *"Your mother."* And he said the same the third time. The fourth time, the answer was: *"Then your father."*[3]

Orphan girls,

who were regarded as without rights and secondary citizens in Arabic society, receive particular protection in Islam.

"Verily,
those who unjustly eat up the property
of orphans, they eat up only a fire into their bellies,
and they will be enduring a blazing fire!"

The Quran, 4: 10

---

1 AL-MUNAWIE: Faydul-Qadier, Beirut 1994, Vol. 3, p. 661.

2 ANNASAII: Assunan, Hadith N°.: 3053.

3 AL-BUCHARI: Assahih, Hadith N°.: 5514, MOSLIM: Assahih, Hadith N°.: 4621.

Islam fought the customs of
some Arab tribes of killing their female newborns, until this tradition was completely abolished.[1]

The second-largest Surah of the Quran bears the title "*An-Nisaa*" (The Women), for it is mainly about women's rights.

Furthermore, when the Quran wanted to give a good example to all Muslims, it spoke of two representative women:

> "*And God has set forth an example*
> *for those who believe,*
> *the wife of Pharaoh, when she said:*
> *'O my Lord!*
> *Build for me, in nearness to you,*
> *a mansion in Paradise,*
> *and save me from Pharaoh and his doings,*
> *and save me from the people who are wrong-doers'*
> *And Mary the daughter of 'Imran',*
> *who guarded her chastity;*
> *and We breathed into her a soul from Us;*
> *and she testified to the truth of the Words of her Lord and*
> *of His Scriptures,*
> *and was one of the obedient (Servants).*"
>
> The Quran, 66: 11-12

The first person to accept Islam was a woman: Khadija, the Prophet's wife. This means that at a specific point in time the Muslim community consisted of only one woman! The first person to die for Islam was a woman: Summayya, who gave her life under the tortures of the Maccans for the sake of Islam.

---

1 The corresponding quote from the Quran is found in Surah 81:8-9.

3.2.2 Prophet Muhammad Speaks About
Women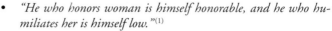

- *"He who honors woman is himself honorable, and he who humiliates her is himself low."*[(1)]
- *"The best one amongst you is the best one to woman."*[(2)]
- *"He who has a daughter and did not bury her alive, and did not offend her, and did not prefer his sons to her, he will be rewarded in Janna because of her."*[(3)]
- *"He who comes up with the living costs of two girls will enter Janna with me like this."* – He held two fingers together.[(4)]
- *"He who has three daughters"* (another time he said: "or three sisters"[(5)]) *"and, even if it is difficult, does not cease to provide for them, regardless of whether they harm him or make him happy, he will be allowed into Janna by Allah because of his mercy."* The Prophet was asked what would happen if one had only two or one (daughter or sister), and the Prophet said: *"Even if she's only one."*[(6)]
- In his Farewell Sermon, he warmly recommended the men to be good to women. He said then: *"Think of Allah when interacting with your wife, for you married her before Allah."*[(7)]

1 **AL- MUNAWIE:** Faydul-Qadier, Beirut 1994, Vol. 3, p. 662.

2 Idem, p. 661.

3 **ABO DAWOOD:** Assunan, Hadith N°.: 4480, **IBN HANBAL,** Ahmad: Al-Musnad, Hadith N°.: 1856, **AL-HAKEM:** Al-Mustadrak, Hadith N°.: 7456, **AL-BAEIHAQI:** Schu-ab Al-Ieman, Beirut 2000, Vol. 6, p. 410.

4 **MOSLIM:** Assahih, Hadith N°.: 4765, **ATTERMEZI:** Assunan, Hadith N°.: 1837, **AL-HAKEM:** Al-Mustadrak, Hadith N°.: 7458.

5 **ATTERMEZI:** Assunan, Hadith N°.: 1839.

6 **IBN HANBAL,** Ahmad: Al-Musnad, Hadith N°.: 8071, **IBN ABI SCHEI-BA:** Al-Musannaf, Beirut 1988, Vol. 6, p. 104 (Chapter: "die Sanftheit mit den Mädchen"), **AL-HAKEM:** Al-Mustadrak, Hadith N°.: 7454.

7 **MOSLIM:** Assahih, Hadith N°.: 2137, **ABO DAWOOD:** Assunan, Hadith N°.: 1628, **AL-BAEIHAQI:** Assunan Al-Kubra, Hyderabad 1925, Vol. 5, p. 8.

The Prophet himself was an example of softness and friendliness towards his wives.

His wife Aisha reported:

"If I drank out of a cup, he would take the cup and lay it on his lips at the same place where my lips had been before and drink. When we ate together, sometimes he would take a bite from his hand to my mouth. He made running competitions with me, but he was always faster than me; it was not until he got older that I could win. One time, we both wanted to step out of the house, and each one of us wanted to step out first, so we wrestled one another. Sometimes, when I was mad, I would push him away from me by his chest. In the worst of cases, I would not speak to him until evening. If we both had insurmountably different opinions we would let my father judge which one of us was right."[1]

He often sought the advice of his wives, even if it was about state affairs and decisions. Sometimes, when one of his wives wanted to ride out with the camel, he would offer his thigh as a step for her. Because of all these respectful and thoughtful behaviors, Muslim scholars of the Sharia, like Al-Imam Malek, stated: *"a Muslim must make an effort to treat his wife in the most loving of fashions."*[2]

3.2.3 Islamic Influence on the Position of Women

As a result of these behavioral basic principles towards women embedded in Islam, women acquired a special position in society. The five-volume book *"Aalam-Anisaa"* by Omar Rida-Kahala talks about famous women in Islamic history, who played important roles in the scientific, religious, political and social fields. Here are some of the points mentioned in his work:

---

1 **AL-MUNAWIE**: Fayd Al-Qadier, Vol. 3, p. 661-662.
2 **AL-MUNAWIE**: Fayd Al-Qadier, Vol. 3, p. 662. In the explanation of Hadith N°.: 4102.

- The second caliph Omar appointed Schifaa Bint Abdullah as director of the central market in Madina.
- Women had a special day during the week when they gathered by the Prophet and received lessons from him.[1]
- Women had the right to freely express their opinion, even if it was a political one against the caliph or an important leader. When caliph Omar spoke to his assembly, a woman interrupted and contradicted him. He let her finish her argument, changed his mind about the subject, and said: *"A woman was right, and a man was wrong."*[2]
- When the Prophet re-conquered Macca, the Muslim woman Ummu-Hanii conceded asylum to two of his enemies. Ummu-Hanii went to the Prophet and declared: *"I have granted both of these men my protection,"* the Prophet replied: *"We grant our protection to those whom you grant your protection."*[3]

Historians and authors described the influence of Islam on the position of women as follows:

Dr. Udo Schaefer said:
"The self-confident, quick-witted and intelligent wife of Muhammad, Khadija, who lived under the public eye, was the model of Arabic aristocracy. At the demand of the Prophet, who sought the education of women, influential jurist and

---

1 **Al-Buchari:** Assahih, Hadith N°.: 99, 1172, 6766, **Moslim:** Assahih, Hadith N°.: 4768, **Ibn Hanbal,** Ahmad: Al-Musnad, Hadith N°.: 10869.

2 **Ibn Hagar:** Fat-hul-Bari, Riyadh 2005, Vol. 11, p. 476, **Al-Mubar-Kafouri:** Tuhfat Al-Ahwazi, Damaskus, n.d., Vol. 4, p. 256.

3 **Ibn Hanbal,** Ahmad: Al-Musnad, Hadith N°.: 25657. And similar in: **Malek,** Al-Imam: Al-Muwatta, Libanon 2004. p. 99, **Al-Buchari:** Assahih, Hadith N°.: 344, 2935, 6592, **Moslim:** Assahih, Hadith N°.: 1179, **Abo Dawood:** Assunan, Hadith N°.: 2382.

magistrate positions were given to women."[1]

Sigrid Hunke said in this regard:

"One saw female jurists appear in the mosques, where they held public speeches and issued laws. Amongst them there was a female expert in constitutional law, the highly acclaimed 'Master of the Jurists'. As 'Sheika', 'Mrs. Professor' and 'Pride of Women', the scholar Shohda was celebrated. After her studies with the most diverse scholars of science, she received a teaching license, and she was lifted to the level of a scholar. Female poets still compete with male poets, as they have always done, and nobody finds this extraordinary."[2]

Dalia Mogahed, advisor for Muslim affairs of the American president Barack Obama

Dr. Gustave Le Bon added:

"If we want to assess the influence that the Quran had on women, we have to take a more precise look at what became of them during the period of Arabic Civilization. The reports of the historians we quote show that their role was equal to the one they played later in Europe, when the gallant Chivalry Code of the Arabs was spread there.

It is from the Arabs – this we have already shown – that the inhabitants of Europe adopted the laws of chivalry, as well as the obligatory respect towards women that these laws demanded.

It was not Christianity, as one generally believes, but rather Islam which raised women up from their downgraded position, where they had remained until that point in time. The noblemen of the Early Middle

---

1 **SCHAEFER, DR. UDO:** Muhammad - ein Lügenprophet? Eine Klarstellung gegenüber des katholischen Glaubens, p. 14, URL: www.udoschaefer.com/pdffiles/muhammad.pdf (Accessed: May 12th 2009)

2 **HUNKE,** Sigrid: Allahs Sonne über dem Abendland, Stuttgart 1962, p. 278.

Ages, who were all Christian, did not express any respect for women. Reading our old chronicles does not leave any doubt about the latter. Before Arabs taught Christians how to interact respectfully with women, they were treated badly by our cruel soldiers in the time of feudalism. The chronicle by Garin de Loherain shows us for instance how women were treated before and during the time of Charlemagne: 'During an argument with his sister, the monarch threw himself at her, grabbed her by her hair and beat her violently and knocked out three of her teeth with one blow of his iron glove, not without, however, having received many blows himself.'

A modern countryman would have presented himself much more gently. The meaning of women during the magnificent period of Arab Civilization is predominantly shown by the amount of renowned women in scientific and literary spheres. In the Orient, under the Abbasids (750-1258), or in Spain, under the Umayyads (756-1031) many women attained great celebrity status. [...] In conclusion, we can thus say, by repeating the text above, that Islam was far from degrading women, but rather that it sought to enhance their status and respect.

A British Policewoman in London

[...] Islam improved the situation of women, and we can add that it was the first religion to do so. The latter is easy to prove by showing how women were mistreated by the religions and nations that preceded the Arabs.

[...]**M. de Amici** also expressed the same about the role of the Oriental woman in the following way: 'after delivering an accusatory speech against polygamy, completely judging from his European viewpoint. She is generally respected, with a sort of obliging politeness. No man would dare to raise his hand to a woman in a public street. No soldier, even during a tumult or insurgence, would dare to mistreat even the most insolent one amongst the women. The husband treats his wife with a sort *of ceremonial reverence. The mother is the object of a special cult.*

There is no man who would dare to let the woman do the work intended for him. It is the husband who provides for the wife: she only brings her dowry and some slaves to his household. In case of repudiation or divorce, the man is obliged to give the woman everything she needs to lead a comfortable life; this obligation prevents him from treating her badly, which would give her the right to leave him.' "[1]

3.2.4 Muslim Women in Today's World

Frequently, while judging the position of women in Islam, it is falsely assumed that the position of women within the tradition of some countries represents the Muslim majority, or they are mistaken for one another, but there is a blatant difference between the religion and the traditions of a culture!

The UN Human Rights reports show that the gender differences and the discrimination against women is a world-wide problem, and that it cannot solely be associated to Islam or Islamic countries:

"Several global surveys suggest that half of all women who die from homicide are killed by their current or former husbands or partners. In Australia, Canada, Israel, South Africa and the United States, 40%-70% of female murder victims were killed by their partners, according to the World Health Organization (WHO). In Colombia, one woman is reportedly killed by her partner or former partner every six days. Hundreds of women were also abducted, raped and murdered in and around Ciudad Juarez, Mexico, over a 10-year period.

[...] Female infanticide, prenatal sex selection and systematic neglect of girls are widespread in South and East Asia, North Africa, and the Middle East. [...] The cost of intimate partner violence in the United

---

1 **Le Bon**, Gustave: La civilisation des Arabes. Paris 1884, Book IV, p. 78ff.

States alone exceeds US$ 5.8 billion per year: US$ 4.1 billion is for direct medical and health care services, while productivity losses account for nearly US$ 1.8 billion. "[1]

In a survey made by the Gallup World Poll Organization in 2005[2], it was attempted to evaluate the position of women in the Islamic world based on more than 1000 people surveyed in eight of the largest Islamic countries. These countries are Egypt, Iran, Jordan, Lebanon, Morocco, Pakistan, Saudi Arabia and Turkey.

According to the survey, the education discrepancy between boys and girls lies at zero in Iran, the same as that in the USA.

(According to the governmental data in Egypt for the year 2005, 49% of the total students in upper school were girls, and in universities one finds the same percentage of 49% of female students.)[3]

The majority of women from the eight surveyed countries think that women can make their own decisions, take on any job they are qualified for, and even serve in the highest governmental offices.

According to the Gallup-Organization, women in the Islamic countries frequently condemn the way women in Western cultures are treated, just like Western women judge the way Muslim women are treated. The answers to the question: *"What is it you most resent about the West?"* speak the loudest and include descriptions of promiscuity, pornography and public indecorousness.

---

1 cp. Anonymous: How widespread is violence against women? United Nations Secretary-General's Campaign, URL: www.un.org/women/endviolence/docs/VAW.pdf (Accessed: May 28th 2009).

2 MOGAHED, Dalia: Perspectives of Women in the Muslim World, The Gallup World Poll Organization, URL: http://media.gallup.com/WorldPoll/PDF/GALLUP+MUSLIM+STUDIES_Perspectives+of+Women_11.10.06_FINAL.pdf (Accessed: May 29th 2009).

3 cp. Anonymous: Stellung der Frauenbildung, Ägyptische staatliche inormationen Service, URL:www.sis.gov.eg/Ar/Women/Society/Education/100303000000000001.htm (Accessed: May 29th 2009).

On the other hand, the use of headscarves is often perceived as a symbol for the inferior cultural status of women in the Muslim world by Westerners. In Muslim societies, the lack of decorum perceived in Western media is seen as a symbol for the degrading of women in their cultural status.

When asked whether women in the Muslim world counted the inequality between genders as one of the largest problems of their society, Jordanian women did not agree, and less than 2% of women in Egypt and Morocco agreed.

In short: Do Muslim men think that women and men should have the same rights? The answer is quite simply "Yes!"[1]

3.2.5 The Headscarf

The headscarf is understood as a symbol of oppression in non-Islamic circles, whereby negative experiences from their own cultural history are projected unto Islam.

In the Bible one finds the demand: *"For if a woman is not covered, let her also be shorn. But if it is shameful for a woman to be shorn or shaved, let her be covered."*[2]

The justification for the latter was that the woman was created for the sake of man, and *"A woman should have a covering over her head to show that she is under her husband's authority."*[3]

In Islam, the headscarf has another explanation. Islam sees man and woman as equal in value, but not equal in their personalities.

The hair of a woman is one of the most important factors of her attractiveness and beauty. But for many women, the bald head of a man does not represent an impediment to finding him attractive.

Therefore, Islam prompts women to cover their hair during their

---

1 cp. MOGAHEAD, l.c.

2 The Bible, WEB, 1 Cor. 11: 6.

3 The Bible, TEV, 1 Cor. 11: 10.

contact with strangers, but not with family or their husband, in order to send out as little sexual stimulus as possible, and to keep a neutral male behaviour.

Thereby, Islam is firstly concerned with the fact that women are respected and their rights are preserved, because they are women and citizens, and they may not be used for any personal intentions.

Some men show attractive women much politeness and helpfulness, not because they respect them as women, but because they desire them as sexual objects. Therefore, they do not act the same towards all women.

In the media, like for instance marketing, the woman is increasingly exploited as object and reduced to her sexual appeal, and therefore she is more and more lowered in status. Islam rejects this and tries to protect women from degradation through the headscarf.

As "right-less and unfree women", female slaves and prostitutes were allowed not to wear a headscarf before the emergence of Islam, and thus Islam defended the use of headscarves as a symbol for the freedom and also as a symbol of respect for women.

3.2.6 The Inheritance of Women in Islam

The Inheritance

In fact, the woman has, in some cases, priority over the man in the Islamic inheritance system, for she is guaranteed a certain percentage of the inheritance.

Apart from the gender, the share of inheritance is differentiated according to certain factors and rules, which are based on the closeness of relationship, generation, financial responsibilities and obligations.

The young generation of the family, which receives life and has to bear financial responsibilities in the future, normally receives more than the "*old*" generation; thus, the daughter of a deceased person receives more than his father.

Through these factors the share of inheritance that women receive is also classified as follows:

- In many cases, man and woman inherit the same, i.e. the father inherits as much as the mother, for they both belong to the old generation.

- In ten cases, the woman inherits more than the man, i.e.: the man died and left two daughters and four brothers. Both daughters receive together two thirds. The four brothers together only receive one third. Another example: a man left 600 hectares worth 300 million euro. The surviving members of his family are his father, mother, wife, daughter and the daughter of one of his sons (the son is dead). According to Islamic law, the daughter will receive 266 hectares, the daughter of the son will receive 88 hectares, as well as each one of his parents, and his wife will receive 70 hectares. The only man, in this case the father, received just as much as his wife, and three times less than a woman, the daughter of the deceased person. If the son's daughter had been a boy, she would have only received 25 hectares, instead of 88 hectares, which means 12 million instead of 44 million.

- Only in four cases does the woman receive less than the man. This has to do with the fact that, in these cases, the man has more financial responsibilities than the woman. If the head of the family dies, for instance, and leaves the unmarried daughter and the unmarried son 150,000 euro, the daughter will then receive only one third of it, while the son will receive two thirds, for when he marries, he must offer his bride a dowry, as well as furniture and facilities for their future common household, which will cost him approximately 25,000 euro. Later, he will also be financially responsible for his family (his wife and kids). His wife must not come up with the sustenance for their family.

- If his sister decides to marry, she will receive a dowry and all the facilities for her household from her groom. She will not have to come up with the living costs of her family after the wedding. This means: the son only has 75,000 euro left and must come up with the living costs for his family, while his now married sister has received 25,000 euro in addition to her 50,000 euro, and she does not have any financial obligations.

Islam freed women from financial responsibilities in order to secure her a safe life, without the danger of being exploited if one day she were to find herself in need.

In summary one can say: there are more than thirty situations in which the woman receives either more than or just as much as the man, or she is the sole beneficiary. In contrast, there are only four cases in which the woman receives less than the man.

3.2.7 Polygamy *Polygamy*

Polygamy is perceived as unwanted in the Sharia (Islamic law). But there is no prohibition regarding polygamy, for in human society there are always cases in which polygamy can be useful, for instance:

- If the wife cannot have any children, but the husband has a strong desire to have children, a second wife is an alternative to divorce.
- After a war, like World War II, when the number of men is massively reduced, polygamy becomes a lawful solution for

the woman to secure her rights and her sustenance and to make having a family possible.

- There are also cases in which the intensive sexual needs of the man far exceed those of his wife, so that a second relationship or "marriage" represents a recognized, official solution that guarantees the rights of both women.

A man that chooses polygamy must be just, first and foremost. The Quran says in this regard:

> *"Marry women of your choice,*
> *two, or three, or four;*
> *but if you fear that you shall not be able*
> *to deal justly (with them), then only one.*
> *[...] That is nearer to prevent you from doing injustice."*
>
> The Quran, 4: 3

The Prophet warned in this regard:
"He who had two wives and did not treat them equally, he will come with a paralyzed half on the Day of Resurrection." [1]

3.2.8 Genital Circumcision

Genital circumcision is not to be brought in relation to Islam. It is part of the tradition of a (mostly African and Asian) culture, and more awareness has still to be raised in this regard in order to stop these cruel practices. Female circumcision is in Islam clearly prohibited, like the Grand Mufti of Egypt, Dr. Aly Goma, has declared several times – e.g. on 01/15/2008. [2]

---

1 **Ibn Hanbal**, Ahmad: Al-Musnad, Hadith Nº.: 8212, 7595, 9707, **Abo Dawood**: Assunan, Hadith Nº.: 1821, **Ibn Magah**: Assunan, Hadith Nº.: 1959.

2 A comprehensive, Islamic explanation to this is found on the governmental website of the Egyptian Fatwa Office at: www.dar-alifta.org.

4 RELIGION, STATE AND CIVILIZATION

Throughout history, we can see two different experiences in relation to the union of state and religion:

- In Europe, the Church was in conflict with science and emancipation, and it was allied to dictatorships. At the time of the Enlightenment (17th and 18th centuries) it came to a bloody revolution against the ecclesiastic and governmental powers, with the purpose, amongst others, of admitting science and progress.

In the French Revolution, the general opinion was that: "*Peoples will only be truly free when the last king is strangled by the bowels of the last priest,*" like the French politician Francois Laignelot (1752-1829) said.[1]

- The Arabs were underdeveloped tribes who worshipped idols, lived in poverty and ignorance, and were at odds with one another. Suddenly, as a result of the adoption of Islam as a religion and state system, they became united and conquered, within 30 years, one third of the known world, and they founded one of history's most powerful and progressive empires. It spanned over the Persian Empire and over half of the Byzantine Empire, over the Middle East, Central Asia, North Africa, and later it spread over Pakistan, India, Southern Italy and the Iberian Peninsula.

Islam spread science, tolerance, freedom of religion, justice and equality everywhere in the world, which had only known dictatorship up to that point. This civilization made a happy life possible for millions of people of all nations. Ninety years after the death of the Prophet, the caliph Omar Ibn Abd Al-aziz[2] could not find a single poor person in the entire Islamic Empire to whom he could give alms.

In other words: when Islam and state were united in the East, people experienced a life of freedom, the preservation of human rights, and the blooming of science. When state and religion merged in the West, people experienced dark times. In the following pages, we will make an overview over the influence of the practice of Islam as a state system on civilization, science and world history.

---

1 **DANZER, G./ RATTNER, J.**: Europäische Moralistik in Frankreich von 1600 bis 1950, 2006, p. 150.

2 Omar Ibn Abd Al-aziz (681-720) was the 13th caliph after the Prophet.

4.1 Knowledge in the Islamic Civilization

If Galileo Galilei had lived in an Islamic country, maybe he would not have been persecuted.

Islam gave science a special position and designated knowledge as the one characteristic with which Adam earned the Sudjud (prostration) of the angels, which thus represents an extraordinary display of respect for the knowledgeable person.

The Prophet expressed in this regard:
"For him who follows the path to increase knowledge God will make the way to Janna easier"[1] *and "Learning is an obligation for every Muslim person (man and woman)."*[2] It is with the help of science that one attains the truth:

"And those
who have been given knowledge
see that what is revealed to you (O Muhammad)
from your Lord is the truth, and guides to the Path of the
Exalted in Might, Owner of all praise."

The Quran, 34: 6

The Quran places scientists on the same level as angels by saying:

"God bears witness
that There is no god but He,
and the angels, and those endued with knowledge
(also give this witness);
(He is always) standing firm on justice."

The Quran, 3: 18

---

1 **Attermezi:** Assunan, Hadith N°.: 20570, **Ibn Hanbal**, Ahmad: Al-Musnad, Hadith N°.: 7965.

2 **Ibn Magah:** Assunan, Hadith N°.: 220, **Attabarani:** Al-Mugam Al-Kabier, Hadith N°.: 10286, **Al-Baeihaqi:** Shu-ab Al-Ieman, Beirut 2000, Vol. 2, p. 254.

Therefore, a learning culture was established in Islamic society, and even today one can hear sayings such as: *"A scholar is stronger against a devil than one thousand devout servants."*

Knowing the value that knowledge has, Muslim conquerors built in every newly subjugated city a school, which was part of the mosque, and thereby they created a centre for worship and education.

Islamic Contributions

4.2 Islamic Contributions to Civilization

Through Islam, the Arabs did not only exert political and economic changes, but they also accomplished even grander successes in the fields of knowledge.

Muslim scientists attained significant progress in medicine, astronomy, engineering and many other fields.

Let us briefly introduce some of the scientists and discoveries, even though it can only constitute a small piece of the entire body of contributions:

Ibn Al-Hytham

In medicine, **Ibn Al-Hytham** (Latinized: Alhazen, 965-1039)

developed the scientific method we still use today (stages of observation, problem description, hypothesis formulation, etc.).

Ibn Al-Hytham (965-1039)

Al-Khawarizmi (ca. 780-850)

In geography, **"Al-Khawarizmi"** (approx.*780-850*) was able to calculate the circumference and the radius of earth. Al-Idrisi (1100-1166) was commissioned to produce a world atlas, in which he used cartography to include territories that had not been discovered yet. By the 15th century, the atlases and maps made by the Muslims represented the only reliable and comprehensive medium for navigation, so much that Vasco da Gama sailed along the coast of Africa aided by Muslim knowledge.

In environmentalism, Muslims such as

Al-Kindi, Al-Razi, Ibn Al-Jazzar

Al-Kindi (800-873), **Al-Razi (864-930)** or **Ibn Al-Jazzar**

(approx. 898-980)

played also the leading roles: they composed treatises about water, soil and air pollution, amongst many others. Toledo, the Spanish city in the Islamic **Al-Andalus**, possessed the first waste containers and waste disposal sites for garbage removal.

In mathematics, we can mention, amongst other Muslim accomplishments, the invention of *"zero"* as a numerical value, of the decimal fraction, or the Arabic numerals, which make calculation easier. In the field of algebra, groundbreaking discoveries took place thanks to Muslims.

Al-Khwarizmi

The Muslim scientist **Al-Khwarizmi (780-850 C.E.), is the pioneer of algebra and algorithms**. From whose name the word algorithm derives and Algebra was named after his book *"Al-Jabr"* which was the first book on algebra.[1]

The book of "*Al-Jabr*" was translated into Latin during the 12ed century by Gerard of Cremona and was the main textbook in the European universities till the 16th century.

J. J. O'Conner and E. F. Robertson

J. J. O'Conner and **E. F. Robertson** wrote in the MacTutor History of Mathematics archive:

"Perhaps one of the most significant advances made by Arabic mathematics began at this time with the work of al-Khwarizmi, namely the beginnings of algebra. It is important to understand just how significant these new ideas were. It was a revolutionary move away from the Greek concept of mathematics. [...] It gave mathematics a whole new development path so much broader in concept to that which had existed before, and provided a vehicle for future development of the subject. Another important aspect of the introduction of algebraic ideas was that it allowed mathematics to be applied to itself in a way which had not happened before." [2]

Carl Boyer

These all and other contributions made **Carl Boyer** say:

"Diophantus is sometimes called 'the father of algebra', but this title more appropriately belongs to al-Khwarizmi." [3]

Thabit ibn Qurra

The theories and contributions of **Thabit ibn Qurra** [4] played an

---

1 MICHEAU, Francoise, "The Scientific Institutions in the Medieval Near East", pp. 992–3, in (Morelon & Rashed 1996, pp. 985-1007)

2 J J O'CONNOR and E F ROBERTSON: Arabic mathematics: forgotten brilliance? URL: www-history.mcs.st-andrews.ac.uk/HistTopics/Arabic_mathematics.html (Accessed: May 25th 2011).

3 BOYER, Carl: The Arabic Hegemony, New York 1991, p. 228.

4 ABU AL HASSAN THABIT BIN QURA (836-901) lived in Baghdad, Iraq. He was a pioneer in geometry, mathematics, astronomy, medicine and music and wrote in these subjects. He was close to the Abbasid caliph AL MUTADID. He also wrote about geometrical quantities, the conic sections, the machines of clocks and the reason of eclipse.

essential role in the development of mathematics. He developed integral calculus and succeeded at determining the surfaces and volumes of different types of bodies. Many centuries later, some scientists started speaking about these processes of integral calculus as their own achievements.

The mathematician Omar Khayyam

The mathematician Omar Khayyam (1048-1123C.E) was the first to find general geometric solutions of cubic equations and laid the foundations for the development of analytic geometry, algebraic geometry and non-Euclidean geometry[1].

He could thus prove that the sum of the four angles of a rectangle equals 360 degrees, while the addition of the three angles of a triangle equals 180 degrees.

Alkindus wrote 32 books and papers about (Spherical Geometry) and (Plane Geometry) and other topics. Muslim scholars applied the geometric rules and theories in different fields of life like the art of Arabic ornamentation (Arabesque).

Muslims are also the founders of chemistry as an empirical natural science. They developed important branches of this discipline. Amongst their inventions are nitric acid, sulfuric acid, aqua regia (nitrohydrochloric acid), silver nitrate, sodium carbonate, iron sulfate, etc. The "bases" were also invented by them, which were introduced in the European languages with the Arabic name "al-kali". Muslims were also the first to apply chemistry to medical treatments and in the production of medicines, and they were also the first to think about the combination of drugs.

The Muslim scientist Addinawari

The Muslim scientist Addinawari (828-895) is considered the father of botany because of his work "*Kitab An-nabat*" (Book of

---

1 J. L. Berggren (1990). "Innovation and Tradition in Sharaf al-Din al-Tusi's equations ", Journal of the American Oriental Society 110 (2), p. 304-309.

Plants). He was the first to use the method of hybrid breeding, through which he could produce new fruits with new characteristics by means of crossing different species. He was also able to obtain new species of flowers by crossing the wild brier with the almond tree. Therefore, Ad-dinawari preceded the Austrian Johann Gregor Mendel in this field who is often credited in the West for pioneering botany.

Stanwood Cobb

In his book "Islamic Contributions to Civilization" Stanwood Cobb[1] **wrote about this subject:**

"*The science of algebra owes much to gifted mathematicians of the Islamic era. Its very name proves the magnitude of this debt, for the name itself is Arabic.*"

"*Another notable feature of the Islamic epoch was the spirit of elan under which science flourished. [...] Every Muslim centre followed the example of Baghdad in founding universities, spreading literacy among the masses, and attracting physicians and scholars to their courts.*"

"*The Universities of Cordova and Toledo were well known to Europeans, and their hospitals were frequented by Christian princes in need of medical care that Christian Europe could not furnish. The first medical schools of Europe were the direct result of this Moorish influence.*"

"*Last but not least of the factors which advanced civilization in the Arabic-Islamic period was the devotion of the people to a common religion, and the devotion of religion to the common people. Islam was simple enough in its theology to be understood by all and demanding enough in its daily ritual of prayer and month-long fasts to enforce a discipline that engendered piety in the daily life. Islam lifted its adherents above consciousness of race or color, establishing an effective brotherhood in the name of Allah.*"

"*Muslim scholars could travel freely between Bokhara north of*

---

1 cp. **Cobb**, Stanwood: Islamic Contributions to Civilization, 1963, URL: www.bahaistudies.net/bahaiworks/cobb.html (Accessed: June 1st 2009).

India, and Cordova. The extent of this Islamic civilization, as well as the progress and achievements of its component parts proved an inspiration to Muslim scholarship and creative arts."

"The Muslim empire was created with the willing collaboration of Greeks, Persians, Copts, Christians, Magians, Sabeans and Jews. But this assistance does not wholly explain what might be called 'the miracle' of Arabic science, using the word miracle as a symbol of our inability to explain achievements which were almost incredible."

"The Oxford History of Technology sums it up as follows: 'There are few major technological innovations between 500 A.D. and 1500 that do not show some traces of the Islamic culture.'"

"Alexander had planned before his death to create from simplified Greek a universal language. Such a plan was actually carried out by the Muslims, and Arabic became the predominant tongue from India to Spain. [...] With the possession of a common language and with a common rule under the aegis of Allah, this Islamic region enjoyed for the first time in history the blessings of peace. Racial energies which had been wasted in internecine warfare were turned into channels which led to prosperity and progress."

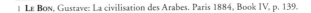
Gustave Le Bon

In his book "La civilisation des Arabes" (The Civilization of Arabs) Gustave Le Bon (1841-1931) says:
"Erase the Arabs from history, writes M. Libri, and the rebirth of science in Europe would have been delayed by many centuries."[1]

Stanley Lane Poole

In his book "Moors in Spain" Stanley Lane Poole says:
"For nearly eight centuries, under her Mohammedan rulers, Spain set to all Europe a shining example of a civilized and enlightened state. [...] Art, literature and science prospered as they then prospered nowhere

---

1 Le Bon, Gustave: La civilisation des Arabes. Paris 1884, Book IV, p. 139.

else in Europe. Students flocked from France and Germany and England to drink from the fountains of learning which flowed only in the cities of the Moors. The surgeons and doctors of Andalusia were in the van of science: women were encouraged to devote themselves to serious study, and a lady doctor was not unknown among the people of Cordova. Mathematics, astronomy and botany, history, philosophy and jurisprudence, were to be mastered in Spain, and Spain alone. The practical work of the field, the scientific methods of irrigation, the arts of fortification and shipbuilding, the highest and most elaborate products of the loom, the gravel and the hammer, the potter's wheel and mason's trowel, were brought to perfection by the Spanish Moors. [...] Whatever makes a kingdom great and prosperous, whatever tends to refinement and civilization was found in Muslim Spain."[1]

The Making of Humanity

Robert Briffault

Robert Briffault wrote in "The Making of Humanity":
"*The debt of our science to that of the Arabs does not consist in startling discoveries or revolutionary theories; science owes a great deal more to Arab culture, it owes its existence. The ancient world was, as we saw, pre- scientific. The astronomy and mathematics of the Greeks were a foreign importation never thoroughly acclimatized in Greek culture. The Greeks systematized, generalized and theorized, but the patient ways of investigation, the accumulation of positive knowledge, the minute methods of science, detailed and prolonged observation, experimental inquiry, were altogether alien to the Greek temperament. [...]*

What we call science arose in Europe as a result of a new spirit of

---

1 **Lane-Poole**, Stanley: The Moors in Spain, Whitefish 2005, p. vii, viii.

inquiry, of new methods of investigation, of the method of experiment, observation, measurement, of the development of mathematics in a form unknown to the Greeks. That spirit and those methods were introduced into the European world by the Arabs."[1]

"Science is the most momentous contribution of Arab civilization to the modern world, but its fruits were slow in ripening. Not until long after Moorish culture had sunk back into darkness did the giant to which it had given birth, rise in his might. It was not science which brought Europe back to life. Other and manifold influences from the civilization of Islam communicated its first glow to European life."[2]

Ibn Sina (Avicenna) (980-1037)

Oliver Joseph Lodge

Oliver Joseph Lodge declared in "Pioneers of Science":
"For more than a thousand years there was not a scientific man of note except in Arabia."[3]

---

1 BRIFAULT, Robert: The Making of Humanity, London 1919, p. 191.

2 Idem., p.202.

3 LODGE, Oliver J.: Pioneers of Science, Whitefish Montana 2003, p. 9.

Fielding H. Garrison

Fielding H. Garrison wrote in "An introduction to the history of medicine":

"The Saracens (Arabs) themselves were the originators not only of algebra, chemistry, and geology, but of many of the so-called improvements or refinements of civilization, such as street lamps, window-panes, fireworks, stringed instruments, cultivated fruits, perfumes, spices."[1]

"How successfully Moslem people of all races pursued the study of astronomy is shown by the fact that for centuries they where its principal supporters. Even now many Arabic names of stars and technical terms are in use."[2]

The Forgotten Legacy

4.3 The Forgotten **Legacy**

Under the title *"Our Arabic Legacy"*, Erika Donner explains that the salvation of humanistic education and European fundamental forces could not have been developed without historical consciousness:

"But what does this historical consciousness look like? It resembles a medieval world map, about whose scope we enlightened people of the 20th century like to mock. For, with the exception of brief side glances to ancient Egypt, Babylon and Byzantium, it is limited to the cultures of Greece and Rome, without taking into consideration the fact that between them and us there was the formidable complex of the

Arabic culture, *which remained unrivaled for 800 years, and whom we owe a considerable part of our occidental culture.*

---

1 GARRISON, Fielding H.: An introduction to the history of medicine, London 1917, p. 110.

2 HIRSCHFELD, Prof. Hartwig: New Researches into the Composition and Exegesis of the Quran, Whitefish 2009, p. 9.

[…] That the Arabs were the leading civilized nation for three quarters of a millennium, and therefore that they flourished for twice as long as the Greeks; yes, that they influenced the West more directly and more diversely than them? That therefore the evolution of our historical consciousness necessarily has to include all that they accomplished and that was only known to a few Orientalists until now?

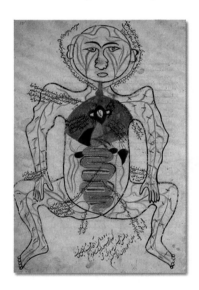

[...] However, up to now, the Arabs were known to play one role to us: as intermediaries of the works of ancient philosophy and science. But the Greeks, the Indians, they were also 'intermediaries' who always used the available knowledge material to continue to work and expand on it.

But one thing sets this accomplishment of the Arabs apart: the Christian church and the monk-hood of the Middle Ages also had the opportunity to save this legacy and expand on it; however, the Greek spirit seemed condemnable to them, so that they not only deprived Europe from it, but they also destroyed it to a great extent.

The accomplishment of the Arabs does not end with the transmission of the Greek and Indian legacies, for they also continued to expand on, complement and clarify the available knowledge material. They are the true founders of experimental research – a field without which the entirety of our modern science would be unthinkable!

While the Greeks practiced theoretical chemistry and natural philosophy, the Arabs created natural science. And they were also the first ones to put chemistry at the service of medicine, to (already in the 8th century) found public drugstores and to have them regularly inspected by officers of the health police.

Who is aware of the fact that, for hundreds of years, countless of our forefathers were attracted, almost absorbed, by the culture of a nation that one likes to represent as a crushing, wild horde of horsemen?

[...] Particularly in Spain, where the Arab culture found its richest unfolding and highest bloom, where Arabs, Jews and Christians lived harmoniously in a paradise of master-builders, singers, poets and scientists; a paradise that was created from nothing, where the dry, apparently sterile hills produced crops like never after the expulsion of the Arabs, where mines were developed and industries established, towns and cities bloomed with baths, hospitals, public schools, high schools and libraries, with cobbled, lit and regularly cleaned streets at a time when beyond the Pyrenees dirt and illiterateness reigned.

Is it a miracle that countless Christians in Spain were irresistibly attracted by this cultural wonder, in spite of the warnings from the north about the 'sorcerers, devil artists and necromancers, about the golden idol Muhammad' that even high Christian dignitaries wore Arabic clothes, had Arabic names, pronounced the gospel in Arabic, which the archbishop John of Seville had translated into the language of the Quran?

That to the young Christian intellectual elite only the language and literature of the Arabs counted, that they constructed large libraries and publicly avowed themselves to this culture?

It was obvious that Arabic was the language of the jurisprudence, diplomacy, government agencies, commerce and traffic, as well as of society.
Within a century it had transformed from a tribal language to a world language; a language that was not only a communication means, but that influenced the entire culture.

The Arabs were especially characterized by one thing: their tolerance towards people of other faiths.

They guaranteed their subjects the practice of their religion and every security, and they even admitted them to their higher public offices. It was not their intention to convert people of other faiths to Islam; they even made the conversion to it difficult because of the poll tax that only non-Muslims paid; but their deep faith and their culture attracted countless voluntary converts, who sought equal ranking for also economic and social benefits.

'He who leaves his herd seeking knowledge strolls the path to God' , says Muhammad, and his disciples gather, study and translate the intellectual resources, so that they can always access them – at a time when, according to Christian conviction, not human reason but divine revelation could enlighten the soul, when scientific efforts were stigmatized as a violation against religion, when the antique libraries of priceless value were plundered, destroyed and burned, when the pillars and stairs of antique buildings were used to build Christian churches, when philosophers were persecuted for magic and witchcraft and thus the last sanctuaries of Hellenic erudition were destroyed, for 'it is not our task in Jesus Christ neither to be curious nor to investigate after the gospel had been announced.'

The passion for books escalates to such an extend that the social prestige of the Arabs between the 9th and 13th centuries are judged based on the amount of books they possess. Small cities have public libraries of 40 000 volumes, every mosque has a library, every hospital disposes of countless works on medicine, and the size of private libraries does not meet their equal in our times.

Not only the experts and scholars, but also the Arabs of all circles are regular customers at the bookstores – equally an invention of the Arabs – which constitute the cultural centre of a city.

While, at the same time, the occidental monasteries keep their dozen books chained.

Naturally, children of all social classes visit primary and secondary schools, whose demanding schedule includes grammar, philology, rhetoric, literature, history, ethnology, geography, logic, mathematics and astronomy.

The mosques are places of highest erudition, where professors (also female ones!) hold public lectures, in which everyone may participate – men and women – where everyone may interrupt the teacher with questions and make comments – what a pressure for the docents to make themselves familiar with the subject and deal with it!

These universities, which counted many secret visitors from the West to their students, became the model for our academic degrees, our faculties and our learning method, and they provided the West with the learning subjects as well.

It is barely necessary to mention that in such an enlightened nation the position of women was different from the one they were given later, that they had the same access to education as men, that they were not oppressed, as long as the Arabic aristocracy was in power, and that even a courtly love cult was dedicated to them, which later spread over the Christian West, where the woman had been given for breeding to man and made into his servant.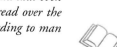

It was with the Persian and Greek female slaves, who shared their lives with the caliphs, that veil and harem found an entrance into Arabic society, but in Arabic Spain they cannot prevent women from participat-

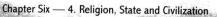

ing in the cultural life of their country.

The gifts that the Arabs brought to us are countless,
all the trade items: *spices, cotton, silk, fine paper, glass, ceramics; and the scientific accomplishments: the Arabic numerals, highly qualified measuring instruments, astronomic discoveries (one of the most significant and famous scientists of that time is an Arab, whose name was later Latinized by Western hand!); and last but not least the creations in art and literature: the arabesque, the ornamentation of buildings: stalactites, ogives, the 'services' to the pillars of our cathedrals – countless elements were adopted, used, transformed and further developed by the Gothic from the Arabs.*

The music, which was not of that foreign monotonousness then, but extraordinarily artful and ornamented, gave important elements to the West, and the poetic arts brought us the end rhyme.

Sigrid Hunke

Sigrid Hunke *draws the conclusion, based on the facts mentioned above, that Europe was drawn back, economically and culturally, by centuries because of its own isolation from the Islamic world, and that it was not until it opened itself to trade with the Orient and adopted the technology and intellectual resources of the Arabs that its spirit awoke again and lead it to a livelier, richer existence.* "[1]

"its spirit awoke again
and lead it to a livelier, richer existence

---

1 **DONNER,** Erika: Unser Arabisches Erbe. 1961. p. 736. URL: www.library.fes.de/gmh/main/pdf-files/gmh/1961/1961-12-a-736.pdf (Accessed: April 12th 2009).

4.4 Downfall

Muslims were, in comparison to other nations, scientifically, economically and politically advanced by centuries under the Islamic state system.

The downfall occurred only after the Islamic political system was abolished. The caliphate became many smaller kingdoms, and slowly new and corrupt kings seized power. These kings increasingly ignored the Islamic state system, for Islam and dictatorship cannot be united together.

The empire, which was based on Islam, lost its identity and was divided into smaller kingdoms, which, in the end, were occupied by the rising European powers. During their occupation, new constitutions were declared, which did not have anything to do with Islam, and led to the division of state and religion, even though Islam offered a comprehensive concept,

A new generation of Muslims came to being, who knew little about their own history, culture and religion. At the end of the occupation, the Islamic countries were predominantly taken over by military regimes, which did not represent the civilized Islam or Western democracy.

An interrogation chair of the Catholic Church in Spain at the time of the Inquisition

4.5 The End
of the Islamic Civilization in Spain[1]

The End of the Islamic Civilization in Spain

In 1469 A.D., when Ferdinand of Aragon married Isabella of Castile, their union struck the death-knell of Muslim power in Spain. The local rulers were no match for this newly evolved Christian power, who conquered Granada in 1492 and so established their powerful rule throughout Spain. [...] they proceeded to destroy the remains of the great Islamic culture in Spain. Moreover, they founded that dread engine of fanaticism, the Inquisition. Forced conversion of the Muslims was inaugurated. Arabic books were withdrawn from circulation, and Arabic manuscripts were burned in huge bonfires.

In 1556 A.D. Philip II proclaimed a strict law forbidding Muslims to practice their worship, language or habits of life. The public baths - so plentiful in Spanish cities because of the abundant water supply from neighboring mountains and so beloved by Muslims and Christians alike -- were destroyed. Henceforth any citizen of Spain overfond of bathing was suspect of heresy and liable to Inquisitional investigations!

In 1609 A.D. Philip III signed a final order of expulsion, and practically all the Muslims then remaining on Spanish soil were forcibly deported. Some three million Moors had been executed, exiled or deported since the fall of Granada in 1492. How different this policy was from that of Alphonso XII of Castile, who in the thirteen[th] century had been a kindly and sympathetic patron of Moorish scholars and artists! The final expulsion of the Moors in the name of Christianity was a racial tragedy.

When the prime minister Lerma, at the instigation of the Church, announced to the king that the exile of the Moriscos had

---

1 cp. **COBB**, Stanwood: Islamic Contributions to Civilization, 1963, URL: www.bahaistudies.net/bahaiworks/cobb.html. (Accessed: June 1st 2009).

become necessary, Philip replied, *"The resolution is a great one. Let it be executed."* *"And executed it was,"* says Buckle in his History of Civilization, *"with unflinching barbarity. About one million of the most industrious inhabitants of Spain were hunted out like wild beasts because the sincerity of their forced conversion to Christianity was doubted. Many were slain as they approached the coast. Others were beaten and plundered, and the majority was in most wretched flight. During the passage the crew in many of the ships rose upon them butchering the men, ravishing the women and throwing the children into the sea."*

In addition to the Moors, all the Jews of Spain were shortly expelled.

[...] If this obliteration of Islamic culture was a disaster to Islam, it was also a disaster to Spain. Agriculture suffered from the loss of Moorish skill and enterprise. The irrigation system fell into disrepair, transforming one of the garden spots of the world into a semi-arid and half-sterile country. The arts of living languished. And the gaiety, carefree spirit, and "joie de vivre" which had characterized Moorish life were lost in the sombre shadow of the Inquisition.

The mines which had always been a source of wealth to Spain were either abandoned or inefficiently worked. The weaving of textiles declined markedly. In Seville, one of Spain's richest cities, the number of looms fell from 16,000 at the peak to 300. Toledo lost almost all of its woolen manufacturing; and also its manufacture of silk which had employed 40,000 persons. The making of gloves, for which Spain had been famous, came to a stop. Trade halted.

Sea-borne commerce and fisheries declined, because the Spanish were not sufficiently versed in navigation.

In fact, the dislocation of the Spanish economy by the expulsion of the Moors and Jews was so severe that want and starvation reigned in many places. *"The Moors were banished,"* says Lane-Poole, in his 'Moors in Spain', *"and for a little while Spain still shone with her borrowed light. Then came the eclipse.*[1]

---

1 cp. **COBB**.

4.6 The Ability to Re-Establish Oneself

The Abilita to Re-Establish Oneself

Shortly after the majority of the Islamic Empire had been destroyed by Mongolian attacks in 1258,[1] the Ottomans adopted Islam and founded the Ottoman Caliphate, which re-established the Islamic civilization and represented it over the following six centuries. Like the Arabs, the Turks were also a group of uncivilized tribes before Islam. After the fall of the Islamic Empire, its slayers, the Mongols, converted to Islam.

5 WHAT IS THE POSITION OF ISLAM TOWARDS PEOPLE OF DIFFERENT RELIGIONS?

The idea that once others did not share one's own "**true**" belief, they could be attacked, punished, and robbed of their rights, reigned in many countries.

Or, like Mary I of England[2] **said:**

"As the souls of heretics are hereafter to be eternally burning in hell, there can be nothing more proper than for me to imitate the Divine Vengeance by burning them on earth."[3]

---

1 The fall of the Islamic capital city of Baghdad was devastating for the humanistic and scientific evolution. The Mongols built a bridge of books over the Tigris.

2 Mary Tudor of England 1516-1558 was the daughter of Henry VIII and had the surname of "Bloody Mary." She married Philip II of Spain and revoked the religious reforms her father had made.

3 Farrar, Frederic William: Mercy and judgment - last words on Christian eschatology, London 1882, p. 116.

In the Islamic world, another concept prevails. The Muslim believes that only God alone may punish the ones who follow the wrong path.

According to Muslim understanding, they believe in the true religion, and therefore they will enter Janna. But it is God's Omniscience also that there are others who do not follow the true path.

> *"If it had been the Lord's Will,*
> *they would all have believed*
> *– all who are on Earth!*
> *Wilt thou then compel mankind,*
> *against their will, to believe?"*
>
> The Quran, 10: 99

Islam considers the differences between people as an inspiration to get to know one another and become closer.

> *"O mankind!*
> *We have created you from a male and a female,*
> *and made you into nations and tribes,*
> *that you may know one another.*
> *Verily the most honored of you in the sight of God is*
> *(he who is)*
> *the most righteous of you."*
>
> The Quran, 49: 13

The Prophet said: *"All people are siblings"*[1] and this is true regardless of their religion.

"All people are siblings"

---

1 **ABO DAWOOD**: Assunan, Hadith Nº.: 1289, IBN HANBAL, Ahmad: Al-Musnad, Hadith Nº.: 18490, **ANNASAII**: Assunan, Hadith Nº.: 9929

5.1 The Position of the Quran

> "*Let there be no compulsion in religion*"
>
> *The Quran, 2: 256*

The American scholar Edwin Calgary wrote about this Quranic verse on the topic of freedom of religion:

"*There is one verse in the Quran that is full of truth and wisdom, and which is known amongst all Muslims. All others should know it as well; it is one that says that there is no compulsion in religion.*"[1]

The preservation of freedom of religion is a strong principle in Islam:

> "*Say, '(This is) the Truth is from your Lord':*
> *Then whosoever wills,*
> *let him believe,*
> *and whosoever wills,*
> *let him disbelieve*"
>
> *The Quran, 18: 29*

The Quran emphasizes that the questioning, the reward or the punishment of man for his belief, and the path he has chosen, is solely God's task:

> "*And whoever invokes (or worships),*
> *besides God, any other god,*
> *he has no authority therefore;*
> *and his reckoning is only with his Lord!*
> *And Surely! the disbelievers will not be successful!*"
>
> *The Quran, 23: 117*

---

1 **QUAILAR**, Young: The Near East: Society & Culture. p. 163-164.

"Verily,
to Us will be their Return;
Then verily,
for Us will be their reckoning."

The Quran, 88: 25-26

"Your duty is only to convey (the Message)
and the reckoning is Our part."

The Quran, 13: 40

The calling of the Quran to just action of Muslims also means that, if need be, they have to act against themselves or those close to them.

"O you who believe!
Stand out firmly for justice,
as witnesses to God,
even though it be against yourselves,
or your parents or your kin."

The Quran, 4: 135

The killing of people is one of the gravest sins:

"If anyone killed a person
not in retaliation of murder,
or (and) to spread mischief in the land
— it would be as if he slew the whole people,
and if anyone saved a life,
it would be as if he saved
the life of the whole people."

The Quran, 5: 32

Non-Muslims are to be treated with justice and benevolence in every situation:

"God does not forbid you
to deal justly and kindly with those
who fought not against you
on account of religion
nor drive you out of your homes.
For God loves those who are just."

The Quran, 60:8

The Muslim scholar Al-Qarafi (died 1283) explains the meaning of the expression *"to deal kindly"* in the verse above:

"[...] Benevolence with the weak, to cover the needs of the poor, to provide the hungry with food and to speak gently to them; all of this out of affection and mercy, and not out of fear or submissiveness. If they do harm unto us as neighbors, we should tolerate it, even if we could stop their behavior. One does this out of benevolence, not out of fear of them. Also to pray for them, so that they receive God's Guidance and thus belong to those who will be happy for all eternity; to give them advice in all worldly and spiritual matters, to protect their reputation, in case they fall victims to badmouthing, and to defend their possessions, their families, rights and interests; to stand by their side in case of oppression, and to guarantee them their rights."[1]

---

1 **AL-QARAFI:** al-Furooq, Beirut 1998, Vol. 3, p. 28-30.

5.2 The Position of the Hadiths

The Position of the Hadiths

The Prophet elevated the equality of mankind to a dogma:

"O mankind, your God is one, your Father is one. The Arabs do not have any priority over others, and the others do not have it over the Arabs either. The whites do not have any priority over the blacks, and the blacks do not have it over the whites either. Priority is achieved only through one's closeness to God."[1]

When the Prophet sat together with his companions, the casket of a Jew was carried by. The Prophet stood up and followed him with his eyes, sadly. One of his companions said to him: "He was a Jew," and the Prophet replied: *"Was he not human?"*[2]

He **emphasized** that it was a great sin to treat a non-Muslim unjustly:

"He who takes from or denies to a Mo-a-had[3] *his rights, or demands from him something that exceeds his capabilities, or takes something from him against his will, will be my opponent on the Day of Resurrection."*[4] And he added: *"Avoid treating someone unjustly, for his supplication, even if he is not a Muslim, will directly reach God."*[5]

The Prophet was generous towards his non-Muslim neighbors, and he exchanged presents with them. They did business amongst

---

1 **IBN HANBAL**, Ahmad: Al-Musnad, Hadith N°.: 22391.

2 **AL-BUCHARI:** Assahih, Hadith N°.: 1229, **MOSLIM:** Assahih, Hadith N°.: 1596, **ANNASAII:** Assunan, Hadith N°.: 1895, **IBN HANBAL**, Ahmad: Al-Musnad, Hadith N°.: 22722.

3 A non-Muslim who crosses the border of an Islamic state with an official permission, or who lives in an Islamic state with a protection contract (Agd Adhimmah).

4 **ABO DAWOOD:** Assunan, Hadith Nr.: 2654, **AL-BAEIHAQI:** Assunan Al-Kubra, Hyderabad 1925, Vol. 9, p. 205.

5 **IBN HANBAL**, Ahmad: Al-Musnad, Hadith N°.: 12091.

one another, and he also visited his neighbors when they were ill to wish them to get better. Amongst his neighboring families there was also a Jewish one, whom he regularly gave donations and even after his death the Muslims kept giving these donations.[1]

He encouraged Muslims to be helpful to all people and said: *"All creatures are the children of God, and God's favorite amongst them is the one who is the most helpful to them."*[2]

He emphasized that taking a human life is a grave sin: *"On the Day of Resurrection, the first ones to be judged will be the cases of homicide."*[3] And he said: *"He who kills a Mo-a-had will not smell the scent of Janna."* (He will not enter Janna).[4]

5.3 In the **Books of Islamic Law (Sharia)**

In the Books of Islamic Law (Sharia)

The rules of Islamic law (Sharia) include:
"That which applies for us, applies for them (the non-Muslims within the Islamic state) (for → rights), and that which lies on us, lies on them (on → obligations)."[5] The latter means that the same rights and the same obligations apply for all the people that belong to the Islamic state.

In the Sharia, one usually finds explanations like *"**The 'Contract of the Charter'** obliges us to guarantee certain rights to the **'People of the Charter'**, for they are in our custody [...] and in the custody of Islam. He*

---

1 cp. **Abo Ubayd**: Al-Amwaal, Beirut 1989, p. 727-728.

2 **Attabarani**: Al-Mugam Al-Kabier, Hadith N°.: 9891, **Al-Baeihaqi**: Schu-ab Al-Ieman, Beirut 2000, Vol. 6, p. 43.

3 **Moslim**: Assahih, Hadith N°.: 3178, **Annasaii**: Assunan, Hadith N°.: 3928

4 **Al-Buchari**: Assahih, Hadith N°.: 2930, **Abo Dawood**: Assunan, Hadith N°.: 2379.

5 **Al-Kasani**: Badaie Assa-naie, Beirut 1986, Vol. 2, p. 37.

who attacks them, be it only verbally, has broken the promise of Allah and His Messenger. "[1]

The famous judge Abo Yusuf (died 805 AD) composed guidelines to govern the State for the Caliph Rashid (786-809 AD): *"May Allah support you, you shall rule softly with the members of the Charter (Ahlud-dhimmah), because this was promised to them in the Charter of your cousin Muhammad, peace be upon him. Watch constantly over them, so that they are not treated unjustly or hurt, so that nothing is demanded from them that they cannot provide. From their money nothing more should be taken than that which corresponds to their obligations.* "[2]

Ibn Hazm

The famous scholar Ibn Hazm stated:

"When one is attacked by an enemy nation, whose target is the people of the Charter who live amongst us, it is our obligation to protect them, completely armed and prepared to die in the battlefield, for these people are under the protection of the Charter of God and His Messenger. To abandon them would be a censurable negligence of the Contract of the Charter. "[3]

According to the Charter contract, non-Muslims paid a yearly tax (jizia) in order to be freed from military service. This yearly tax was however much lower than the amount of taxes that a Muslim had to pay (zakah), and it was removed as soon as a non-Muslim exerted a military role. The poor and the old were spared from it, and in case of death their surviving family members were compensated.

---

1 **AL-QARAFI:** al-Furooq, Beirut 1998, Vol. 3, S. 28-30.

2 **ABO YOUSUF,** Al-Qadi: Al-Charag, Kairo 1962, S. 124-125.

3 **AL-QARAFI:** al-Furooq, Beirut 1998, Vol. 3, S. 28-30.

The judge Al-Mawardi[1] wrote about this jizia in the Sharia book Al-Ah-kam Assul-tanyya:

"Through the jizia the 'people of the Charter' are guaranteed two rights: not to be touched and to be protected by us."[2]

When Muslims feared that they could no longer guarantee their safety during a battle, the leader Abu Ubayda wrote to his commanders that they should send the money that they had collected as jizia to the Syrians with the following message:

"We are reimbursing you your money, for we have heard news about awaiting armies. The condition of our agreement was that we would protect you, and now we are not capable of doing so. If God bestows victory upon us, then we will keep our promise."

The Syrians replied to the latter:

"May God bring you safely back to us. May He grant you victory. If the Byzantines had stood in your place, they would not have reimbursed anything, and they would have taken everything we have."[3]

---

1 Abul-Hasan Al-Mawardi (Latinized Alboacen) (born 972 in Basra- died1058 in Bagdad), is a famous Islamic law scholar (faqih) and the most significant judge of the late Abbasid period. His writings about Islamic Law are still relevant today, amongst others his book: "Al-Hawii Al-Kabeer" about Islamic law, which is composed of 20 volumes. The Abbasid Caliph al-Qaim bi Amr Allah appointed him as his ambassador, and sent him to many different countries.

2 AL-MAWARDI, Abul-Hasan: Al-Ah-kam Assul-tanyya, Kuwait 1989, p. 182.

3 ABO YOUSUF, Al-Qadi: Al-Charag, Kairo 1962, p. 139.

5.4 The Practical Interaction with People of Different Religions

Jesus said: *"You will know them by their fruits."* How Islam dealt with other religions shall be judged based on a simple test: How did Muslim monarchs behave for over a thousand years, when they had the power to *"spread the religion with the sword"*?[1] For more than a thousand years, when Islam was practiced as a state system, Muslims, Christians, Jews and peoples of other religions lived together in peace. Tolerance and freedom of religion were so developed that Jews and Christians possessed their own courts of justice and did not have to accept Islamic law.

---

1 **Averny**, Uri: Mohammeds Schwert. URL: www.uni-kassel.de/fb5/frieden/themen/Islam/avnery2.html#orig (Accessed: August 15th 2009).

Adam Mez

Adam Mez[1] writes in his book "*Renaissance of Islam*" about it:

"*As the Muslim Law was only meant for Muslims, people of other faiths were left to seek remedy in their own courts. These courts, so far as we are aware, were exclusively ecclesiastical. The heads of the churches acted as Judges and, in fact, published several law books. Their jurisdiction extended not merely to marriage and inheritance but also to most of the disputes occurring among Christians. With these disputes the State did not concern itself.*"[2]

5.4.1 Protection and Preservation of Other Religions

Protection and Preservation of Other Religions

The centuries-long existence of non-Muslims throughout the Muslim world, from Moorish Spain and Africa, south of the Sahara, to Egypt, Syria, India and Indonesia, is a clear proof of the religious tolerance of Islam towards people of different religions. This tolerance even led to the annihilation of Muslims, like in Spain, where the remaining Christians took advantage of the Muslim weakness. The Christians attacked them there and practiced forced conversions, expulsion and murder until the last Muslim was exterminated.

Etienne Denier

Etienne Denier wrote about the Christians in Islamic states:
"*They preserved their religion in complete safety during the eight centuries that the Muslims governed their lands. Some of them held*

---

1 Professor Adam Mez (1869-1917) comes from Freiburg in Breisgau. He is considered the actual founder of Islamic studies in Basel. In 1894 he received the venia docendi for Semitic languages and literatures, and before the turn of the century he received the extraordinary and later the ordinary professorships.

2 **MEZ**, Adam: The renaissance of Islam, London 1937, p.43.

high positions in the palace in Cordoba, but when those same Christians attained power over the land, suddenly their first wish was to exterminate the Muslims."[1]

Sir Thomas Arnold

The British Orientalist **Sir Thomas Arnold** wrote about the latter:
"*We hear nothing of any organized attempt to force the acceptance of Islam on the non-Muslim population, or of any systematic persecution intended to stamp out the Christian religion. Had the Caliphs chosen to adopt either course of action, they might have swept away Christianity as easily as Ferdinand and Isabella drove Islam out of Spain, or as Louis XIV made Protestantism penal in France, or as the Jews were kept out of England for 350 years. [...] the very survival of these Churches to the present day is a strong proof of the generally tolerant attitude of the Mohammedan governments towards them.*"[2]

Gustave le Bon

Gustave Le Bon summarizes this topic as follows:
"*The first conquests of the Arabs could have easily bedazzled them and led them to injustices, like the ones usually committed by conquerors. The latter includes, primarily, treating the defeated badly and violently forcing the new belief onto them, which they intend to spread over the entire world [...] – the Arabs avoided this diligently; [...] whichever region they invaded, if Syria or Spain, they treated the people with utmost gentleness by leaving them their laws, their institutions and their religion [...]. Never before had the world known conquerors with such tolerance or with such gentle a religion.*"[3]

Many historical facts are known to us about how Islam practiced acceptance and respect towards other cultures and religions, which range from decrees on "foreign affairs" to private affairs of non-Muslims. Some of them will be presented in the following subchapters, divided chronologically.

---

1 **Denier**, Etienne: Muhammad The Messenger Of God. p. 332.

2 **Arnold**, Thomas: The Preaching of Islam, London 1913, p. 79, 80.

3 **Le Bon**, Gustave: La civilisation des Arabes, 1884, Book VI, p. 169.

5.4.2 Examples from the Time of the First Caliph

Examples for the Time of the First Caliph

Like he declared it in his first speech, the principle of the first Caliph Abu Bakr as-Siddiq[1] was: "*The strong one amongst you is weak before me, until I have taken from him the rights of others. The weak one amongst you is strong before me, until I have given him his rights.*"[2]

Abu Bakr ensured Christians a peaceful and protected coexistence with Muslims, and he composed the following security contract for the city of Najran:

"*In the name of Allah, the most merciful. This is the written declaration of God's slave Abu Bakr, the successor of Muhammad, the Prophet and the Messenger of God. It guarantees them the rights of a protected neighbor, in themselves, their lands, their religious communities, their richness, their liegemen and servants, those of them who are present or abroad, their bishops and monks, their monasteries, and everything they possess, be it large or small. They shall never be robbed of any of it, and they shall always have full control over it.*"[3]

5.4.3 Examples from the Time of the Second Caliph

Examples for the Time of the Second Caliph

In the security contract of the second Caliph Omar Ibn Al-Khattab (died 644 AD) for the inhabitants of Jerusalem it says:

"*This is the security that is ensured by the slave of God, Omar, the Commander in Chief of the believers, the people of Iliya (Jerusalem): Security is guaranteed to them, for their possessions, churches, crucifixes,*

---

1 Abu Bakr (born 634), was the first caliph after the Prophet. He was his closest companion, known for his righteousness. He died at the age of 63 and was buried beside the Prophet.

2 **ABDURRAZZAQ:** Al-Musannaf, Hadith N°.: 20701.

3 **ABO YOUSUF**, Al-Qadi: Al-Charag, Cairo 1962, p. 73.

and everyone therein, whether sick or healthy, and for everyone in their community. Their churches will neither be occupied nor destroyed, nor will they be robbed of anything: neither furniture, nor crucifixes, nor money. They will not be forced to abandon their religion, or come to harm because of it. They will not be occupied by the Jewish settlers in Jerusalem." [1]

Caliph Omar

On his deathbed, Caliph Omar emphasized:
"I entrust to the next caliph the People of the Charter of the Messenger of Allah (non-Muslims). He shall maintain the 'Contract of the Charter' and fight to preserve their protection, and nothing should be demanded of them that they cannot fulfill." [2]

Dr. Lohtrop Stoddard

The American author **Dr. Lothrop Stoddard** explained that Caliph Omar was obviously concerned about the preservation of the integrity of the Christian holy places, and that those who would succeed him as caliphs would follow his footsteps. [3]

Caliph Omar Ibn Al-Khattab

His Justice towards People of Other Religions
A well-known principle of Caliph Omar Ibn Al-Khattab was: "Nothing can limit justice, even if it is exercised against a relative or during hard times." [4]

The Egyptian Christian Fartuna complained to Caliph Omar about his representative Amr Ibn Al-Aas and said that he had forcefully evacuated her from her house, where he built the extension of a mosque. The Caliph demanded a written explanation from his

---

1 ATTABARI: Attariech, Leiden 1879, Vol. 3, p. 159.

2 AL-BUCHARI: Assahih, Hadith N⁰.: 1305.

3 DR. STODDARD, Lothrop: The New World of Islam, London 1922, p. 11.

4 ATTABARI: Attariech, Leiden 1879, Vol. 3, p. 86.

representative. The latter defended himself by saying that the mosque was too small for the growing number of Muslims, and that he did not have any other choice but to integrate the surrounding houses into the building. In spite of a large compensation, the woman refused to give up her house. The caliph considered this explanation insufficient and ordered him to deconstruct this part of the mosque and to rebuild the house of the woman.[1]

The caliph found an old, blind Jew begging at a house and asked him: *"Why are you begging?"* And the Jew replied: *"Old age, need and jizia."* The caliph took his hand and led him to his own house, gave him some money and issued a decree in which this Jew and other similar cases were exonerated from jizia and commented:

"It is not fair that we take jizia from him in his youth and then abandon him in his older years. Allah said: 'Truly, alms are only for the poor, and those in need,' etc., and this man is a person in need."[2]

In Syria he found some ill Christians and ordered that they were given alms from the state treasury.

People Are Born Free

At the horse races in Egypt, the horse of an Egyptian man was faster than that of the son of the representative of the Caliph.

The latter hit the Egyptian with his whip and said:

"Take this from the son of the noblest people!" The Egyptian complained to the caliph and the caliph called for his representative and his son.

The caliph gave the Egyptian his whip and told him:

"Hit the son of the noblest people!"

The Egyptian hit him until he had had enough, and then the caliph said:

"Now hit on the bald head of his father, for his son would not have

---

1 **Dr. Assiba-Ie**, Mustafa: Rawaie Hadaratina, Cairo 1998, p. 85.

2 **Abo Yousuf**, Al-Qadi: Al-Charag, Cairo 1962, p. 126.

done this without his power."

The Egyptian said:

"I am satisfied, and I have hit him who hit me,"

then the caliph said:

"Since when have you enslaved men, even though their mothers have born them free?"[1]

5.4.4 Egypt *Egypt*

In every country that Muslims entered, the inhabitants were freed from religious oppression and absolutism:

Amr Ibn Al-aas

When the Arabic leader Amr Ibn Al-aas reached Egypt in 640 AD, a time of terrible persecution of Christians reigned. The Egyptian pope Benjamin had been hiding for some years in the desert because of it. The Romans tried to convert the brother of the pope by torturing him, and they drowned him. Churches and monasteries were transformed into torture prisons, and many thousands met their deaths there. The historian and Coptic Christian Sawiras Ibn Al- Moqanna reports:

pope Benjamin

"Sanotius, a leader of the Egyptian Church, told the Arabic leader Amr that the Egyptian pope Benjamin had been hiding for thirteen years in an unknown place. Immediately, Amr distributed in all of Egypt an advertisement, on which it said: 'Wherever the Coptic pope Benjamin is – there is the promise of security and peace of Allah for you. Come back calm and safe, lead your church and take care of your community.' Pope Benjamin heard of the integrity and reliability of the Arabs and returned with Muslim escort."[2]

---

1 **AL-MUTTAQI AL-HINDI:** Kanz Al-Ommal, Beirut 1989, Vol. 12, p. 660, **AL-ABSCHIEHI:** Al-Mustatraf, Beirut 1986, Vol. 1, p. 239.

2 **ASSALABI,** Dr. Ali Muhammad: Faslul-Khitab Fi Sirat Ibn Al-Khattab, p. 593.

Michael of Syria

In Syria the situation was not much different. **Michael of Syria**, who at this time was the bishop of Antakya, said:

"The Lord of Vengeance brought the sons of Ismael from the South to free us from Roman hands."

Caliph Ali

The **Caliph Ali** said to his governor in Egypt, **Malek Al-Ashtar**: *"Feel mercy for your subjects, love and benevolence, for they are two groups – either a brother for you in religion, or an equal in the Creation."* It is also reported that the shield of the Caliph disappeared, and that it was found at the house of a Jewish fellow citizen. The Jew however said: *"This is my shield."* The Caliph accused him in front of the Court of robbery. The judge Shuraeih[1] made them sit both together and spoke to Caliph Ali: *"The shield is in the possession of this man, and it is your duty to prove that it is yours."* The Caliph invited his son and his servant as witnesses. Finally, the judge decided in favor of the Jew because of lack of proof, and argued: *"A son would never declare against his father."*[2]

5.4.5 One Century after the Prophet

The 13th **Caliph Omar Ibn Abdul Aziz** (720 AD) wondered why non-Muslims did many things in public which were clearly forbidden to Muslims. He thus composed a letter to the scholar **Al-Hassan Al-Basri**[3] to ask for his judicial assistance:

---

1 The Muslim judge Shureih ibn Al-Harith Al-Kindi was judge of the city of Kufa in Iraq for 60 years. He was a scholar of hadiths and a poet.

2 **ABO NO-EIM**: Hilyatul Awliya, Beirut 1988, Vol. 4, p. 139.

3 Hasan al-Basri was born in Basra in 642 AD as son of a slave, and he was freed from his captivity by the Prophet's minister Zaid Bin Thabit. He became the most renowned scholar of the second generation of Muslims. Hassan was one of those who transmitted many hadiths about the Prophet. His mother had the honor to serve in the household of the Prophet's wife Umm Salama.

"How is it possible that the previous caliphs of the non-Muslims preserved all these forbidden things in the state, like marrying close relatives, having swine and drinking wine?"

Al-Hasan replied:

"This is the Islamic Law, they (the non-Muslims*) must be left to the practices of their religion, and you may only follow the Islamic Law, but you cannot re-invent it."*[1]

Years later, the Muslim general Qutayba occupied the city of Samarkand. The inhabitants of the city complained to the Caliph and said that Qutayba had occupied their land without them knowing their rights and without allowing them to negotiate to avoid the war. Omar ordered the governor of the city to give the city back to the people and to negotiate with them. Amazed by this demonstration of immediate justice, many inhabitants of Samarkand voluntarily converted to Islam.[2]

5.4.6 Examples since the 10th Century

Examples

A Christian monk came to the palace of **Ahmad Ibn Tulun** (the deputy Caliph in Egypt 868-884) to complain about his governor, who had taken 300 dinars from him. Ibn Tulun consequently called the monk and the governor to him. He asked the governor: *"Do you have the need that entitles you to take from others?"* Ibn Tulun deposed him from his office and asked the monk again, how much was taken away from him exactly. He replied: *"300 dinars."* Ibn Tulun replied: *"It is a pity that you did not say 3000. He needs a higher punishment, but it must correspond to your statement."* The monk was given his money back.[3]

---

1 **MAUDUDI**, Abul-Aala: The Rights Of The People of Covenant In The Islamic State, Beirut 1984, p. 22.

2 **TANTAWI**, Ali: Qasas Minat-Tarikh, 2. Edition, Cairo n.d., p. 197 ff.

3 **IBN HAMDOUN**: At-Tazkira al-Hamduniyya, Beirut 1996, Vol. 3, p. 200-201.

In negotiations, a Tartar leader agreed to release those of his prisoners who were Muslims. Ibn Teimiya however replied: *"We will not be satisfied until the last of the Jews and the last of the Christians are freed, for they are members of the Charter."*[1]

The famous Islamic principle: **"God gives the just State victory, even when it does not believe in Him, and He supports no unfair State, even if it is Muslim"**[2] comes from **Ibn Teimiya**.

The deeds of Ibn Teimiya (1263-1328) are further examples of how Muslims fought for and defended the rights of non-Muslim citizens.

5.4.7 Under the Ottoman Caliphate (1299-1923)

Richard Stebbins spoke about the experiences of Christians under Turkish rule: *"They (the Turks) allow them all, Roman-Catholics and Greek-Orthodox, to keep their religion and follow their conscience as they chose; they allowed them to have their churches in Constantinople and many other places to conduct their sacred rituals. This is in opposition to that which I witnessed after twelve years in Spain; not only did we have to sit through their pontifical ceremonies, but our lives and the lives of our grandchildren were equally in danger."*[3]

Thomas Arnold mentions that at that time there were many people in Italy who longed for the Ottoman rule. They wished to be ensured the same freedom and tolerance that the Ottoman rulers gave their Christian subjects. Desperate, they attempted to demand this from their Christian rulers. Many Jews found refuge in Ottoman Turkey during their persecution in Spain at the end of the 15th century.[4]

---

1 **Dr. Al-Qaradawi**, Yusuf: Ghayr al-Muslimeen fil-Mujtama, Cairo 1992, p. 10.

2 **Ibn Taymeya**: Al-Fatawa, Cairo 2005, Vol. 28, p. 63.

3 **Dr. Al-Qaradawi**, Yusuf: Al-Aqaliyyat ad-Diniyya wal-Hal al-Islami. 1st Edition, Cairo 1996, p. 51-52.

4 **Arnold,** Thomas: The Preaching of Islam, Westminster 1896, p. 135.

5.4.8 Aid and **Support for the Jews**

Aid and Support for the Jews

The Israeli writer and journalist Uri Avnery wrote:

"There is no evidence whatsoever of any attempt to impose Islam on the Jews. As is well known, under Muslim rule the Jews of Spain enjoyed a bloom the like of which the Jews did not enjoy anywhere else until almost our time. Poets like Yehuda Halevy wrote in Arabic, as did the great Maimonides. In Muslim Spain, Jews were ministers,

Uri Avnery

poets, and scientists. In Muslim Toledo, Christian, Jewish and Muslim scholars worked together and translated the ancient Greek philosophical and scientific texts. That was, indeed, the Golden Age. How would this have been possible if the Prophet decreed the 'spreading of the faith by the sword'?

What happened afterwards is even more telling.

When the Catholics re-conquered Spain from the Muslims, they instituted a reign of religious terror. The Jews and the Muslims were presented with a cruel choice: to become Christians, to be massacred or to leave.

And where did the hundreds of thousand of Jews, who refused to abandon their faith, escape?

Almost all of them were received with open arms in the Muslim countries. The Sephardic ("Spanish") Jews settled all over the Muslim world, from Morocco in the west to Iraq in the east, from Bulgaria (then part of the Ottoman Empire) in the north to Sudan in the south. Nowhere were they persecuted. They knew nothing like the tortures of the Inquisition, the flames of the auto-da-fe, the pogroms, the terrible mass-expulsions that took place in almost all Christian countries, up to the Holocaust.

[…] Every honest Jew who knows the history of his people cannot but feel a deep sense of gratitude to Islam, which has protected the Jews for fifty generations, while the Christian world persecuted the Jews and tried many times 'by the sword' to get them to abandon their faith."[1]

---

1 **AVNERY**, Uri: Mohammeds Schwert. URL: www.uni-kassel.de/fb5/frieden/themen/Islam/avnery2.html#orig (Accessed: August 26th 2009).

On November 2nd 2007, the Jewish-American photographer Norman Gershman held an exhibition in the Holocaust Memorial of Jerusalem in Yad Vashem. This exhibit documented how the Muslims of Albania in the period of 1943-45, in spite of all dangers, provided hundreds of Jews from many countries protection from the Nazis, gave them hideouts in their homes and thus saved them. From the published documents from Albania one can see that practically all Jews who sought refuge in the country were saved.

The journalist Christine von Kohl wrote about this:

"In spite of all the horror that the Liberation and Civil war presupposed for the Albanian people, no Jew was delivered to the Germans. The report of Mark Menahem, who found shelter with a family in Tirana attests, amongst many others, to the latter. When the Germans knocked on the door, the lady of the house, whose husband was not home at that moment, put Mark in her bed and presented him as her ill husband."[1]

---

1 **Sahm**, Ulrich W.: Nur die Albaner widerstanden der Nazi-Mordmaschine, ULR: http://europenews.dk/de/node/2345 (Accesed: June 8th 2009)

6 JIHAD, A FREE TICKET FOR SUICIDE BOMBERS?

In Arabic, the term *"Jihad"* has many peaceful meanings, and amongst Muslims it is a beautiful-sounding word and popular name for girls and boys. However, since September 11th 2001, their beautiful names were associated with predominantly one thing through the mass media: with terror, death and a war (supposedly) in the name of God.

Other terms such as *"Madrasa"*, which in Arabic simply means *"school"* were also twisted, misinterpreted and deformed to *"place of terrorist formation"*. *"Hewala"*, which means *"money transfer"*, suddenly was synonymous of *"financing of terrorist attacks."*

Let us get back to the term *"Jihad"*, which grammatically is the infinitive of the verb *"jaa-had"*, which simply means *"to strive for something"*. Because of its polysemy in Islam, the Prophet was once asked: *"What kind of Jihad is the best one?"* The Prophet said: *"A true word before an unjust governor."*[1] Jihad also means **"To explain the truth by means of the Quran"** *(The Quran, 25:52)*, and it further means simply **"Prayer"**. A woman asked the Prophet: *"Teach me a good deed to perform."* He replied: *"Perfect the prayer, because it belongs to the best of Jihads."*[2]

"Jihad" also means to fight one's own human weakness[3] and it is also used in the sense of **"giving Alms"**.[4]

Finally, almost all kinds of worship in Islam include a type of Jihad; things that require effort.

Jihad can also mean **"to fight"**, but not in the sense of attacking, but solely in the sense of defense of – religion (1), justice (2), oneself (3) or civilians (4).

Without the fight, the Quran explains, the freedom of religion would have been abolished, and the churches and synagogues destroyed:

> *"Had it not been
> that God checks one set of people
> by means of another,
> monasteries, churches, synagogues, and mosques,
> wherein the Name of God is mentioned
> much would surely have been pulled down.
> Verily, God will aid those who aid His (cause).
> Truly, God is All-Strong,
> All-Mighty."*
>
> The Quran, 22: 40

---

1 IBN HANBAL, Ahmad: Al-Musnad, Hadith N°.: 18076, ANNASAII: Assunan, Hadith N°.: 7834.

2 ATTABARANI: Al-Mugam Al-Kabier, Hadith N°.: 20867.

3 cp. AL-BAEIHAQI: Azzuhd Al-Kabier, Beirut 1987, p. 165.

4 The Holy Quran, 37: 11.

History shows the justice and freedom that are not preserved by force are fragile. There were always states and groups of people who tried to reach their goals through injustice. In many places of the world, except for where there are strong armies that protect peace and justice, people are murdered. The Muslim protects justice, even if he has to fight against Muslims to protect it:

> *"If two parties among the Believers*
> *fall into a quarrel,*
> *then make peace between them,*
> *but if one of them rebels against the other,*
> *then fight you (all) against the one that which rebels*
> *till it complies with the Command of God;*
> *then if it complies,*
> *then make reconciliation between them justly,*
> *and be equitable.*
> *Verily! God loves those who are fair (and just)."*
>
> The Quran, 49: 9

The Quran encourages the Muslim to defend himself when he is treated unjustly, but it makes a difference between defending oneself justly and bringing harm to innocents through this defense.

> *"And those who,*
> *when an oppressive wrong is done to them,*
> *they take revenge.*
> *The recompense for an evil is an evil like thereof,*
> *but whoever forgives and makes reconciliation,*
> *his reward is due from God.*
> *Verily, He likes not those who do wrong.*
> *And indeed whosoever takes revenge*
> *after he has suffered wrong,*
> *for such there is no way (of blame) against them.*
> *The way (of blame) is only against those who oppress men*

and wrongly rebel in the earth,
for such there will be a painful Penalty.
And verily, whosoever shows patience and forgives,
that would truly be an exercise of courageous will
and resolution in the conduct of affairs."

The Quran, 42: 39-43

"And if you punish (your enemy),
then punish them with the like of that
with which you were afflicted.
But if you show patience,
that is indeed the best (course) for those who are patient."

The Quran, 16: 126

In order to defend and protect civilians in case of an attack, the Quran encourages Muslims as follows:

"And why should you not fight
in the Cause of God
and of those who, being weak, are ill-treated and oppressed?
Men, women, and children whose cry is:
'Our Lord! Rescue us from this town,
whose people are oppressors;
and raise for us from You one who will protect;
and raise for us from You one who will help!'"

The Quran, 4: 75

He who dies in a battle by defending his wife or his religion is a Shahid (martyr), and thus he receives a high level in Janna. The Prophet said: *"He who dies for his religion, his life, his family or his possessions is Shahid."*[1]

---

1 **ABO DAWOOD:** Assunan, Hadith Nº.: 4142, **ATTERMEZI:** Assunan, Hadith Nº.: 1341, **ANNASAII:** Assunan, Hadith Nº.: 4027, **IBN HANBAL,** Ahmad: Al-Musnad, Hadith Nº.: 1565.

It should be emphasized, once more, that Islam diligently strives for peace, and only accepts and justifies war in the extreme case of self-defense.

> *"But if the enemy inclines towards peace,*
> *do you (also) incline towards peace,*
> *and trust in God.*
> *He is the All-Hearer, the All-Knower."*
>
> The Quran, 8: 61

When the Prophet came to Madina, he concluded a peace treaty with the Jews. This peace treaty is the first one of its kind in history, and people of different religions came together to sign a treaty that should guarantee them a peaceful coexistence, tolerance and freedom of religion.[1]

Like the Prophet explained, the most negative personal names in Arabic culture are *"Harb"* (war) and *"Murrah"* (bitter).[2]

A Quranic Surah (chapter) is called *"Victory"*; this victory is however not related to the success of a war, but it refers to the success of closing a peace treaty.

---

1 **Ibn Sayed Annas:** Uyoun Al-Athar, Beirut 1986, Vol. 1, p. 261, **Ibn Kathier:** Assyra, Beirut 1971, Vol. 2, p. 322.

2 **Ibn Wahb:** Al-Gamee, Saudi-Arabia 1996, Vol. 1, P. 122, **Assu-Youti:** Tanwier Al-Hawalik, Damaskus 2005, Vol. 2, p. 557.

6.1 The Morality of Battle in Islam

Islam sets criteria for clean and purposeful battle:

- It is forbidden to murder children, women, old people and those who are not fighting, for it is only against those who fight that one may fight.
- It is forbidden to destroy the religious houses and places of worship.
- It is forbidden to bother and kill animals.
- It is forbidden to cut down trees.

 When the Prophet sent the army to battle, he gave the following instructions:
"Do not kill any old man, any child or any woman."[1]
And he frequently said: *"Do not kill those who are in religious sites."*[2]

Caliph Abu Bakr

When, in 634 AD, the first Caliph Abu Bakr decided to appoint Yazid Ibn Abi Sofian as leader of his army, he gave him 10 guidelines:

"Do not kill any women, children or old people, and do not cut any trees, do not destroy any inhabited houses, do not kill any sheep or camel but to eat them. Do not burn any date trees, do not let anybody drown and do not take money from people without having the right to."[3]
When he was bidding his army farewell he said: *"You will pass by monks in religious buildings; leave them and do not destroy their buildings."*[4]

---

1 **Ibn Abi Shei-ba**: Al-Musannaf, Beirut 1988, Vol. 7, p. 654.

2 Idem, p. 656.

3 **Malek**, Al-Imam: Al-Muwatta, Libanon 2004, p. 258-259.

4 **Al-Waqidi**: Futuh Asch-scham, Kalkutta 1854, Vol. 1, p.7-8.

Nowadays, civilians are attacked with a multitude of justifications by states that declare that they are only bringing an end to terrorist attacks. These attacks are also carried out by terrorists, who declare that they want to end the attacks of certain states against their countries. From a purely Islamic perspective, the Muslim refuses both. Any justification for murdering civilians is rejected.

- Clergymen are to be protected.
- The corpses of dead people may not be harmed, but they are to be buried honorably.
- A war prisoner is a person in a weaker situation; therefore, he must be treated well, and he may not be caused psychological or physical pain.

Amongst the war prisoners after a battle were two girls. On the way to the Prophet they encountered the corpses of their relatives and they began to cry horribly. The Prophet was very angered by this, and told the soldier who had brought them:

"Was mercy taken out of your heart, that you could not avoid to lead the two girls by the corpses of their relatives?!"[1]

The Prophet forbade the hitting and torturing of war prisoners to gain information from them[2] and remarked many times that a Muslim may not mutilate people.[3]

War prisoners were brought to the mosques and the Muslims were encouraged to provide them with nourishment and water. The Quran places providing the ones in need as one of the most important characteristics of a good Muslim, and war prisoners clearly belong to those who have to be taken care of:

---

1 IBN KATHIER: Assyra, Beirut 1971, Vol. 3, p. 374, IBN KATHIER: Al-Bedaya Wannehaya, Beirut 1988, Vol. 4, p. 224.

2 ABDURRAZZAQ: Al-Musannaf, Hadith N°.: 9727.

3 AL-BUCHARI: Assahih, Hadith N°.: 2294, 5092, IBN-HANBAL, Ahmad: Al-Musnad, Hadith N°.: 17991, 17993, IBN ABI SCHEI-BA: Al-Musannaf, Beirut 1988, Vol. 5, p. 277, ATTABARANI: Al-Mugam Al-Kabier, Hadith N°.: 3777.

"And they feed,
for the love of God,
the indigent, the orphan and the captive — (saying),
'We feed you for the sake of God alone:
No reward do we desire from you,
nor thanks.'"

The Quran 76: 8-9

The summing up of the latter is found in Stanwood Cobbs' summary:

"That peace is a necessity for cultural advance is a special lesson that the history of Islam teaches us. The regions which the Arabs first conquered had been eroded by constant warfare. Under Arab administration, in the name of Allah and the Quran, peace was established throughout the whole empire, eventually reaching from India to the boundaries of France. Under Islam merchants as well as scholars could travel from Samarkand to Spain. Trade brought a wealth to the rulers and merchants which could be devoted to the creation and spread of culture. Science, technology and the arts of daily living began to flourish greatly. Never before, in fact, had the common people lived so well; and the luxury of the upper classes was legendary."[1]

How Does a Person Become a Muslim?

The only thing that has to be *"done"* in order to become a Muslim is to pronounce the following two phrases with conviction:

"I declare that there is no god but Allah, and that Muhammad is the Messenger of Allah."

– in Arabic it is: *"Ash-hadu Alla-ila-ha illa Allah, wa Ash-hadu Anna Muhammadan rasulu Allah."*

---

1 cp. **Cobb**, Stanwood: Islamic Contributions to Civilization. 1963, URL: www.bahaistudies.net/bahaiworks/cobb.html (Accessed: June 1st 2009).

Final Remarks on **Chapter Six**

1. A basic problem in the Islamic and secular world is the different interpretations of the Quran and the Sunnah, which are often taken out of context and thus lead to misunderstandings.

2. Many verses of the Quran are subject to many ways of interpretation, which utterly lead to false statements in those who lack a comprehensive knowledge and do not take into consideration the Sunnah.

3. The chapter represents a – even though only small – look into the understanding of true Islam, like the one represented by many scholars who are authorities in the matter.

4. In order to comprehensively discuss some of the problems addressed in this chapter, many more books are required, which must pick up each problem and then truly and contextually discuss it.

5. The existing multitude of spoken and written words, images and sounds about Islam (let us think of the approx. 400,000 video clips in a large internet video portal) present those who are interested in Islam with a large challenge. In order to differentiate amongst each contribution and to be able to make a meaningful judgment, it is necessary for the recipient himself to have previous knowledge of their authors, their fundamental interpretation of Islam, as well as knowledge of the Quran, the Sunnah and the Sharia. Certainly an unreachable endeavor to someone who, for instance, wants to simply inform himself without previous knowledge of the matter.

6. But how and where does one find reliable sources? Here are some helpful references for continuative information:

Websites:

Subject-specific and personal questions about Islam:
www.dar-alifta.org (the Egyptian Fatwa Bureau).

Islamic questions and personal advice:
www.hemaya.info (the personal homepage of the author),
www.musafira.de

Courses: www.sunnipath.com

General: www.radicalmiddleway.co.uk

Books:

- Dr. Murad Wilfried Hofmann (former German ambassador): Islam: the alternative, ISBN: 978-9695190074
- Muhammad Asad: The Road to Mecca
  ISBN: 978-1887752374
- Sohaib Sultan: The Koran for Dummies,
  ISBN: 978-0764555817

7   This book aims at showing the reader that Islam is a beautiful religion that strives for harmony and justice. The fact that Islam is the fastest growing religion[1] and that the majority of its followers lead a peaceful and tolerant existence while striving for a life in reverence to Allah and His Prophet Muhammad (peace be upon him), as well as in love to their fellow men speak for these characteristics.

---

1   **YOUNG**, Gayle: Fast-growing Islam winning converts in Western world, URL: www.cnn.com/WORLD/9704/14/egypt.islam (Accessed: June 10th 2009), Anonymous, The List: The World's Fastest-Growing Religions, URL: www.foreignpolicy.com/story/cms.php?story_id=3835 (Accessed: June 10th 2009).

The central points of Islam *The central points of Islam*

God created everything. He created man, so that he worships and loves Him. He wants him to live happily and peacefully in this limited life on earth. In order to continue his bliss with body and soul until eternity, God created Paradise.

God sent Messages to man with Prophets in order to enlighten him about the Hereafter and the eternal bliss, and to announce what is demanded of him in his worldly existence.

Abraham, Moses and Jesus are some of these Prophets. They always brought the same message, but in different versions. This one message – *"Islam"* was finally sent by God as the last version with Prophet Muhammad (peace be upon him), and it applies to all people and until the end of this life.

This Message consists of the Quran, which is *"The Last Testament"*, and the *"Hadith"* (the explanations of the Prophet), which explain the details of Islam.

This message explains what God wants from man regarding:

- matters of faith,
- worship,
- and the interaction with other people.

In terms of faith, the Message announces that **there is only one God** who created everything, including Heaven and Earth. He knows all, sees all, and hears all. He is capable of everything and He is the most merciful. His existence has neither a beginning nor an end, and His Being is absolutely independent of all things. He was not born, He has no children, and He resembles none of His creatures. The human brain cannot visualize God, nor comprehend His Majesty.

The belief in God and His Prophet Muhammad is considered the main condition for the entrance into Paradise.

Death is not the end of human existence, but only a phase in between. Man continues to live during it, enjoys or suffers, until the Day of Resurrection. On this day, God will re-create the human body and will bind it to its soul. Man will be held accountable for his deeds, and the consequences for his eternal fate will be declared.

In addition, this Message comprises information about what will happen to man after this life until the Day of Resurrection, what will finally happen on the Day of Resurrection, and what life in Janna is like, what he will find and see there.

In the field of worship: prayer, fasting and charity are required.

When it comes to interaction with other people, honesty, justice and mercy are demanded.

To be benevolent to others, and to treat them just as one wants to be treated, is also part of this life.

A Muslim may not punish a person of different faith because of

his religion, and there is no compulsion to believe.

All people are equal – regardless of the color of their skin or their nationality. The best one before God is the one who comes closest to Him.

Judgment: *Judgment:*

He who believes in God and accepts his Prophet Muhammad (peace be upon him) is a Muslim.

Afterwards, the faithful one receives a positive point for each good deed towards God or another person. This positive point is called *Hasana (pl. Hasanat)*. On the contrary, for every bad deed he receives a *Sayye-ah (pl. Sayye-aat)*, a sin point.

For every Hasana, the Muslim receives a reward, while for the redemption of a Sayye-ah the prayer for forgiveness is required. A Muslim who dies with Sayye-ah without asking for its forgiveness will likely be punished. Those who commit Sayye-aat and thus violated not only God's Rights but also the rights of other people must not only ask for forgiveness, but also restore the rights to the affected people.

Each Hasana is registered tenfold by God, while each Sayye-ah is only counted once and can even be forgiven.

The level in Paradise is determined in accordance with the amount of **Hasanat**, just like the level of torture in Hell is determined in accordance with the amount of **Sayye-aat**.

The greatest Hasana is to accept the Message of God and His Prophet, and the greatest Sayye-ah is, accordingly, to ignore or reject Him and His Prophet.

Sayye-aat   *Hasanah*

– – – –   +++

In Islam, it is not expected that man is flawless and does not commit any sins, but rather that he comes back to God and asks for forgiveness.

Asking for forgiveness of a Sayye-ah takes place between man and God, without any other intermediaries. God hears what we say, knows what we do, has a merciful disposition towards us and loves those who come back to him asking for forgiveness.

Man does not inherit any sins, but he is born pure and will only be held accountable for his own deeds.

The Message of God teaches us that this life, in actuality, is only a limited trial period, and, according to our deeds in it, our fate in the eternal life will be decided. There will be no repeating or erasing.

"O my Servants
who have transgressed against themselves!
Despair not of the Mercy of God:
for God forgives all sins:
for He is Oft-Forgiving, Most Merciful.
And turn in repentance
and in obedience with true Faith to your Lord
and submit to Him, (in Islam),
before the Penalty comes upon you,
then you will not be helped.
And follow the best
of that which is sent down to you from your Lord
(i.e. this Quran),
before the Penalty comes on you suddenly
while you perceive not! –
Lest a person should (then) say:
'Ah! my grief that I was undutiful to God,
and I was indeed among those who mocked!' –
Or (lest) he should say:
'If only God had guided me,
I should certainly have been among the righteous!' –
Or (lest) he should say when he sees the Penalty:
'If only I had another chance
I should certainly be among those
who do good!'"

The Quran, 39: 53-58

Glossary

Hadith

A Hadith is a report about the Prophet (peace be upon him) that recounts his speeches, his lectures, his actions or a situation at the time of the Prophet. The Hadiths were recorded and transmitted with great efforts and highest attention.

They were memorized and transmitted by the Prophet's companions. In every generation after the Prophet, these Hadiths were written down, compared and tested for their accuracy by numerous famous compilers. No Hadith was transmitted without the complete information about their journey from the Prophet and each of its transmitters: his loyalty, his accuracy, his attention and strength while memorizing, if he received these Hadiths written or only verbally, if other compilers also transmitted the same Hadith. Through this way, many large special branches of science were created in Islam, each one of them with databanks which contain precise information about the history and the circumstances around each Hadith, each transmitter and each compiler. For every Hadith there is a "Sanad" (chain), which contains all of its transmitters until the Prophet, and the special branch of science dedicated to this is called "Ilm Al-Asanieed" (discipline of the chains of transmission).

The special branch of science "Ilm Arri-gal" (branch of science of the transmitters) occupies itself with the precise information about the transmitters and their characteristics, their different levels, strengths, weaknesses and lacks.

In order to achieve a comprehensive overview over the entirety of laws, circumstances, kinds, levels and regulations for the transmission of a Hadith there is the branch of science called "Ilm Al-Mustalah."

Remarks

- <u>Muslims consider it important and a sign of politeness that one says or writes, when speaking or writing the name of Prophet Muhammad: salla Allahu aleihi wa sallam "May Allah praise him and grant him peace." Or shortly: "Peace be upon him".</u>

- The citation of the Hadith sources in this book was composed as they are known in Arabic. In Arabic, most of the names of the Hadith-compilations are linked to the name of their compilers, and therefore very well-known, which is why no further information about their authors is necessary.

- Since every Hadith-compilation has countless editions in all Arabic and Islamic countries, here we mostly cite only the Hadith number.

- With the number information, one can easily find the Hadith through the processing software "Al-Maktabah Ash-shamelah". "Ashamelah" is an Arabic searching engine that comprises over six thousand Islamic books, and it is available for free at: **www.shamela.ws**.

Janna (Paradise)

Janna is the place of reward that God created for those who accepted his Message. Multiple but similar versions of this Message were sent by God with many prophets. Each Prophet (amongst others Noah, Abraham, Moses and Jesus) was sent with a version that was composed for certain people at a certain time. In the end, God sent the last prophet, Muhammad, with the newest version of the Revelation for all people. From the Day of Resurrection until eternity one leads an unimaginably blissful, beautiful life in Janna, materially, physically and psychologically. The sum and beauty of the objects, rewards and bliss there, and the degree of luxury, were described by the Prophet one day and at the end of his description, the Prophet said that there are things there that eyes never saw, ears never heard and man never imagined.

Jahannam (Hell)

Jahannam is the place of punishment that God created for those who rejected His Message. From the Day of Resurrection until eternity, they will suffer unimaginably cruel physical and spiritual tortures in the fire, while being completely conscious. More under the title *"The Description of Jahannam."*

Sharia (Islamic Law)

Sharia is composed of precepts, laws and practical morality derived from the Quran, the Sunnah and their rules and basic principles.

iman

ieman or iman: The belief in God, His prophet and the Afterlife, which deeply rooted in one's heart.

References

1. Alt, Franz: Kampf gegen Mädchenmorde. Fokus, Nº. 9/2001.
2. Andrae, Tor: Mohammed, Sein Leben und Glaube. New York 2000.
3. Andrews, C. F.: The Genuine Islam. Singapore 1936.
4. Arberry, Arthur J.: The Koran Interpreted. London 1964.
5. Arnold, Thomas: The Preaching of Islam, Westminster 1896 and London 1913,
6. Al-Gesr, Nadeem: Kissatul-Ieman, Tripoli, n.d.
7. Al-Mausili, Abu Yala: Al-Musnad (Hadith Collection), Damascus 1984.
8. Abu Dawood: Assunan, (Hadith Collection), electronic version from "Al-Maktabah Asch-schamelah" V. 3.24
9. Abdurrazzaq: Al-Musannaf, (Hadith Collection), electronic version from "Al-Maktabah Asch-schamelah" V. 3.24
10. Addaraqutni, Abul-hasan: Arru'ya, (Hadith Collection), electronic version from "Al-Maktabah Asch-schamelah" V. 3.24
11. Abu No-eim: Marifatus-sahaba, Riyadh 1998.
12. Abd Ibn Humeid: Al-Musnad, (Hadith Collection), electronic version from "Al-Maktabah Asch-schamelah" V. 3.24
13. Abu Noeim: Hilyatul-Awli-yaa, Beirut 1988.
14. Abu Ubayd: Al-Amwaal, Beirut 1989
15. Abu Yousuf, Al-Qadi: Al-Charag, Cairo 1962.
16. Al-Abschiehi: Al-Mustatraf, Beirut 1986.
17. Adahabi: Se-yar Aalam Annobalaa, Beirut 2001.
18. Addoulabi: Al-Kuna wal-Asmaa, Hyderabad 1904.
19. Al-Baeihaqi: Azzuhd Al-Kabier, Beirut 1987.
20. Al-Baeihaqi: Assunan Al-Kubra (Hadith Collection), Hyderabad 1925.
21. Al-Beihaqi: Dalail Annu-bowwa, Cairo 1988.
22. Al-Baeihaqi: Schu-ab Al-Ieman (Hadith Collection), Beirut 2000.
23. Al-Buchari: Al-Gamie As-sahih (Hadith Collection), electronic version from "Al-Maktabah Asch-schamelah" V. 3.24
24. Al-Buchari: Al-Adab Al-Mufrad, Beirut 1989.

25. Al-Berti: Musnad Abdurrahmad Ibn Auf (Hadith Collection), Beirut 1993.
26. Al-Hakem: Al-Mustadrak (Hadith Collection), electronic version from "Al-Maktabah Asch-schamelah" V. 3.24
27. Al-Muttaqi Al-Hindi: Kanz Al-Ommal, Beirut 1989.
28. Al-Marwazy, Muhammad Ibn Nasr: Tazim Qadr Assalah, al-Madína al-munawwara 1987.
29. Al-Waqidi: Futuh Asch-scham, Calcutta 1854.
30. Al-Qudaie, Asch-schihab: Al-Musnad (Hadith Collection), Beirut 1985.
31. Al-Asbahani, Abu Asch-scheich: Amsaal Al-Hadith, electronic version from "Al-Maktabah Asch-schamelah" V. 3.24
32. Al-Fayrous Aa-bady: Al-Kamoos Al-Muheet, Beirut 1999.
33. Al-Kasemi, Gamaluddin: Mau-isat Al-Mu'mnieen, Beirut 1995.
34. Al-Kasani: Badaie Assa-naie, Beirut 1986.
35. Al-Mawardi, Abul-Hasan: Al-Ah-kam Assul-tanyya, Kuwait 1989.
36. Al-Munawie: Al- Munawie: Faydul-Qadier, Beirut 1994.
37. Al-Mubar-kafouri: Tuhfat Al-Ahwazi, Damascus n.d.
38. Al-Qarafi: al-Furooq, Beirut 1998.
39. Al-Qurtubi: Attafsier, Beirut 1985.
40. Dr. Al-Qaradawi, Yusuf: Ghayr al-Muslimeen fil-Mujtama, Cairo 1992.
41. Dr. Al-Qaradawi, Yusuf: Al-Aqaliyyat ad-Diniyya wal-Hal al-Islami. 1st edition, Cairo 1996.
42. Attermezi: Assunan (Hadith Collection), electronic version from "Al-Maktabah Asch-schamelah" V. 3.24
43. Annasaii: Assunan (Hadith Collection), electronic version from "Al-Maktabah Asch-schamelah" V. 3.24
44. Assu-youti: Tanwier Al-Hawalik, Damascus 2005.
45. Assafadi: Al-Wafi bil Wafiyyat, Beirut 2000.
46. Attermezi: Asch-schamail, Beirut 1996.

47. Attabarani: Al-Mugam Al-awsat (Hadith Collection), Cairo 1995.

48. Attabarani: Al-Mugam Assagier (Hadith Collection), Beirut 1985.

49. Attabarani: Al-Mugam Al-Kabier (Hadith Collection), electronic version from "Al-Maktabah Asch-schamelah" V. 3.24

50. Attabari: Attariech, Leiden 1879.

51. Arruyani: Al-Musnad (Hadith Collection), Cairo 1995.

52. Assalabi, Dr. Ali Muhammad: Faslul-Khitab Fi Sirat Ibn Al-Khattab.

53. Assalhi: Subul Al-Huda War-raschad, Beirut 1993.

54. Bediüzzaman Said Nursi in his work "Rasael Annour." (several-volumes).

55. Besant, Annie: The Life And Teachings Of Mohammed, Madras 1932.

56. Blachère, Régis: Introduction au Coran, Paris 1959.

57. Bosworth Smith R.: Mohammed and Mohammedanism, London 1874.

58. Brewster, D.: Life of Sir Isaac Newton, London 1831.

59. Briffault, Robert: The Making of Humanity, London 1919.

60. Bucaille, Dr. Maurice: The Bible, The Qur'an And Science, Paris 1976.

61. Bucaille, Dr. Maurice: The Qur'an and Modern Science, Raleigh (North Carolina) 1997.

62. Croswell, Ken: The Alchemy of the Heavens Searching for the meaning of the Milky Way, New York 1995.

63. Carlyle, Thomas: On Heroes, Hero-Worship and the Heroic in History, California 1993.

64. Carlyle, Thomas: Heroes and Hero Worship and the Heroic in History, Nebraska 2008.

65. de Lamartine, Alphonse de: Histoire De La Turquie, Paris 1854.

66. The Holy Quran.

67. The Bible, Contemporary English Version (CEV Bible), Editor American Bible Society 1995.

68. The Bible, Elberfelder Bibel (1905) (German).

69. The Bible, Hoffnung für Alle (German).

70. The Bible, King James Version

71. The Bible, Lutherbibel (1912) (German).
72. The Bible, Neue evangelistische Übersetzung. (German).
73. The Bible, Today's English Version.
74. Darwin, Charles: On The Origin Of The Species, London 1859.
75. Danzer, G./ Rattner, J.: Europäische Moralistik in Frankreich von 1600 bis 1950, n.l. 2006.
76. Denison, John-Hopkins: Emotion as the basis of civilization, New York and London 1928.
77. Denier, Etienne: Muhammad The Messenger Of God.
78. Dorman, Harry G.: Towards Understanding Islam, New York 1948.
79. Durant, Will: The Story of Civilization, New York 1935-75.
80. Draper, John William: A History of the Intellectual Development of Europe, London 1875.
81. Dr. Assiba-ie, Mustafa: Rawaie Hadaratina, Cairo 1998.
82. Encyclopaedia Britannica, Chicago 1921/22.
83. Einiger, Christoph: Die schönsten Gebete der Menschheit, Munich 1964.
84. Erckmann, Rudolf: Der Einfluß der arabischspanischen Kultur auf die Entwicklung des Minnesangs, Darmstadt 1933.
85. Gage, Matilda J.: Woman, Chruch and State, New York 1893.
86. Farrar, Frederic William: Mercy and judgment - last words on Christian eschatology, London 1882.
87. FERRIS, Timothy: The World Treasury of Physics, Astronomy and Mathematics, London 1991.
88. Fielding H. Garrison: An introduction to the history of medicine, London 1917.
89. Gibb, H. A. R.: Arabic Literature – An Introduction, Oxford 1963.
90. Gibbon, E./ Ocklay,S.: History of the Saracen Empire, London 1870.
91. Gibbon, E.: The Decline and fall of the Roman Empire, n.l. 1823.
92. Haidar, Bammate (George Rivoire): Visages de L' Islam, Lausanne 1946.
93. Hart, Michael H.: The 100: A Ranking Of The Most Influential Persons In History, New York 1978.
94. Hawking, Stephen: A Brief History of Time, New York 1988.

95. Hess, Frances: Earth Science, New York 2002.

96. Hirschfeld, Prof. Hartwig: New Researches into the Composition and Exegesis of the Qoran, Whitefish 2009.

97. Hitti, Phillip Khuri: History of the Arabs. London 1937.

98. Hoyle, Fred: The Universe. Past and Present Reflections, Engineering and Science, n.l. 1981.

99. Hunke, Sigrid: Allahs Sonne über dem Abendland, Stuttgart 1962.

100. Hurgronje, C. Snouck: Mohammedanism. n.l. 2007.

101. Irving, Washington : Mahomet And His Successors, UK 2007.

102. Ibn Hamdoun: At-Tazkira al-Hamduniyya, Beirut 1996.

103. Ibn Teimiya: Al-Fatawa, Cairo 2005.

104. Ibn-Hibban: Assahih (Hadith Collection), electronic version from "Al-Maktabah Asch-schamelah" V. 3.24

105. Ibn Hanbal, Ahmad: Al-Musnad (Hadith Collection), electronic version from "Al-Maktabah Asch-schamelah" V. 3.24

106. Ibn Al-Qayyim: Arruh, Beirut 1982.

107. Ibn Hagar: Fat-hul-Bari, Riyadh 2005

108. Ibn Abi Osama, Al-Harith: Bughyat Al-Bahith, Cairo, n.d.

109. Ibn Hagar: Al-Matalib Al-Aaliya, Riyadh 1998.

110. Ibn Khuzayma: Attawhid, Riyadh 1988.

111. Ibn Al-Mubarak, Abdullah: Al-Musnad (Hadith Collection), Riyadh 1987.

112. Ibn Rajab: Gami Al-Ulum Wal-hikam, Cairo 2004.

113. Ibn Sayed Annas: Uyoun Al-Athar (Hadith Collection) Beirut 1986.

114. Ibn Wahb: Al-Gamee (Hadith Collection), Saudi Arabia 1996.

115. Ibn Abi Shei-ba: Al-Musannaf (Hadith Collection), Beirut 1988.

116. Ibn Abi Aasim: Assunnah, Riyadh 1988.

117. Ibn Kathier: Attafseer. n.l. 2002

118. Ibn Kathier: Assyra, Beirut 1971.

119. Ibn Kathier: Al-Bedaya Wannehaya, Beirut 1988.

120. Ibn Magah: Assunan (Hadith Collection), electronic version from "Al-Maktabah Asch-schamelah" V. 3.24

121. Ibn Al-Gawzi: Sefat Assafwa, Alexandria, Egypt n.d.

122. Ibn Hagar: Al-Isaba, Egypt 1960 (Attaba Assalafya).

123. Ibn Hagar: Al-Isaba, Calcutta 1856.

124. I-yad, Al-Qadi: Aschifaa, Beirut 1988.

125. J.G. Cotta'schen Buchhandlung (Editor): Goethe's Werke, Stuttgart and Tübingen 1828, Vol. 6.

126. Jung, C. G.: Modem Man in Search of a Soul, New York 1933.

127. Kenny, Anthony: The Five Ways, New York 1969,

128. Kerrod, Robin: Encyclopedia of Science Heavens 2, New York 1997.

129. Kurth, Dieter: Das Ältere Egypt, Nurnberg 2000.

130. Lane-Poole, Stanley: The Moors in Spain, Whitefish 2005

131. Le Bon, Gustave: La civilisation des Arabes, Paris 1884.

132. Leipoldt, J.: Jesus und die Frauen, n.l. 1921.

133. Leonard, Major A.: Islam, its Moral and Spiritual Values. London 1909.

134. Le rouge, Raymond: Vie de Mahomet, Paris 1939.

135. Linde, Andrei: The Self-Reproducing Inflationary Universe. Scientific American, November 1994.

136. Lodge, Oliver J.: Pioneers of Science, Whitefish Montana 2003.

137. Malek, Al-Imam: Al-Muwatta, Lebanon 2004.

138. Maududi, Abul-Aala: The Rights Of The People of Covenant In The Islamic State, Beirut 1984.

139. Maurois, André: Le peseur d'âmes, Paris 1931.

140. Mez, Adam: The renaissance of Islam, London 1937.

141. Michener, James A.: Islam.The Misunderstood Religion. In: Reader's Digest (American Edition), 05/1955.

142. Minkel, J.R.: Mystery of Galaxies Full of Dark Matter Solved. Scientific American, edition of 02/16/ 2007.

143. Montet, Edward: La Propaganda Chretienne et Adversaires Musulmans, Paris 1890.

144. Moore, K.L. et al: Human Development as Described in the Quran and Sunnah [Human Evolution as described in the Quran and the Sunnah].

145. Moore, K.L./ Persaud, T.V.N.:The Developing Human. Clinically Oriented Embryology, 1993.

146. Moore, Patrick: The International Encyclopedia of Astronomy, New York 1981.
147. Morris, Mark: "The Milky Way." The World Book Encyclopedia, Chicago 2002.
148. Moslim: Al-Gamie As-sahih (Hadith Collection), electronic version from "Al-Maktabah Asch-schamelah" V. 3.24.
149. Muhammad Ibn Nasr: Tazim Qadr Assalah, al-Madína al-munawwara 1987.
150. Naidu, Sarojini: Speeches and Writings of Sarojini Naidu, Madras 1918.
151. Nursi, Said: Rasael Annour, 3rd Edition, Cairo 2002.
152. Anonymous: Soul has weight, physician thinks. New York Times, edition of 03/11/1907.
153. O'leary, De Lacy: Islam At Crossroads, London 1923.
154. Anonymous: Indiens Frauen und der Hinduismus. Neue Zürcher Zeitung (2001), Nº.100.
155. Anonymous The Sunday Telegraph, 10/18/1992
156. Parrinder, Geoffrey: Mysticism in the World's Religions, New York 1976.
157. Peale, Norman Vincent: Beyond Death There Is Life, Reader's Digest, October 1957; Vol. 71, Nº. 426.
158. Quailar, Young: The Near East: Society & Culture.
159. Rai, Anita: Muhammad, Uncovering the True Story, n.l. 2007.
160. Sale, George: The Koran.The Preliminary Discourse, London and New York 1891.
161. Schrefler, Harald: Das traditionelle Frauenbild gemäß den brahmanischen Gesetzgebern, University of Vienna 2003.
162. Sharbel, Moris: Das Jenseits unter Wissenschaftlichem Licht, n.l., 1998.
163. Shulamith, Shahar: Die Frau im Mittelalter, Königstein 1981.
164. Smith, Prof. Huston: The Illustrated World's Religions. A Guide to Our Wisdom Traditions, New York 1995.
165. Spencer, Herbert: Descriptive Sociology of England. in: Gage, Matilda J.: Woman, Church And State, New York 1893.

166. Stoddard Lothrop, Ph.D.: The New World of Islam, London 1922.
167. Streit, Prof. Dr. Bruno: Biozahl 2006 – 2 Millionen-Grenze erreicht, in: Natur und Museum Vol. 136, Frankfurt am Main 2005/06.
168. Scott, S. P.: History of Moorish Empire in Europe, Philadelphia 1904.
169. Thompson, S. P.: The Life of William Thomson. Baron Kelvin of Largs, London 1859.
170. Travis, John: Could a Pair of Cosmic Strings Open a Route Into the Past?, Science Magazine, New York Avenue 04/10/1992.
171. Tritton, Arthur Stanley: The People Of The Covenant In Islam.
172. Timothy Ferris: The World Treasury of Physics, Astronomy and Mathematics, London 1991.
173. The Sunday Telegraph, 10/18/1992.
174. Tantawi, Ali: Qasas Minat-Tarikh, 2nd edition, Cairo n.d.
175. Veccia Vaglieri, Laura: Apologie de I'Islamisme. n.l. 2002.
176. Von Braun, Werner in: James Perloff: Tornado in a Junkyard, Arlington 1999.
177. von Sydow, Momme: Darwin – A Christian Undermining Christianity? On Self-Undermining Dynamics of Ideas Between Belief and Science, Burlington 2005.
178. Watt, William Montgomery: Mohammed At Mecca, Oxford 1953.
179. Watt, William Montgomery: Muhammad At Medina, Oxford 1956.
180. Weil, Dr. Gustav in: Brockelmann, Carl (Editor): History of the Islamic Peoples, Cornwell 1947.
181. Winternitz, Moriz: Die Frau in den indischen Religionen. in: Hirsch, M (Editor): Archiv für Frauenkunde und Eugenetik (1915-1916), Berlin 1916.
182. Young India (periodical), 1st edition 1924, Nº. 8.

Internet References

183. Avnery, Uri: Muhammad's Sword. URL: www.globalresearch.com (Accessed: 09/26/2006).

184. Cain, Fraser: Sun Orbit, URL: www.universetoday.com/guide-to-space/the-sun/sun-orbit (Accessed: 02/18/2010).

185. Dr. Craig, William L.: The Teleological Argument and the Anthropic Principle, URL: www.conservapedia.com/Evidence_for_intelligent_design_in_cosmology (Accessed: 11/21/2009).

186. Dr. Craig, William Lane: Does God Exist?, www.leaderu.com/offices/billcraig/docs/craig-pigliucci1.html (Accessed: 12/01/2009).

187. Caxton, William: Famous Prefaces. The Harvard Classics 1909–14, Epilogue to Dictes and Sayings of the Philosophers, First Edition (1477), URL: www.bartleby.com/39/4.html (Accessed: 0/01/2009).

188. Cobb, Stanwood: Islamic Contributions to Civilization. n.l.1963, URL: www.bahaistudies.net/bahaiworks/cobb.html. (Accessed: 06/01/2009)

189. Craig, William L.: How to Know God Exists -The Argument From Design, URL: www.comereason.org/newsletters/feb01.htm(Accessed: 04/25/2009).

190. Donner, Erika: Unser Arabisches Erbe. 1961, URL: www.library.fes.de/gmh/main/pdf-files/gmh/1961/1961-12-a-736.pdf (Accessed: 04/12/2009).

191. Gallagher, Jonathan: The Universe and the existence of God, URL: www.pineknoll.org/jg/45-god-in-other-words/173-jonathan-gallagher-the-universe-and-the-existence-of-god (Accessed: 04/25/2009).

192. Gill, N.S.: Evidence about greek women in the archaic age (2009). URL: http://ancienthistory.about.com/od/greekwomen/p/022900ArchGkwom.htmAbout.com (Accessed: 05/29/2009).

193. Groll, Tina: Ohne Ehemann kein Recht auf Leben (2006). Frauenseiten Bremen, URL: http://www.bremen.de/sixcms/detail.php?id=3860580 (Accessed: 06/01/2009).

194. J J O'Connor and E F Robertson: Arabic mathematics: forgotten brilliance? URL: www-history.mcs.st-andrews.ac.uk/HistTopics/Arabic_mathematics.html (Accessed: 25/05/2011).

195. Gayle Young: Fast-growing Islam winning converts in Western world, URL: www.cnn.com/WORLD/9704/14/egypt.islam (Accessed: 06/10/2009),

196. Haley, Alex: The Autobiography of Malcolm X., as well as cp.: URL: www.malcolm-x.org/docs/let_mecca.htm

197. Lara, B.: Evolutionsfaktoren, ULR: www.webmic.de/evolutionsfaktoren.htm, home.arcor.de/paflitschek/ppt/Selektion_und_Gendrift.ppt (Accessed: 09/05/2009).

198. Lefkowitz, Mary R./ Fant, Maureen B.: Women Life in the in Greece & Rome, Husbands' punishment of wives in early Rome, URL: www.stoa.org (Accessed: 04/12/2009).

199. Mogahed, Dalia: Perspectives of Women in the Muslim World (2006). The Gallup World Poll Organization, URL: http://media.gallup.com/WorldPoll/PDF/GALLUP+MUSLIM+STUDIES_Perspectives+of+Women_11.10.06_FINAL.pdf (Accessed: 05/29/2009)

200. Moore, James: Evolution and Wonder - Understanding Charles Darwin.Speaking of Faith (2006) in: (Podcast) American Public Media, URL: http://speakingoffaith.publicradio.org/programs/darwin/transcript.shtml (Accessed: 04/25/2009).

201. Moore, Keith L.: Video1, einsehbar unter URL: http://www.dies-ist-die-wahrheit.de/video/index.htm (Accessed: 04/25/2009).

202. Morrison, A. Cressy: Seven Reasons Why a Scientist Believes in God, URL: www.dlshq.org/messages/sciblgod.htm (Accessed: 04/25/2009).

203. Anonymous: Belief. Historical essay, What did Darwin believe?, URL: www.darwinproject.ac.uk/content/view/130/125/. (Accessed: 05/09/2009).

204. Anonymous: How widespread is violence against women? United Nations Secretary- General's Campaign, 2008, URL: www.un.org/women/endviolence/docs/VAW.pdf (Accessed: 05/28/2009).

205. Anonymous: The List: The World's Fastest-Growing Religions, URL: www.foreignpolicy.com/story/cms.php?story_id=3835 (Accessed: 06/10/2009).

206. Anonymous: Stellung der Frauenbildung, Ägyptische staatliche inormationen Service, URL: http://www.sis.gov.eg/Ar/Women/Society/Education/100303000000000001.htm (Accessed: 05/29/2009)

207. Anonymous (BBC): Women in Ancient Athens (2007). URL: http://www.bbc.co.uk/dna/h2g2/A23428659 (Accessed: 05/30/2009)

208. Anonymous: Wußten Tiere von dem Tsunami?, URL: www.china-intern.de/page/wissenschaft-neue/1104343167.html (Accessed: 04/25/2009).

209. Anonymous: Zehn Millionen Mädchen in Indien gezielt abgetrieben (2006), URL: www.3sat.de/dynamic/sitegen/bin/sitegen.php?tab=2&source=/nano/news/87449/index.html (Accessed: 05/31/2009)

210. Ross, Dr. Hugh: Design and the Anthropic Principle, in: Origins, URL: www.origins.org/articles/ross_designanthropic.html (Accessed:11/21/2009).

211. Rybka, T.: Hieroglyphen. URL: http://www.siltry.de/artikel.htm (Accessed: 05/25/2009) and cp. Kurth, Dieter: Das Ältere Ägypten. Vol. 070, p. 16.

212. Sahm, Ulrich W.: Nur die Albaner widerstanden der Nazi-Mordmaschine, ULR: http://europenews.dk/de/node/2345 (Accessed: 06/08/2009)

213. Schaefer, Dr. Udo: Muhammad - ein Lügenprophet? Eine Klarstellung gegenüber des katholischen Glaubens, p. 4. URL: www.udoschaefer.com/pdffiles/muhammad.pdf (Accessed: 05/12/2009)

214. 2Thompson, James B.: Legal status of women in ancient Rome (2005). URL: www.womenintheancientworld.com (Accessed: 06/01/2009).

215. Zverev, A.: Melatonin. 2005, URL: www.egbeck.de/melatde.htm, (Accessed: 04/25/2009).

List of Illustrations

- Image P. 027 - (1st Image from left) – Image credit: NASA/ JPL-Caltech.
- Image P. 027 - (2nd Image from left) - Image credit: NASA/ JPL-Caltech.
- Image P. 027 - (3rd Image from left) - Image Credit: NASA/ JPL-Caltech/T. Pyle (SSC).
- Image P. 027 - (4th Image from left) - Copyright: PlanetariumHH, created with Sciss Uniview.
- Image P. 028 - modified image / Isaac Newton.
- Image P. 046 – This image is based on the image "DNA orbit animated.gif" from Wikipedia, the free encyclopedia, and it is under the GNULicense for public use. Original uploader: Richard Wheeler (Zephyris) at en.wikipedia.org.
- Image P. 053 - (3rd Image from left) – Credit: NASA, JPL-Caltech, Galex Team, J. Huchra et al. (Harvard CfA).
- Image P. 073 – Illustration Credit: NASA/CXC/M.WeisP.
- Image P. 160 - Credit: Library of Congress, Prints & Photographs Division, Look Magazine Photograph Collection. Call number LOOK – Job 61-9343. All rights released per Instrument of Gift. Author: James Hansen.
- Image P. 180 – Image credit: NASA/CXC/JPL-Caltech/PSU/ CfA.
- Image P. 181 – Illustration by: NASA/JPL-Caltech/R. Hurt (SSC/Caltech).
- Image P. 228 (down-right) - Image Credit: NASA/JPL.
- Image P. 231 – Author: coskun80, "the shade of myself", permission was obtained from the author.

- Image P. 238 – Library of Congress (www.loc.gov), public domain image.
- All images P. 272 – are from the artist Mr. Lars Hörl. A licence was awarded from him to the author.
- All images P. 274 – are from the artist Mr. Lars Hörl. A licence was awarded from him to the author.
- Image P. 298 – This image is based on the image "Abu Abdullah Muhammad bin Musa al-Khwarizmi.jpg" from Wikipedia, the free encyclopedia, and it is under the GNULicense for public use. Original uploader: Chris 73 at en.wikipedia.org.
- Image P. 333 (down) – Author: Uri Avnery, public domain image.
- Illustrations P. 003 (above), 022, 023, 030, 031, 033, 036 (1st right), 036 (left), 049, 052, 053 (1st Image from left), 053 (4th Image from left), 055, 056, 057, 058, 059, 061, 064, 068, 069, 078, 079, 080, 085, 088, 105, 110, 124, 128, 129, 142,166, 167, 175, 176, 184 (above), 187, 194, 195, 197, 210, 214, 218, 220, 221, 223, 224, 225, 234, 245, 248, 249, 252, 265, 294, 311 (above), 336, 323, 333 (above) and 346 are the property of the author.
- Illustrations P. 024 (right), 47, 230, 159 , 190 and 266 are by Interior Designer Asmaa M. Hemaya.
- Illustrations P. 003 (down), 024 (left), 036 (2nd right) and 053 (2nd Image from left) are by Ahmad M. Hemaya.
- Images P. 037, 044, 081, 082, 134, 137, 144, 155, 156, 164, 184 (down), 192, 236, 228 (above- right), 232, 267, 269, 270, 275 and 311 (down) are Public domain images.

Notes

Notes